Poet, Madman, Scoundrel

189 Unusual Irish Lives

Poet, Madman, Scoundrel

189 Unusual Irish Lives

David Slattery

ORPEN PRESS

Orpen Press
Lonsdale House
Avoca Ave
Blackrock
Co. Dublin
Ireland

e-mail: info@orpenpress.com
www.orpenpress.com

ISBN: 978-1-871305-70-8
ePub ISBN: 978-1-871305-96-8
Kindle ISBN: 978-1-871305-97-5

Printed in Ireland by Colorman Ltd.

Acknowledgements

Our libraries remain a constant valuable national resource while everything else changes around them. I want to thank the several fabulous libraries that gave me essential help with the research for this book. Thanks to Dr Jason McElligott, keeper of Archbishop Marsh's Library, which, along with being a source of historic treasure, was founded in 1701 and is itself an historical institution. Some of the books still bear bullet holes from the Easter Rising of 1916. Jason was a great help in pointing me towards interesting Cromwellians, rebels and scandalous law cases.

Thanks are also due to the helpful staff at the Royal Irish Academy who gave me access to their vast collection, including the definitive guide to who currently counts in Irish history – *The Dictionary of Irish Biography from the Earliest Times to the Year 2002*. This vast tome is edited by James McGuire and James Quinn, and is published by the Royal Irish Academy and Cambridge University Press. It is the principal source for the lives I have included in this book. My thanks to those hundreds of expert contributors to the dictionary who provided the biographical details for the thousands of historical figures. The Royal Irish Academy has also the best reading and writing space in Ireland. I also thank the National Library, which continues to provide the entire population with a fabulous free historical resource and a glorious reading room.

Thanks also to Piotr Sadowski for his suggestions and to Tomás Clancy for sharing with me both his legal erudition and extraordinary grasp of the history of Irish law.

Special thanks to my editor Elizabeth Brennan for the original ideas, predictably good advice and constant support.

Contents

Preface

When I told friends that I was writing an Irish history, most of them shuddered with the memories of school history that had emerged from the murky depths of their unconscious. I persisted by explaining that, in order to write a fun history of Irish people, I had decided to forget, or repress, what I learned in school, and that *my* Irish history wasn't intended to be traumatising. In fact, it was actually intended to be enjoyable because it would be a history of unusual Irish people, as opposed to the usual suspects who populate Irish school history.

So be reassured that this book is about only interesting Irish people. If you've never read any Irish history, I assure you that we are all interesting.

Poet, Madman, Scoundrel is a chronicle of how 189 unusual Irish individuals chose to live – the professions they followed, their interests and passions, and the risks they took for their ambitions. I haven't embellished the documented details of their lives in any way. I have merely interpreted that information, which anyone writing history should try to do, and I've tried to present it in an entertaining way. While it was often tempting to change the ending of many lives to make them happier, nastier, more miserable or even more successful, I have stuck rigidly to the facts. I say this because I am sure that, like me, you will ask yourself, "Is this really true?" at certain points in the stories. Suffice to say at this point that, yes, it is all true.

Have I covered exactly 189 lives in this book? Have I counted them accurately? The answer is not simple – it depends on the way you count. If you are a mathematical genius like some of those in Chapter 7, you will know – even if I don't – what is meant by 189 being a complex number, part real and part imaginary, because who decides what counts as one life anyway? I can also imagine you asking, "Why 189?" The answer would be easy if there were only 189 unusual people in the whole of Irish history, but that is definitely not the case. My 189 are just the tip of a human iceberg. To help you count them I have included birth and death dates only for the Irish lives portrayed in this book. I don't intend for those people omitted from the book to be viewed as dull. I chose the most interesting histories that caught my attention in our national archives during one particular period of research. I recommend searching out others for yourself.

Irish history is like a well-trodden path through an overgrown wood with who knows what scary monsters hiding in the gloom. Where the path is worn, it's very worn. Just off the path the darkness increases quickly. I have chosen to explore the less travelled areas of this vast forest of Irish lives. Some of those I include in this book lie partially on the well-worn path so that their names will be familiar to many of us. Others lived far from the limelight and some, while famous or notorious in their own time, have since fallen out of focus.

I have concentrated on those who might have been interesting or even dangerous to know, especially if they were experimenting with the law, chemicals, bombs or quack cures. I have chosen to include the following: a selection of our less successful rebels because we have so many; some saints because we are famous for them, but I have also included sinners for moral balance; soldiers of both sexes because, while the Irish started very few wars in history, once a good conflict was under way, anywhere involving anyone, we were happy to join in and take our chances; a variety of sporting heroes of a range of shapes and sizes because so many of us enjoy watching and playing sport; sailors and explorers because we live on an island and love the sea; and writers and their inspirations because we write almost as much as we talk. I finish with our scientists and thinkers of varying degrees of rigour. Though we do not have an international reputation for our scientific achievements, we have had interesting experimenters and several people who were good at sums.

*

My interest in former times is anthropological rather than historical in the traditional sense. I am interested in our social history, much of it involving individual tragedies and triumphs, rather than the history of our well-established national heroes who, when they do feature in this book, tend to be spear carriers in someone else's play. L.P. Hartley famously tells us in the opening line of his novel, *The Go-Between*, that, "The past is a foreign country: they do things differently there." Who am I to judge these foreigners from our past? Where we have presidents, they had kings. Where we have the internet, they had pamphleteers. Where we have hygiene, they had prayers. Where we have television they had – actually – nothing. But we do have much in common with these foreigners. Like us, people in the past hoped for the best. They had ambitions for themselves and their families. They lay awake at night worrying, probably about fleas.

If people from 200 or 300 years ago could travel forward in time they would be astonished to see us driving around in our horseless carriages while apparently talking to our own hands (on our mobile phones). But it is just as amazing and challenging for us to imagine what life was like in the past because so much changes over time. There are fashions in cars, horseless or otherwise, clothes, diseases and careers. For example, the Black Death, gangrene, leprosy, tuberculosis, smallpox, melancholia and syncope were once highly fashionable diseases. Syncope is itself an historical term for fainting, which ladies used to do frequently in the past, especially when there were wealthy gentlemen on hand to catch them.

Similarly, in the area of careers, the professions of saint, quack, eccentric, physiognomist and pamphleteer are now out of vogue. Unfortunately, nowadays, fancy professions such as highwayman or pirate, or being the proprietor of a laboratory in a castle basement (where you dissected the brains of just-dead criminals) are obsolete.

Many forms of entertainment have also declined in popularity from earlier times, such as fantastic free public entertainments like hangings, beheadings and dissections. Before cinema ruined it, the travelling Waxwork Show was popular in Ireland. With a simple change of clothes, hair added or taken away, or a nose lengthened or squashed, the museum proprietor could keep up with contemporary celebrities without fuss or expense. A wax figure that started out as Napoleon could become Robert Emmet with a simple change of uniform, or Enrico Caruso with the addition of hair. If a blaze melted your exhibits they could simply become other celebrities. This once happened in Skibbereen, Co. Cork, where a melted Mayor of Cork became a circus clown. Technology has killed this form of entertainment. But such constant change makes all travel through time exciting.

People tell me that I am living in the past. That is not true. I would like to live in the past, which is a completely different matter. Oh, for a time machine! I am currently building one in my garden shed. But until I have perfected my technology, I have history.

To the memory of Adele Farrell

1

The Rebellious Irish:
It'll Be All Right on the Night

We know from George Orwell's *Animal Farm* that all victorious revolutionaries end up looking and acting exactly like those they have overthrown. Therefore, there is nothing implicitly tragic about a failed revolution. However, revolutionary protocol demands that we morally support the underdogs, just so long as they remain losers. Fortunately, since Irish history has many examples of failed rebellions, we have a comprehensive range of revolutionary failures that we can root for. Irish political rebels tended to leave much to chance, and few were motivated by an attention to detail. They were often more interested in the justification for their cause than the pragmatics of successful organisation. It seems that things were almost guaranteed to go wrong on the actual night.

One of our most famous revolutionaries, Wolfe Tone (1763–1798), even missed his own rebellion when it eventually happened. But we can forgive him because he was a gentleman and a dilettante rebel. Any self-respecting dilettante must be fashionably late.

A Missing Revolutionary

Tone's life acts as a template for the typical Irish would-be revolutionary because it has all the insurrectionist components, including pamphleteering,[1] public executions, fancy uniforms, dissections, poor punctuality, the to-be-expected untimely storms at sea and, of course, failure.

Wolfe Tone was the eldest of eighteen children. His father had entered a lengthy litigation with his own brother, resulting in the inevitable near-ruin of both families. Wherever there is a reference to attorneys[2] in Irish history, it usually occurs in the context of "lengthy litigation" because any worthwhile application of the law should be protracted. Lengthy litigation usually precedes the litigants "being

---

[1] Pamphleteering was the popular habit of putting thoughts on any subject into the public arena in the form of a brochure, usually paid for by the author. The best pamphlets were written as self-justifications for the most outrageous actions, opinions, inventions, remedies, cures or beliefs. A pamphlet war frequently broke out when a pamphleteer attacked the sentiments of another, forcing a pamphlet response in kind. Vitriolic pamphlet wars were popular with the reading public.

[2] The term "attorney" is derived from the Anglo-Norman French *attorner*, which means to turn or to put in the place of, or to substitute one for another. The term was used in Ireland as a generic description for all those involved with the law (except the accused or the litigants) between 1541, when the Kings' Inns was founded, and 1877 when an Act of the Supreme Court of Judicature (Ireland) united court structures by amalgamating the state courts and the chancery courts, which had their origins in religious jurisdiction. After 1877 a stringent naming rule was confirmed, assigning definite separate roles to barristers and solicitors. This had the added benefit of allowing lawyers to generate law cases against each other for misuse of these new terms. As most of the lawyers in this book predate 1877, I use the term "attorney" for them, and "barristers" or just "lawyers" after that date. America never had a legal amalgamation because they never had a split between state and religious jurisdictions, and this is why we still have attorneys in American television dramas.

left penniless" and "ending their days in the poorhouse" because of the legal fees incurred. Such fees are the reason why being an attorney has remained a fashionable career throughout Irish history. Lengthy litigation was also known by the expression "thrown into chancery". If property was thrown into chancery (that's a pun) there was no hope of benefit to the "interested parties", also known as the victims.

In 1781, to keep his father happy, Tone entered Trinners,[3] where he was a talented but lazy student. He was suspended for a year for his involvement in a duel in which a student was killed. Unfortunately, the student duel has now passed into obsolescence. He finally graduated in 1786, having established a scenic route through the college that was popular with many who came after him. He won three medals from the debating society, the College Historical Society, which had been founded in 1747 by Edmund Burke (1729–1797). Burke was a notable statesman, author, orator, political theorist, philosopher and, importantly, a Trinity alumnus who wasn't hanged. He was such a model of traditional propriety that a statue of him was erected in front of the college. He was a critic of the French Revolution and argued against abstractions, such as the rights of men; instead he advocated the virtues of tradition. In other words, the kind of ideas that merit a statue in front of Trinners.

From his diaries we learn that Tone loved Shakespeare, liked irony and self-deprecation, and disliked humbug, though, while many promoted it, it is hard to find people in history who admit to actually liking the latter. He had an embarrassing relationship with a married woman, Eliza Martin. So embarrassing was it that he was determined

---

[3] I refer throughout to Trinity College Dublin by its popular name "Trinners". As the oldest university in Ireland, it is the institution from which many people in Irish history graduated, were expelled or just dropped out.

not to embarrass himself with Martha Witherington, aged fifteen. He did the proper thing by running away to marry her against her parents' wishes. They had four children together. Being married disqualified Tone from a fellowship at Trinners, so he decided to become an attorney at Middle Temple in London.

It tells us much about Tone's well-balanced mind that he was bored stiff studying the law. While supposed to be studying, he dabbled in or day-dreamed about journalism, non-embarrassing adventures with women and a military colony in the Sandwich Islands.[4] He even day-dreamed about joining the East India Company's army because he fancied himself in uniform. He also wrote a novel that appeared as *Belmont Castle*, published in 1790. However, he stuck it out at Middle Temple before returning to Ireland in 1788.

He was called to the Bar in 1789 where he could have remained as just another historically anonymous villain, but he didn't. From 1790 to 1791 he became a pamphleteer, which was a fashionable pastime. He described his own first pamphlet scribblings as mediocre. In his pamphlets he advocated Irish non-participation in the war effort against revolutionary France. This political position gave him some notoriety, while ruining his chances of a respectable law practice and a seat in Parliament. But his writing improved with practice because, by 1791, he wrote what would become the most famous pamphlet in Irish history – *An Argument on Behalf of the Catholics of Ireland*. This circular sold well.

In 1791, on the strength of his new fame as a pamphleteer, he travelled to Belfast to meet Thomas Russell (1767–1803). From Tone's diary we learn that the two spent most of their time drinking or treating their hangovers. Tone loved debate fuelled by alcohol. So did Russell. Tone supported the principles of the French Revolution. So did Russell. Together

---

[4] Now known as the Hawaiian Islands.

they formed the United Irishmen,[5] which they modeled on the new French republicanism. The ironically named United Irishmen provide us with an extensive cast of rebellious *dramatis personae*. Unlike the French, they never experienced the inconvenience of success.

Most of the leadership of the United Irishmen became fascinated as teenagers with the American Revolution, which had radicalised them. The most prominent of the United Irishmen travelled to Paris once the French Revolution was under way, either to work together to bring about a French invasion of Ireland or to work on creating splits within their own ranks. The sense of excitement and possibility in Paris in 1792 would have been similar to that in Berlin in 1990 following the fall of the Berlin Wall.

Some of the first United Irishmen, who were Protestant, had reservations as to whether or not Catholics were capable of managing their own liberty, so the cracks began to appear from the beginning. Furthermore, Irish Catholics were suspicious of the Irish Presbyterians, and instead looked to all religions in England for support. From both a pragmatic point of view and for the sake of precision, Tone could have named this society the Disunited Irishmen, but, happily, the United Irishmen were anything but pragmatic.

Back in Dublin, Tone was bored again after the high life in Belfast. But the boredom ended when his revolution began to get under way – with the arrest for treason in 1794 of the Reverend William Jackson, a French agent in Ireland. Following this capture, the United Irishmen were outlawed because England was then at war with France. In return for his co-operation with the authorities, it was agreed that Tone could leave Ireland for America, the traditional solution for

---

[5] The United Irishmen were a political alliance formed by the Catholic and Presbyterian middle classes. The union was initially created to bring about political reform but evolved into a military organisation.

Irish troublemakers. He sold up and, with £796,[6] he and his wife, children, and younger brother and sister sailed for Philadelphia.

Tone hated life and politics in America. He particularly hated George Washington. However, he bought a farm for his family near Princeton, New Jersey. In 1796 the French agreed for Tone to travel to Paris to argue his plan for a French invasion of Ireland. He sailed under the name "James Smith", leaving the authorities in Dublin Castle believing that he was still in America. While away, Tone was tormented by the fear that his daughter, Maria, might marry an American. However, he quickly grew to love France so much that he arranged for his family to join him there. Finally, in 1796, Tone was appointed *chef de brigade* in General Louis Lazare Hoche's army, thereby achieving his boyhood ambition of becoming a soldier with access to fancy uniforms.

---

[6] About €53,000 in contemporary currency values. It is difficult to calculate relative monetary value over centuries. Economists try because we like to ask "How much would that be worth now?" Some economists use the notion of buying power where they compare, for example, the number of sheep we could buy then and now for a given amount of money. But sheep can fluctuate in price and are not as central to our shopping list as they once were. Others use wages where we can compare how many days of a weaver's time we might expect for an amount of money then and now. But it is difficult to imagine how well-off a weaver is compared to, say, an attorney or a plumber. I have relied on currency value rather than buying power or comparative wages throughout this book. Currency value gives an interesting, if unscientific, idea of the amounts involved. Considering economists disagree amongst themselves over the notion of value, calculations should be treated with caution or even skepticism because amounts have to be transformed from imperial into decimal currencies, across regions, and then across currencies from pounds into euro where rates are also subject to fluctuations. I have included a value because I like to know how much a pound from hundreds of years ago is worth today, especially when someone is buying a wife or paying a fine!

In December 1796, a French fleet left Brest for Ireland with 14,450 French soldiers and Tone on board. The fleet was scattered by a storm and only a few ships reached Bantry Bay. However, since the soldiers on these ships were unable to disembark, they sailed back to Brest. The mission was a complete failure. When Hoche died unexpectedly, hope of another armada seemed to die with him.

Tone met General Napoleon Bonaparte in December 1797. In terms of his military plans, Napoleon was actually interested in the Mediterranean, but he strung Tone along as a diversion. However, on 17 June 1798 rebellion broke out in Ireland, catching both Tone and the French unawares. Tone immediately sailed to the fight on board the *Hoche*. But his ship was intercepted at sea by a British squadron. Following a furious six-hour battle, the *Hoche* surrendered. When Tone was taken ashore at the obscure town of Buncranna, Co. Donegal, whom should he meet but an old classmate from Trinners. This classmate had unfortunately remained loyal to the Crown and immediately recognised him. We have all had the experience of running into old classmates at the most inopportune times. Tone was promptly arrested and sent to Dublin to be tried as a traitor.

Technically, because Tone was a French army officer with his own line in fancy French uniforms he should not have been tried for treason. For his trial he wore a blue uniform embroidered with gold and a tricolored cockade hat. His court martial took over an hour to convict him. He offered no defence except to read a declaration to the court. He requested that he be shot rather than hanged. His request was refused. However, Cornwallis, the lord lieutenant,[7] being both humane and urbane, considerately waived, in

---

[7] The lord lieutenant of Ireland, also known as the viceroy, was the British monarch's representative and effective head of the Irish Government.

Tone's case, the subsequent beheading and posting of the head on a prominent spike which was the fate of many hanged for treason at the time.

Several of Tone's friends from Trinners tried to get him off by delaying the case, hoping that the passage of time would save him. An injunction was in fact granted to prevent his execution, but by then Tone had slashed his throat and lay dying in gaol. It is unclear whether or not he meant to actually kill himself, or to simply cause a delay, because in those days you weren't supposed to be hanged if you had a cut throat. As he neared his death, he remarked cryptically, "I am sorry I have been so bad an anatomist." This could mean that he was either sorry he cut too deep or not deep enough. Understandably, he was suffering from that historic malaise, melancholia. His final words were, "What should I wish to live for?" He had missed his own rebellion.

His family returned to America, a country they soon learned to enjoy a lot.

Dis-United Irishmen

Once the word "united" was used in the title of the revolutionary organisation, it motivated the perverse amongst their ranks to act according to the opposite principle. Think how well they might have done by calling themselves The Disparate Irishmen. James Napper Tandy (1737–1803) brought about one of the inevitable official splits amongst the United Irishmen by seeking French support for his own invasion of Ireland. He was also in Paris when Tone was there. The French Directory[8] was happy to confirm the split by recognising two camps. They made Napper Tandy a *générale de brigade*, despite his lack of any military experience.

---

[8] The French Directory was the Executive Government of the First French Republic from 1795 to 1799, when Napoleon toppled the Directory and replaced it with the Consulate with himself as First Consul.

Napper Tandy, who also missed the start of the rebellion in Ireland, sailed to Rutland Island in Donegal on the *Anacréon* in 1798. He disembarked on one of the remotest parts of the country to deliver a "liberty or death" speech to a few of the local sheep that had gathered around him to see what was happening. He had to get back on board due to a chronic lack of local rebels.

He sailed from Donegal to Norway and was eventually handed over to the English, who, despite sentencing him to be hanged, in turn handed him back to the French. In 1803 he died in the arms of his mistress, Marie Barriére, leaving her his estate and thereby facilitating a lengthy litigation between her and his son. At last an Irish rebel had succeeded in changing the lives of others for the better: two attorneys.

Made in France

Another leading light in the 1798 Rebellion was Lord Edward FitzGerald (1763–1798). FitzGerald had also moved to Paris for the French Revolution, where he shared lodgings with Thomas Paine[9] in 1792. He embraced the revolution by changing his name to "le citoyen Edouard FitzGerald" because being called "Lord" just wasn't the thing. He cut his hair short in the fashion of the French revolutionaries, and married Pamela Sims, who allegedly was the daughter of the Comtesse de Genlis and the French King's revolutionary cousin, Philippe Égalité, duc d'Orléans.[10]

---

[9] Thomas Paine had a typical mix of competencies. He was a pamphleteer, journalist, inventor and revolutionary. Author of the influential *Rights of Man*, he can also be regarded as the father of the American Revolution.

[10] Louis Philippe Joseph d'Orleans, who was King Louis XVI's cousin, actively supported the French Revolution. He adopted the name "Equality Philip" to demonstrate his republican credentials. Despite

When FitzGerald returned to Ireland after his stay in Paris as a revolutionary skinhead, his radical reputation was such that he featured on jugs in Belfast as "the man of the people". He rejected the main form of transport, horse riding, as being too aristocratic. He also refused to wear black mourning clothes when the French revolutionaries chopped his father-in-law's cousin's head off in January 1793. He learned to play the uilleann pipes, took up step dancing and charmed his way through the pubs of Kildare. The locals adored him. FitzGerald came to be regarded as the most charismatic of the rebels because he was the most charismatic man in Ireland, if not the world, at that time.

FitzGerald was the fifth son of the Duke of Leinster. His mother was the daughter of the Duke of Richmond. Fitz-Gerald was his mother's pet. He was educated by his tutor Ogilvie – who later married his mother – in the spirit of the teachings of the radical French philosopher Rousseau.[11] During his life, FitzGerald, influenced by his Rousseauian education, transgressed barriers of class, nationality and race, amongst others.

As a younger son, FitzGerald had to pursue a career in the army. He was commissioned into the Green Howards regiment as a lieutenant. Despite his ideals, he sailed from Cork to South Carolina to fight against the American revolutionaries, arriving in Charleston in June 1781. One of his American prisoners wrote of the experience of being captured by FitzGerald: "[I] never knew so loveable a person, and every

---

his great courage as a noble revolutionary, he was guillotined during the Reign of Terror in November 1793.

[11] Jean-Jacques Rousseau's political philosophy directly influenced the French Revolution because in his 1762 treatise *The Social Contract* he argued for the legitimacy of republicanism. He also provided a radical philosophy of education, arguing that right and wrong was learned from experience rather than custom. This philosophy of education came to life in FitzGerald.

man in the army, from the general to the drummer, would cheer at his expression ... an idol to all who served him."

FitzGerald was badly wounded in September 1781 and left for dead. But he was rescued by Tony Small, a South Carolina slave, and nursed back to health by him. FitzGerald formed a close relationship with Small. They travelled everywhere together and were inseparable until FitzGerald's death. In 1786 FitzGerald finally resolved to send Small to London to become a hairdresser (let's not make too many assumptions here), but when the time came for Small to actually board the ship, FitzGerald couldn't let him go.

FitzGerald travelled widely in North America and Canada with Small. A hundred and seventy years before the social revolution of the 1960s, he embraced the ideal of "the brotherhood of man", but without the drugs. He befriended the Native American Indians. He came to believe that the human race was "all one brother" or, as the Indians told him, "all one Indian". He travelled south from Canada through the American wilderness and down the Mississippi River as far as New Orleans, remarking that Ireland would be too small for him when he got home. Joseph Brant, the Irish-Indian Mohawk leader, inducted FitzGerald into the Seneca nation, one of the six tribes that formed the Iroquois League,[12] as a chieftain with the name "Eghnidal".

Back at home in Ireland his family was trying to find him a suitable bride, but two of their marriage proposals were thwarted, probably because FitzGerald was a younger son with limited prospects rather than the product of an eccentric education. Disenchanted with European culture, he

---

[12] The Iroquois League, better known from Western films as the Six Nations, and less known by the name they call themselves, the Haudenosaunee, were formed from a confederation of six tribes of indigenous people of North America, which included the Seneca nation and Mohawk tribes.

wrote to his mother: "I really would join the savages .... Savages have all the happiness of life. There would be no ... fortune for children; no separations in families; no devilish politics; no fashions, customs, duties or appearances ...." In this we can detect a prototype John Lennon. In a different age, FitzGerald could have become a Beatle.

He also travelled in the West Indies, England, Germany, Switzerland, Portugal, Spain and France. Back in Ireland in 1784, he entered Parliament. But he was quickly bored with talking politics. He rejoined the British Army in Canada in 1788 as a major. He was offered the rank of lieutenant colonel in 1790, but to accept he would have had to commit himself to William Pitt, the British prime minister. As he couldn't swear loyalty to what he considered to be an archaic regime, his army promotions stalled.

Counter-Revolution

It is impossible to have a revolution without those you are attempting to overthrow putting up some form of resistance, even for the sake of appearances. What is the point if compliant tyrants just politely agree that they should step down? Such regimes wouldn't be worth overthrowing. Irish counter-revolutionaries usually have bad reputations just because they were better at their jobs than the revolutionaries themselves. That was hardly their fault.

Lord Edward FitzGerald fell into the hands of the counter-revolutionary Major Henry Sirr (1764–1841), who was the chief of police. Sirr enjoyed a reputation for being able to appear in two places at the one time. He was an effective and efficient counter-revolutionary and the nemesis of the United Irishmen. He ran a stable of informers and bespoke perjurers, who were also known as witnesses. He learned to speak Irish while stationed in Munster, which was to prove useful in his rebel-busting career in Dublin.

In 1796 FitzGerald became one of the leading United Irishmen, and the society's most important military strategist. With the poor judgement or typical bad luck that beset the members of the society, he invited Thomas Reynolds to join the United Irishmen, and quickly promoted him to colonel. When Reynolds promptly betrayed the society, FitzGerald had to go into hiding. But he didn't flee to America, declining to leave his followers.

Francis Mangan was an attorney who believed that the law wasn't bad enough for him on its own: he had to supplement it. For a reward of £1,000, he betrayed FitzGerald's hiding place. At 7.00 p.m. on 19 May 1798, Sirr, accompanied by an arrest party, burst into an upstairs room at 151 Thomas St, Dublin, where FitzGerald was hiding. Fitz-Gerald killed one of the guards with a dagger before taking a bullet in the shoulder from Sirr's gun at point-blank range. Wadding, the material wrapped around the musket ball to keep it in place in the gun barrel, embedded itself in the wound, causing septicemia and tetanus. FitzGerald died in extraordinary pain on 4 June in Dublin's Newgate Prison. In this way, one of the most genuinely fascinating men in the world at that time passed out of life and into Irish history.

A Poet in a Bomb Factory

With the death of the charismatic FitzGerald, the United Irishmen hadn't yet run out of charming revolutionaries for Sirr to chase: they still had Robert Emmet (1778–1803). At school, Emmet studied oratory, fencing, astronomy and music. Surprisingly, this syllabus proved to be a poor preparation for revolution. He entered Trinners where he became a swot, coming top of his class. Worryingly, in 1795 he entered the King's Inns with the intention of becoming an attorney. But he really wanted to be the Irish George Washington.

He joined the United Irishmen in 1796, and wrote a poem about Irish independence that was published in the United Irishmen's newspaper, *The Press*. His eventual rebellion was so inept that it could qualify as the first-ever student demonstration. It had everything you might expect of a revolution organised by a student of literature, including poetry. He should have been given a million lines – "I must not rebel" – rather than being hanged. The punishment showed a paltry appreciation of student life on the part of the authorities at the beginning of the nineteenth century.

Emmet became a leading speaker in both debating societies[13] at Trinners. As now, students were encouraged not to discuss relevant topics or current affairs at debates. But Emmet had a genius for getting round the rules and became an annoyance to the college authorities. They were so upset with him that they persuaded a former student to return to challenge Emmet to a debate. Debates were judged according to what extent the speaker could keep his head and project a calm demeanour. Emmet lost his head and thus the argument. In short, the former student wiped the floor with Emmet.

Emmet was then expelled in 1798 for being a member of the proscribed Society of United Irishmen. After the failure of the rebellion that year, he was given the job of writing a report on what had gone wrong. His own later catastrophic rebellion makes this one of the most ironic assignments in the history of employment. In 1800 he was made secretary of a United Irishmen's delegation to France.

---

[13] One, the College Historical Society (the Hist), mentioned earlier in this chapter, claims to be the oldest student society in the world, tracing its origins to 1747. The other is the University Philosophical Society (the Phil), which also considers itself to be the oldest student society in the world, tracing its origins to 1683. I will leave them to debate the issue amongst themselves.

In Paris, unlike his illustrious predecessors, he became disillusioned with French politics, preferring to hang out with Irish and English visitors. At this time yet another split happened amongst the United Irishmen over the question of the sincerity of the French promise of aid to Ireland.

Emmet returned to Dublin in 1802. His father died leaving him £2,000,[14] which he used to finance his rebellion. He made a practical start. He rented depots around the city for the manufacture of weapons, establishing a bomb factory, a rocket factory and a factory on Thomas St for the production of a special pike[15] of his own invention. He wasn't content to manufacture just any old pikes. He designed a hinged model that could be concealed under a coat. This folded pike could be taken out from under a rebel's coat at an opportune moment, and instantly opened out to full length for stabbing and lancing purposes – a flick-pike, if you like. While experimenting with weapon design and opening munitions factories seemed a promising start, the more prosaic aspects of revolution were soon neglected because Emmet fell in love and became embroiled in the important task of writing love letters and poems.

Imagine falling in love while organising a revolution. Only a true poet could achieve this. While visiting a friend from Trinners, Richard Curran, Emmet fell madly in love with his sister Sarah Curran (1782–1808). This was a particularly stupid infatuation, even by Emmet's standards, because Sarah's father, who came to despise Emmet because of his relationship with his daughter, was the most effective defender of political rebels in court. Emmet should have known that he was soon going to need the best attorney available.

---

[14] About €80,000 in contemporary currency values.

[15] A pike is a long spear that was used by infantry soldiers. It was not intended to be thrown. Instead, it was used to thrust at individual cavalry soldiers or in large formations against a cavalry charge.

Sarah had an unhappy life. When she was ten years old her sister Gertrude fell out the window of their home and died. When Sarah was thirteen, her father threw her mother out – through the door – when she became pregnant with someone else's child. Sarah was a talented singer, harpist and pianist. Anticipating her father's hostility, she kept the affair with Emmet hidden, and they only met in secret to sing, recite poetry and play music together.

Emmet did realise that he needed experienced revolutionaries to support him. Amongst others, he turned to Michael Dwyer (1772–1825). Dwyer was a guerilla leader of considerable talent and experience. He was the antithesis of Emmet in that he was an exceptionally practical rebel without opportunity or inclination to write poetry. He had been fighting five years in the field by the time he met Emmet. He was not impressed but agreed that if Emmet could capture Dublin Castle he would support him. He said of Emmet that if he "had brains to his education, he'd be a fine man". As it turned out, Dwyer fought on until 1806, three years after Emmet's rebellion, when he finally surrendered on the agreement that he could go into exile in Australia with his family, where he became a farmer. In 1807 he was arrested on suspicion of sedition and, though acquitted by a jury, he was nevertheless sent to the penal settlement on Norfolk Island at the insistence of Governor William Bligh, one-time Captain Bligh of HMS *Bounty*.[16] This injustice contributed to

---

[16] Captain William Bligh (1754–1817) of "Mutiny on the *Bounty*" fame came to Dublin, between mutinies, in 1800. He spent three months in the Hibernian Hotel on Dawson St while he mapped Dublin Bay as part of an engineering project that ultimately made the port safe for navigation. Through popular portrayals in films, Bligh has become a by-word for cruelty and tyranny. But in reality he was a man of extraordinary abilities. Bligh was an exceptional cartographer, an extraordinary navigator, a naturalist, a scientist and an illustrator. But he did have anger management issues because he set himself

the second mutiny against Bligh by the New South Wales Corps and Dwyer's return to his farm in 1809.

The date was set for Emmet's rebellion – 23 July 1803. In historical terms, on that day Emmet may have pulled off the most inept rebellion in the history of revolution. The bomb factory on Patrick St blew up by accident on 11 July but, surprisingly, the authorities didn't think too much of it. They either weren't prepared for a rebellion led by a poet or Dublin was filled with exploding bomb factories at that time. However, the explosion unnerved Emmet's co-conspirators. It added to both their stress and whatever insecurities about their leader they were already trying to suppress. To soothe their fears, he put on his specially made fancy green uniform and regaled his men with tales of his planned achievements. Then he wrote more love letters.

On the day of the rebellion Emmet planned to deploy his most effective weapon: his rockets. These were guaranteed to shock and awe the authorities into immediate submission. Frustratingly, no one remembered to bring along the fuses for them or, in fact, to even make them, which was a contributing factor to the rocket factory escaping the fate of the bomb factory. The rebels also forgot to collect all the guns they went to such pains to produce and, of course, bombs were in short supply following the explosion in the factory. A prominent aide, who had been sent to purchase supplies, wisely ran off with the funds. Hard men with revolutionary experience, who'd arrived from Kildare, took one look

---

high standards. On the *Bounty* he was recorded as saying "infamous scoundrel", "audacious rascal", "vagrant", "you are a disgrace to the service", "God damn you, sir what are you about?" and, the worst, "dastardly villain". All this was enough to utterly demoralise any crew member, especially if they were pining after the scantily clad ladies of Tahiti that Bligh had unreasonably insisted they leave behind, instead taking his precious cargo of breadfruits. No wonder there was mutiny.

at the flick-pikes, the general student-like disorganisation, the still-smoldering munitions manufacturers, and Emmet in his special green uniform and went home again. Emmet had been expecting 2,000 rebels to turn out on Thomas St, but on the day just 80 turned up, almost all of whom were plastered having gone to the pub to fuel their courage and deal with their stress.

The rebellion was due to officially get underway at 11.00 a.m. However, the start time had to be brought forward to 9.00 a.m. because of a false alarm, so some of the rebels were late, which actually wasn't their fault. At 9.00 a.m., Emmet, in his distinctive green uniform, read the proclamation of the provisional government to his eighty drunken men, who weren't really listening because they were too busy playing with their new flick-pikes. His proclamation commendably called for the lenient treatment of prisoners and the maintenance of order at all times, because this was to be a polite rebellion. His men were too drunk to listen. In fact, they booed him. He had drawn up sophisticated plans on paper, which included blocking streets, rocket attacks, ambushes involving lobbing bombs from different directions, seizing strategic locations, firing actual guns and flick-piking a variety of specific authority figures. All these plans were abandoned, as he was, when most of his men ran down the street in a drunken riot. He attempted a charge on Dublin Castle but this failed miserably when most of his few remaining men wandered back to the pub.

When his drunken rebels dragged Lord Kilwarden, Lord Chief Justice of the King's Bench for Ireland, and his nephew from their carriage and flick-piked them to death, Emmet gave up the polite rebellion and fled to the Wicklow Mountains. Lord Kilwarden, Arthur Wolfe, was regarded as an agreeable chap because he had signed the stay of execution for Wolfe Tone in 1798. His murder was viewed as the single most shocking event in Emmet's shockingly awful rebellion.

Following a period of depression-inspired poetry in the mountains, Emmet returned to Dublin, renting a room under an assumed name in Harold's Cross so that he could be near his girlfriend. Major Sirr searched the house as part of a routine hunt for the rebels. I assume Emmet wasn't wearing the green uniform at this point but with him it is difficult to know for sure. In any case, Emmet panicked during the rummage around and started to act suspiciously. Not able to take the stress of it anymore, he knocked out a guard and ran from the house. He was chased and caught by Sirr, who apologised for roughing him up because this was a polite rebellion. Emmet told him that it was okay because "all was fair in war".

Emmet was taken for questioning to Dublin Castle, where the farce continued. On arrival, he tried to bribe a gaoler, who he thought might be sympathetic to him, to help him escape. The gaoler immediately reported him to Sirr. Emmet wouldn't talk until finally the authorities showed him two love letters from Sarah Curran. Sirr thought that these two maudlin compositions must have been coded messages from his co-conspirators. He couldn't imagine that two people would actually communicate in this way. Emmet thought that they were going to arrest Sarah, so, wishing to protect her, he promised to talk and pleaded for a deal. Sirr was surprised by his sudden change of heart. He was probably disappointed that they were actual love letters and not secret documents. Ah, love in a time of rebellion.

Back in his cell, Emmet wrote a letter of apology to Sarah and handed it to the same gaoler whom he trusted, asking him to secretly deliver it to his lover. The gaoler duly handed it to Sirr. Next day, Sirr and his men raided the Curran house. When Sirr arrived, he found Sarah alone in her bedroom, in bed. Some historians believe that he allowed her to burn her love letters, or that he even burned them himself because by now Sarah had had convulsions and had collapsed. A soldier raiding the bedroom of an unmarried woman while she was actually in bed constituted a scandal significantly greater than the rebellion itself. Sarah's father was so angry that he refused to represent Emmet, not even for money. Following his usual way of dealing with all his domestic crises, he kicked Sarah out of the house.

Curran's reaction meant that Emmet had to hire his own defence team. He chose Peter Burrows and Leonard MacNally, the latter being one of Sirr's secret informers. To rescue his rebellion from disaster, Emmet decided to go back to what he was competent at – making speeches. He decided to vindicate his efforts rather than defend them. His trial took place at Green St Court. He refused to offer any defence, though I imagine that a plea of insanity would have had a sympathetic hearing from the judge. Before the death sentence was pronounced, he was invited to speak from the dock. His speech gained international recognition as one of the all-time exceptional speeches from a dock. It is for this, rather than his organisational skills, that Emmet is remembered today. No definitive version of the speech exists; however, we are assured it was an awesome one. Judge Norbury even had to tell him to shut up several times.

On his way to the gallows, Emmet discussed politics and theology with two clergymen. He arrived at 2.00 p.m. at Saint Catherine's Church on Thomas St, where the scaffold had been erected. This was gratuitous torture because we can imagine that Emmet never wanted to see Thomas St, again. The authorities, perhaps fearing a resurgence of his rhetorical powers, only allowed him to say, "My friends, I die in peace and with sentiments of universal love and kindness towards all men." He shook hands with his guards and helped to put the noose around his own neck. But, being back in student mode, he hesitated three times when the hangman asked him if he was ready. Finally, the hangman kicked the plank from under his feet. He was then beheaded and his head shown to the huge crowd. No one knows where he is buried because his relatives were too afraid to claim his body.

Sarah Curran was devastated after Emmet was executed. Homeless, she moved to Cork where she met Captain Robert Henry Sturgeon of the Royal Staff Corps. He would have had colourful fancy uniforms like Emmet. They married in 1805 and travelled together to Italy. Their son died soon after birth, and Sarah herself died in 1808. Her father refused to bury her beside her sister Gertrude, who had fallen out of the window.

The Vincible Invincibles

One of the most sensational trials in nineteenth century Ireland was that of sixteen members of the Irish National Invincibles, who were a secret society of Fenian assassins. This society was a splinter group of the Irish Republican Brotherhood (IRB). The IRB was itself a secret oath-bound organisation whose affiliates were dedicated to the establishment of an independent democratic republic in Ireland. The members of both groups were commonly referred to as Fenians.

In 1883, a number of Invincibles were tried for the infamous Phoenix Park Murders. The previous year, an Invincible, James Carey (1845–1883), had decided to assassinate the Under Secretary of Ireland, Thomas Henry Burke. Carey came up with the idea of using knives as weapons. He imported these from London and hid them in his own house. As Burke walked in the Phoenix Park with the newly appointed Chief Secretary, Lord Frederick Cavendish, Carey identified him to the waiting assassins wielding the knives. They stabbed Burke and Cavendish to death, making

Cavendish surely the unluckiest new arrival in Ireland since Bishop Palladian.[17]

Joseph Brady was first of the accused into the dock. Brady was taken from Kilmainham Gaol by car to Green St Court under heavy armed guard. In a second car, also heavily guarded, was James Carey, who had just become the main witness for the prosecution. Judge William O'Brien, popularly known as "Hatchet Face", presided.

James Carey had joined the IRB in 1861 and took part in the Fenian uprising of 1867. He had inside information on the art of informing because at one time he acted as head of the vigilance committee of the IRB to detect and eliminate informers. He split from the IRB in 1878, disillusioned with infighting and splits. In 1881, he was sworn into the Invincibles.

By January 1883 the police had enough on Carey to arrest him and sixteen others, including his brother Peter, in connection with the murders. Carey's arrest as a leading Invincible caused a public sensation because he was a town councillor. In those days being a councillor meant that he was generally regarded as a virtuous citizen. He was also highly respected for his piety. Carey was persuaded that some of his fellow conspirators were about to spill the beans, so he decided to get in first with the bean spilling. He agreed to inform on the others in return for a reprieve. Carey told the jury at Brady's trial all about the meticulous preparations for the murders. Brady, who was godfather to one of Carey's children, was found guilty and sentenced to death by hanging.

The English hangman William Marwood[18] hanged Joseph Brady at Kilmainham Gaol. The trials of Tim Kelly, Michael

---

[17] See the opening of Chapter 2 – Saints and Sinners of the Irish Tradition – for more details on Palladian's very brief missionary career in Ireland.

[18] Marwood appears at another hanging in Rope for Humanity in Chapter 2.

Fagan and James Fitzharris followed that of Brady. According to Carey, Kelly was active in the murders but the jury were confounded because he was so young and innocent looking. At one time he had sung in the church choir so he was, literally, a choirboy. He had to be tried three times before a jury could be assembled who could agree on his guilt. The night before Marwood hanged him, Kelly sang "The Memory of the Past" in his prison cell. A cousin of the murder victim Mr Burke was a nun, and she came to the gaol to listen to him sing and to comfort the ex-choirboy. It would have been interesting to be a fly on that cell wall.

For Michael Fagan's trial, two journalist artists who could identify him in connection with the murders had to be threatened with twelve months in gaol in order to force them to give evidence. Busy Marwood also hanged Fagan.

James Fitzharris was next into the dock. He was known as "Skin the Goat" because at one stage he owned a fine goat, and, desperate to raise funds for drink, he killed the goat and sold the skin. Fitzharris winked at everyone in the courtroom who caught his eye: witnesses, the judge and members of the jury alike. An English court reporter wrote that he had the appearance of having been "badly battered by contact with a traction engine". He was sentenced to penal servitude for life. Marwood must have been disappointed. He was released after a few years and we learn that he led a saintly life from then on.

Carey came to be regarded with contempt by both his fellow Fenians and the police. His tenants refused to pay their rent and he was removed from Dublin Corporation. He quickly became the most hated man in Ireland. The authorities decided to send him away for his own safety. He was the first Irishman to go into a prototype witness protection programme. These were the early days when the authorities would experiment with aspects of such programmes, often with fatal consequences. He was shipped off to Natal in South-East Africa. He sailed on July 1883 on the *Kilfauns Castle* under the name "James Power".

For disguise, he shaved off his beard. In the evenings he visited the ship's bar and drank with Fenians and ranted against the English while drinking too much. Overall, it was a skillful disguise on his part. He became friendly with a fellow passenger, Patrick O'Donnell, who was a Fenian sympathiser. They met regularly in the bar for a drink and a rant.

At Cape Town in South Africa, O'Donnell was shown a portrait of Carey and immediately recognised him to be his new friend Power. Carey and O'Donnell sailed on together on the *Melrose* to Port Elizabeth in South Africa. When they met in the bar that evening, O'Donnell drew a pistol and shot Carey three times, killing him. O'Donnell was arrested and put on trial in London, out of Marwood's reach. He was executed in Newgate Prison in 1883, not having pleaded insanity. A marble monument was sent from New York to Glasnevin Cemetery in Dublin, where it was erected to his memory.

The Wrong Place at the Right Time

The effective revolutionary knows how to be in the right place at the right time. The ineffectual ones, like Tone, don't. But you can also get into Irish history by being in the wrong rebellion at the right time. This is what happened to the Dublin hack reporter Frank Power (1858–1884), better known to his many friends as Ghazi.

J.B. Hall of the *Freeman's Journal* tells us that Ghazi became historically noteworthy for a short period by being the "one man who, from the lowest rung of the journalistic ladder, became in a few months the most talked of man in the whole world."[19] This was a considerable achievement in an age

---

[19] Hall collected a selection of his (Hall's) journalism in *Random*

before reality television or the internet. Ghazi was a writer, an artist who exhibited at the Royal Hibernian Academy and a linguist. Above all, he was a fantasist *par excellence* whose dreams came true in the most grizzly fashion. A fellow journalist wrote of him, "in the history of journalism, never were so many or exciting tales of military prowess told with so much modest audacity." Unfortunately for Ghazi, his improbable revolutionary imaginings became real.

Ghazi was a penny-a-liner journalist who, when not scribbling for the *Freeman's Journal*, was persuading himself that he had saved the life of Osman Nuri Pasha during the Franco-Russian War[20] of 1877. Pasha was an Ottoman Turkish field marshal. He was also known as Gazi Osman Pasha, where *gazi* means hero, a title he got when he was wounded in hand-to-hand fighting at the Siege of Plevna when the Russians outnumbered the Turks by five to one. Ghazi got his nickname from claiming to have fought beside Pasha. Ghazi told everyone he met that he killed four Russians with his pistol in the act of saving Pasha's life.

On another occasion during the height of the Land League,[21] he made his way into Morrison's Hotel in Dublin to warn the leader of the Irish Parliamentary Party,[22] Charles

---

Records of a Reporter (The Fodhla Printing Company, Dublin 1928). Hall wrote for the *Freeman's Journal*, or the *Journal* as it was popularly called, which was Ireland's oldest nationalist newspaper and was in print from 1763 to 1924.

[20] This conflict was known outside of Ireland as the Russo-Turkish Wars.

[21] The Irish Land League was a nineteenth-century political organisation that campaigned for the transfer of landlords' estates to their tenant farmers who actually worked the land.

[22] Also known as the Home Rule Party, this political party sought to establish an Irish Parliament, as a constituent part of the United Kingdom, to exercise a range of powers devolved to it from Westminster. While Home Rule was a legally complex proposal that

Stewart Parnell (1846–1891), that he was about to be arrested. Ghazi told Parnell that he had heard of the imminent arrest directly from the indiscreet drunken Attorney General, with whom Ghazi believed he had been dining that evening. Parnell was so impressed with Ghazi's information that he went to the offices of the *Freeman's Journal* to consult with the editor Edmund Gray, Ghazi's boss. To both embroider and authenticate his account, Ghazi claimed to have been shot and wounded in the arm while rapidly cycling to get the news to Parnell in his hotel. He rolled up his sleeve in the newspaper offices to show off a bleeding bullet hole in his arm. This wound was identified as a bloody boil by the night watchman "Old King", who may have been working as a "doctor"[23] during the day.

After what we assume must have been a swift kick in the pants from his boss, Ghazi drifted to London where he became a pavement artist. A few weeks later, he turned up in Khartoum, Sudan just before a crisis point in that city's history. Muhammad Ahmad bin Abd Allah had declared a holy war against the Egyptian authorities in Sudan in 1883 and he and his Mahdist Sudanese forces surrounded Khartoum, which was a small British outpost. Just before the siege Ghazi had abandoned Khartoum with General Hicks's army but had to return when he got dysentery. He thus avoided being massacred with Hicks.

Recovering in Khartoum, he found himself in charge of the most perilous political and military situation on the planet at that time because everyone with political or military experience had fled. He was made both the *Times* correspondent and Her Majesty's Consul at Khartoum, a role beyond

---

made many attorneys happy, in the Irish context it usually simply meant independence.

[23] A career in Irish history often involved quotation marks. Being a "doctor" is a recurring historical profession in Ireland.

even his wildest imaginings. He occupied the Government House, pending the arrival of General Gordon's defending forces. He communicated officially with London every day. Despite the siege, transport remained open on the Nile and the telegraph worked, so Ghazi got his vital reports out. He must have been happy despite the threat of massive enemy forces outside the walls.

Every night in Westminster Parliament, Prime Minister Gladstone would provide the House with updates from Ghazi, the consul of Khartoum. Political position papers would be enlivened with accounts of his shooting a thousand "fuzzy-wuzzies" off the walls of the city with his pistol. "Fuzzy-wuzzy" was the nickname given to a member of the Hadendoa tribe, one of Ahmad bin Abd Allah's allies, by British forces in Sudan. It was based on their traditional hairstyle, which was, well, fuzzy. The members of Parliament would anxiously ask, "What does Mr Power say?" and, "What does Mr Power think we should do?" The city eventually fell to the Mahdists on 28 January 1885 when General Gordon was killed fighting to lift the siege. Fuzzy-wuzzies killed Ghazi on the banks of the Nile when his boat hit a rock. I imagine that he died happy, already having reached a fantasist's heaven.

The 1916 Battle for the Biscuits

The IRB organised the next major rebellion in Ireland, the 1916 Rising. This began, as was usual for Irish rebellions, behind schedule – on Easter Monday at midday. Every Irish rebellion demands a split or falling out amongst the rebels before it can properly commence. The 1916 split didn't occur until the last minute. It was a close thing; for a while it seemed there might have been no split, but I imagine the rebels would have delayed until such time as a split had taken place.

In order to offset any impression of unity, the splitters ran a notice in the *Sunday Independent* paper that seemingly countermanded the order for three days of "Easter manoeuvres" that were originally planned for the Sunday. "Easter manoeuvres" was the term chosen as a cover for the Rising. Therefore, many of the rebels went to the annual Easter horse races at Fairyhouse. The rebels who were not actually at the races made their way to their appointed targets or strategic strongholds in Dublin on the Monday. The rebellion got underway just one day late. One platoon of rebels, with their guns and ammunition in tow, boarded a tram into the city. Their officer insisted on buying valid tickets for all those in his charge, because this was to be another conscientious revolution in the style established by Emmet.

The first clashes occurred in the Phoenix Park with a failed attempt to blow up the Magazine Fort. An Irish Citizen Army[24] raiding party then stormed Dublin Castle. On the north side of the city, the rebels seized the Four Courts and the General Post Office. On the south side, the South Dublin Union and St Stephen's Green were taken.

At exactly midday, Major John MacBride (1865–1916), strolling with a cane and smoking a cigar, accompanied Thomas MacDonagh (1878–1916) and his brother John to Jacob's biscuit factory on Bishop St, which was their assigned target. A large crowd of mostly local women, who had gathered to see what was happening, were pushed back at bayonet-point as a rebel force of 150 men and women occupied the factory. The door to the factory was locked so some

---

[24] The Irish Citizen Army was a group organised from trade union volunteers, specifically for the protection of workers from the police during labour demonstrations. It was formed by James Larkin (1876–1947) and Jack White (1879–1946). It took part, along with the Irish Volunteers (a nationalist military organisation) and the IRB, in the 1916 Rising.

rebels climbed in through a window to open the door from the inside. One rebel discharged his shotgun by accident, blasting a hole in the ceiling and almost blowing MacBride's mustache off. MacBride asked the man to be more careful.

The local women outside in the street shouted abuse at the rebels as they marched into the biscuit factory, encouraging them to "Go out and fight the Germans."[25] Some policemen and detectives refused to leave the street, so Thomas MacDonagh thought that it might be necessary to shoot a few of them as proof positive that hostilities had commenced for possession of the biscuit factory.

John MacBride had fought with the Boers in the Irish Commando (brigade) during the Second Boer War (1899–1902). After the war he travelled to Paris and became involved with a group of nationalist ex-patriots who were under the influence of Maud Gonne (1866–1953).[26] He married Maud in 1903, despite advice from everyone he knew not to marry her. At the time she said that she thought she was marrying Ireland. Gonne was soon accusing MacBride of drunkenness, molesting her daughter, cruelty and infidelity. They separated in 1906. During the divorce proceedings he was accused of having been drunk on one occasion during the marriage. This seems petty from someone who, in her own words, had "married Ireland". William Butler Yeats (1865–1939) described him as "a drunken vainglorious lout".

Back in Dublin after his marriage breakdown, MacBride wasn't taken seriously as a rebel until he stumbled by

---

[25] The 1916 Rising took place in the middle of the First World War, 1914–1918, which provided the wider backdrop to events in Ireland.
[26] See A Musing in Chapter 6 for more details on Maud Gonne and her relationship with the poet and playwright William Butler Yeats (1865–1939), who was obsessed with her. Gonne was an English-born Irish revolutionary, feminist and actress. She turned down at least four proposals of marriage from Yeats, so he greatly resented her marrying MacBride.

accident into the 2nd Battalion of Thomas MacDonagh, who appointed him second-in-command of the assault on the biscuit factory.

Thomas MacDonagh had at one time prepared to become a priest, but he had a crisis of faith and became a teacher, poet, writer and revolutionary instead. He changed from Christianity to neo-Platonism, spurning what he considered to be the piety and humourlessness of the Irish language movement with whom he was involved. He became a poet, a career move that was helped along by a thwarted love affair. As a commander of men, he was famous for his congenial humour and indecision. He kept changing his mind and dithering. Such indecision can be stressful for control freaks in a conflict situation. On Easter Monday 1916, his men disobeyed his direct order and fired on a small advance party of British troops, destroying the chance to ambush the main party bringing up the rear and inflict heavy casualties. But most of the time his men drank tea and ate biscuits.

On their first evening in occupation of the factory, a plain-clothes policeman stood outside taking copious notes. This being a civilised revolution, he was politely asked to move away but he refused, so he was fired on and killed.

By now, crowds of spectators were gathering at the various rebel strongholds to watch the rebellion as it unfolded. When the rebels in the biscuit factory made an occasional sortie outside they were often booed and pelted with rubbish by the local women, many of whom had husbands and sons fighting in the British Army against the Germans. For the rest of the time they remained barricaded in the biscuit factory, where they were effectively besieged by the locals. At one stage, when the mob outside was at its worst, an old priest appeared and blessed the walls of the factory, one side at a time. The crowd became silent, joining in the prayers and eventually melting away quietly.

At night all the rebels withdrew into the factory building. While the rebels crowded at the Bishop St entrance to the factory to get through a barricaded door guarded by their comrades, a mob of women would regularly attack them with kitchen utensils, beating them around their heads and knocking their hats off. The mob would then try to break through the door while the frantic rebels squeezed inside. When the rebels sallied out during the day, scuffles broke out between them and the locals. A local man, who wanted a gun to shoot the rebels, was shot while trying to grab a rifle from one of them.

The women of the Coombe threw their arms around the necks of policemen taken prisoner by the rebels, hugging and kissing them to the disgust of both the rebels and the prisoners themselves. Every day, one of the smallest and youngest of the rebels, armed with a shotgun, escorted two huge policemen prisoners to their assigned job, which was to peel spuds for the dinner of the rebel troops.

In the weeks before the Rising, MacDonagh had refined his tactics for the factory with James Connolly (1868–1916), the commander of the Dublin Brigade of the Irish Citizen Army, whom he would meet in the Kevin St public toilets so they could plot rebellion together. Despite this, MacDonagh kept changing his mind about his orders during the week in the factory. He couldn't commit to making a sortie out to relieve his comrades in the many battles raging in the other rebel strongholds around the city. The factory seemed impregnable, if strategically unimportant, so he stayed put.

The bored rebels had formed a book club in the library on the top floor of the factory, which had a glass roof and windows. The book club had a particular interest in quoting military aphorisms from *Julius Caesar*. At one point during the week, a rebel went to the library to get a book to read. A bullet came through a library window while he was browsing for a distracting read, so he retreated downstairs. On another floor, there were piano recitals. To pass the time, a dance was organised and dancing partners were found amongst the women of Cumann na mBan[27] and the Clan na Gael[28] girl scouts. There was a gramophone with a record of "God Save the King". This was played when MacDonagh and MacBride made their tours of inspection.

The rebels became increasingly bored as the week passed. As a distraction, they searched the factory and gorged themselves on tonnes of crystallised fruit and chocolate, and dreamed of plain bread. A Fianna[29] boy ate an entire fruitcake and became so violently sick that his comrades encouraged him to go home to his mother. He refused.

By the weekend the biscuit factory garrison knew that the Rising would soon be over. From the roof they could see the General Post Office burning across the river. But they had resolved to fight to the death. Early on Sunday morning, MacDonagh swore he would never surrender. By 3.00 p.m. he agreed to surrender after the commander of the British forces in Dublin, General Lowe, personally gave him a graphic description of what would happen if he didn't surrender. But they had plenty of food and could hold out for months so maybe they shouldn't surrender. No, they were not surrendering.

---

[27] There is a mesmerising range of republican organisations in Irish history because new ones were springing up all the time, splitting, reforming and merging with others. Some were just for women. Cumann na mBan (the Irish Women's Council) was a republican organisation formed in 1914 as the women's branch of the Irish Volunteers.

[28] Clan na Gael (the Family of the Gaels) was formed in the late nineteenth century in America as the successor to the Fenian Brotherhood – see Beneath the Green Waves in Chapter 5 for details on some of the activities of the Brotherhood.

[29] The Fianna was not another organisation. It is used as another name for the Irish Volunteers.

Then another priest, Father Monaghan, arrived to beg the men in the factory to go home. So they thought that maybe they should surrender. MacDonagh decided to put it to a vote. He promised that he would definitely go with the majority decision, maybe. The debate raged on amongst the rebels. When they eventually decided to surrender, MacDonagh cried, probably having changed his mind again. Widespread weeping, wailing and hysteria amongst the ranks followed. A woman from Cumann na mBan fainted when she received the order to surrender.

Those not in uniform were encouraged to drift away into the crowds outside, but most stayed. At last, the doors opened and, lining up outside, they marched out in formation to surrender. The crowd outside formed a cordon that led to the British forces that were awaiting them. Some rebels blended into the crowd or were pulled in by their mothers and disappeared home with a clout across the ear. However, the officers felt honour-bound to hand themselves over. They were escorted into prison. The leaders of the Rising, with the exception of Constance Georgine Markievicz (1868-1927), Eamonn de Valera (1882-1975) and Thomas Ashe (1885-1917),[30] would be executed by the authorities.

In Kilmainham Gaol awaiting execution, MacBride told a fellow prisoner that he had said three Hail Marys every day since the Boer War that he would not die until he had fought the British again. His prayers had been answered, so he died happy when he was executed the following morning.

---

[30] The reason why Markievicz was not executed is explained in Only Men Go Out with a Bang below. There are several controversial suggestions as to why de Valera was not shot but one plausible reason was the fact that he was an American citizen, which may have saved his life. It is unclear why Ashe was not shot. One theory is that he was amongst the last to be tried and by then the authorities had tired of shooting people. In any case, he died in September of the following year after being force-fed on hunger strike in Mountjoy Gaol.

When stood in front of the firing squad, he refused a blind-fold, stating that he had looked down the barrels of guns all his life.

On 3 May, on the morning of his execution, MacDon-agh came down the stairs to the courtyard of Kilmainham Gaol whistling a tune. The firing squad was so nervous that, according to a witness, they could hardly aim and were waving their guns around "like a field of corn". Yeats, in criticising MacDonagh's poetry, argued that he was just finding his true poetic voice when he was shot.

Meanwhile, while marching a crowd of rank and file rebels down Ormond Quay to be put onto ships and sent to prison in Britain, soldiers pushed a tiny old man sitting on some steps into the group of prisoners and marched him away. He was a Russian sailor just off a boat in the port. He ended up in prison in Knutsford in England, getting himself unexpectedly into Irish history because he was in the wrong place at the wrong time.

Only Men Go Out with a Bang

When it came to shooting women, the British were shame-less sexists. Constance Georgine Markievicz (1868–1927) was one of the many women who took part in the 1916 Rising. Markievicz was the daughter of the explorer Sir Henry Gore-Booth of Lissadell, Co. Sligo. She was born in London and had a privileged upbringing, receiving private tuition at home in the essential rebel syllabus of music, art and poetry. In 1886 she undertook a Grand Tour of Europe with her governess. She was presented to Queen Victoria in 1887.

While studying Art in Paris, she met and married fellow art student Count Dunin-Markievicz in 1900. They had a daughter, Maeve, whom they gave to her grandparents to raise, as you do, while they enjoyed the cultural scene in Dublin. They painted, talked about painting and acted in plays at the Abbey Theatre,[31] which was the thing to do, especially if you had no gift for acting. The Markieviczes separated in 1909.

Markievicz joined Sinn Féin and Inghinidhe na hÉireann[32] in 1908. In 1909 she formed a paramilitary organisation that instructed children in the use of firearms. By 1913 she was a strike advocate in the lockout[33] of that year, and she organised soup kitchens in the Dublin slums. She supported a split within the rebels over the issue of Irish participation in the First World War.

During the Easter 1916 Rising, Markievicz was second-in-command with the rank of colonel at St Stephen's Green park under Michael Mallin (1874–1916), and thereafter at the Royal College of Surgeons when the park had to be abandoned. Markievicz was the only female member of the Irish Citizen Army to wear breeches to the rebellion. In general, she enjoyed wearing uniforms and carrying sidearms.

On their first night in St Stephen's Green, the rebels slept satisfied with having held the park for an entire day. Initially, they had had difficulty persuading the people relaxing in the park that they should get out because they needed it for a revolution. However, thus far this rebellion compared very favourably with Emmet's, which had lasted just two hours. In defence of Emmet, he did set achievable standards for

---

[31] The national theatre founded in 1903 by W.B. Yeats and Lady Augusta Gregory (1852–1932). The theatre's agenda was to invest in and promote Irish writers and artists.

[32] Sinn Féin (We Ourselves) is a republican political party founded in 1905 by Arthur Griffith (1872–1922). Inghinidhe na hÉireann (Daughters of Ireland) was a radical nationalist women's organisation led by Maud Gonne from 1900 until 1914, when it merged with Cumann na mBan.

[33] The Dublin Lockout was an often violent industrial dispute involving 300 employers and 20,000 workers that lasted from August 1913 until January 1914, when the beaten workforce went back to work.

future rebellions. While the rebels were asleep, the British placed a machine gun in the Shelbourne Hotel, which overlooked their positions in the park. In the morning when they awoke to the sound of rapid gunfire, the rebels had to retreat to the nearby Royal College of Surgeons. There they found skeletons and organs in jars under the supervision of the caretaker and his wife. Markievicz had an epiphany during the week amongst the skeletons and converted to Catholicism without the inconvenience of understanding its doctrines.

After a week of heavy fighting, Markievicz surrendered and was confined in Kilmainham Gaol with the other leaders while awaiting sentencing. She was found guilty by a court martial and sentenced to death by firing squad. Her sister Eva was working frantically behind the scenes in Dublin to save her. Her brother Sir Josslyn was working significantly less frantically behind the scenes in London. Her fellow Anglo-Irish aristocrat Lord Powerscourt, who seemed committed to equality, was begging the authorities to shoot her. Her sentence was commuted to penal servitude for life because she was a woman. She told the officer who brought her this verdict, "I wish you had the decency to shoot me." This indelicacy was typical of the meanness of the British authorities of the time. They would never oblige anyone. She was eventually released from prison on general amnesty in 1917.

Markievicz was the first woman ever elected to Westminster Parliament, but she did not take her seat. She was also the first woman in the world to be chosen as a cabinet minister when she became a member of the new Irish Free State Government. Again, she didn't take her seat.

Following periods in gaol, boycotting Parliament and on the run, her health broke down in 1927. She was elected to the Dáil that same year but she died in hospital as a self-declared pauper before she could take up her seat. Her posh

Anglo-Irish connections combined with her being a woman had often caused her republican comrades to distrust her. She knew that they would have to trust her if she was shot. Think how happy she could have been if the British had shot her in 1916. Think how happy some of her posh relatives would have been.

Murder in a Time of War

You might imagine that if you were going to murder people you could do so with impunity during a battle. Who is going to make a fuss about a few extra bodies? But that is not always the case. Apparently, even in the middle of a rebellion you can't just shoot whoever you like. John Colthurst Bowen-Colthurst (1880–1965) discovered this inconvenience during the 1916 Rising.

Bowen-Colthurst, born into landed gentry in Co. Cork, fought on the side of the British Empire in the Second Boer War and was taken prisoner in 1900. He received the Queen's Medal with four clasps for his service to South Africa. He then served in India between 1901 and 1908, taking part in Francis Younghusband's invasion of Tibet in 1904, for which, on this occasion, he received a medal with only one clasp.

In India he underwent a religious conversion, as you do, and became a fanatical Christian. This was before it was fashionable to become a fanatical Buddhist after touring Tibet or India. Except for his religious views, Bowen-Colthurst seems to have been quite sane before the First World War, refusing to shoot fellow Irishmen during the Curragh Mutiny[34] in the summer of 1914. In September of that year, while fighting

---

[34] This was the name given to the mass resignation of commissions by British Army officers stationed in Kildare when apparently ordered to march against Ulster Unionists. The British Government backed

in the First World War, he made a frenzied attack without orders on a German position during the Battle of the Marne. He was wounded in the chest and arm and was beaten back. When he was discharged from hospital he was suffering from "nervous exhaustion", which was the common medical term used in 1914 for being buck mad. He was posted back to a barracks in Ireland, where it was assumed he could do little harm.

During the Easter Rising of 1916 he was back in a frenzy of activity directed at attempting to singlehandedly put down the rebellion. When his barracks came under attack, he sallied forth, firing at silhouettes in windows, believing them to be snipers, and randomly lobbing bombs into shops and buildings. He led a raid on a tobacco shop belonging to J.J. Kelly – who was a Home Ruler and thus most definitely not a rebel – because he believed the shop belonged to Tom Kelly or maybe even Seán T. O'Kelly[35] – who definitely were rebels.

On the way to the raid on the wrong Kelly's shop, Bowen-Colthurst shot dead a man whom he'd stopped outside a church, apparently to ask directions. He lobbed a bomb into Kelly's tobacco shop and took captive two customers who were inside at the time. These customers happened to be journalists. One of the journalists, Patrick McIntyre, wrote for the conservative newspaper *The Searchlight*, and not the rebel paper *The Spark*, as Bowen-Colthurst seemed to believe.

The next morning he ordered the shooting of the two journalists and Francis Sheehy-Skeffington (1878–1916), all of whom were in military custody. The evening before, Sheehy-Skeffington was on his way home from having organised a group to prevent the looting of shops when he was arrested

---

down, claiming the original order had been misinterpreted by the commanding officer.
[35] Seán T. O'Kelly (1882–1966) became the second president of Ireland in 1945.

for crossing a bridge. Okay, maybe Sheehy-Skeffington was asking for it because as well as being a writer, a supporter of women's suffrage and a school friend of James Joyce (1882–1941),[36] he was also a pacifist. He shouldn't have been out and about during a rebellion since he couldn't fight back. Later that day, Bowen-Colthurst shot Labour Councillor Richard O'Carroll, leaving him to die in the street.

At Portobello Barracks, Major Sir Francis Fletcher Vane, Bowen-Colthurst's commanding officer, protested to the barracks commander that Bowen-Colthurst was just not playing cricket with the rebels. Bowen-Colthurst responded by claiming that Vane may himself be a rebel because he had been against the shooting of civilians during the Boer War, and should be shot himself. General Sir John Grenfell Maxwell, in supreme command in Dublin after martial law was declared following the Rising, thought that Bowen-Colthurst was just a "hot-headed Irishman" and should be left alone to play cricket with the locals whatever way he liked. Eventually, Herbert Kitchener[37] himself ordered Bowen-Colthurst's arrest.

He was court-martialed in Dublin in 1916, and found guilty but insane. He was committed to Broadmoor Hospital for the criminally insane. Insanity was a recurring condition amongst the rich in Irish history. While the poor couldn't afford even a diagnosis, a private asylum was *de rigueur* for the insanely rich, with prompt release into the arms of their nervous relatives being common. In Irish history, insanity is a state of social status rather than a state of mind. Witnesses testified that Bowen-Colthurst had tried to falsify evidence

---

[36] For more on Joyce see Sticking with Joyce in Chapter 6.
[37] Herbert Kitchener (1850–1916) was an Irish-born British field marshal who became Secretary of State for War during the First World War. His was the face on the famous British "Wants You" war recruitment poster.

that could have undermined his insanity plea because, according to the M'Naghten Rules[38] on insanity, to qualify as insane you should either be ignorant of the nature of your actions or be unaware that they were wrong. Shell shock was accepted as a legal defence if you were an officer. However, an ordinary soldier claiming shell shock as a defence would naturally be shot because the ranks couldn't suffer from shock – they were too obtuse.

When his family moved Bowen-Colthurst to a private asylum in January 1919 he was soon released as sane, and was encouraged to emigrate to Canada. His family home in Cork was understandably completely destroyed by the IRA in 1920 to prevent him returning home. Obviously, the IRA had little faith in psychiatric medicine at that time.

You Would Have to Be Mad to Rebel

An urbane madman whose name we don't know was detained in the Richmond Lunatic Asylum in Dublin for a single unspecified form of insanity in the late nineteenth century. It was commonly believed that he was a failed revolutionary who wisely played the insanity card in court. This lunatic was an actor before his singular insanity set in. When his former friend and fellow thespian, the most highly regarded Mr Mollison, came to the Gaiety Theatre to perform his famous Hamlet, he begged Dr Connolly Norman, the resident medical superintendent, for temporary release to attend an evening performance.

The doctor relented and three seats were reserved in a box: one for the lunatic and one each for his two minders

---

[38] Daniel M'Naghten gave his name to these tests for insanity, which must have pleased him. He had attempted to assassinate the British Prime Minister in 1843. If you pass the tests you may be found "not guilty by reason of insanity" or "guilty but insane".

from the hospital. While the hamming on stage got under-way, the two minders retired to the theatre bar for a drink. Realising that prices were much higher in the theatre, they retreated down the road to a cheaper pub and settled into the snug for all five acts and twenty scenes of *Hamlet*.

When the final curtain came down and the theatre emptied out after three standing ovations, our lunatic found himself all alone. Just before panic or madness could set in, his minders came staggering through the front doors, completely inebriated. After chastising them, the revolutionary lunatic forced them into a cab and begged them to make an effort to appear sober to prevent them being fired. They reached the safety of the lunatic asylum without further incident.

*

The history of Irish rebellion leaves me with one question – where would we be now if our rebels had heads and our attorneys had hearts?

2

Saints and Sinners of the Irish Tradition

Pity Palladius, the first Christian bishop to come to Ireland. He was fascinated by the subtleties of theological heresy but, when he landed in Ireland, he immediately found himself armpit deep in unsophisticated pagans. Who can blame him for dying on his first day on the job? He probably expired from dismay.

Someone whose name we don't know followed him to Ireland. We can assume that he was also theologically effete because he didn't last long either, and probably died from pagan-related shock. Patrick was the third, and perhaps last, choice because it was clearly time for a lowbrow Christian. Patrick was more robust than Palladius and his anonymous successor. On his own, he managed to convert the lot of us and also banish our snakes.

Patrick (c.420–490?) is our national saint. We know quite a lot about him because he wrote an autobiography called *Confessions* at the end of his life as a defence against his critics. In this opus he tells us about his life as a slave and his undemanding brand of religion, and he bemoans his poor education. He never recovered from his resentment that his studies had been cut short by being kidnapped, which must be one of the better student excuses of all time. He details his escape from Ireland back to his home and his ultimate return to Ireland to convert us. He tells of his disappointment when he initially failed to become a bishop. Patrick also wrote the *Epistole* as an open letter of excommunication against the soldiers of Coroticus, who was either a fearsome Briton warrior or a Roman soldier living in Ireland, who had killed some of Patrick's converts. But there are several significant gaps, or missing years, in Patrick's story.

We do know that Patrick was born in Roman Britain. He came from a comfortable background with land, houses and his own slaves. But during his lifetime, and for centuries afterwards, no one cared about his trip to Ireland because the Western Roman Empire was collapsing under an onslaught of barbarian hordes. Everyone was trying to keep their heads – literally. Not only was Patrick unrecognised in his lifetime, he was also quickly forgotten both inside and outside Ireland shortly after his death. It wasn't until the seventeenth century that he acquired the baroque clothes of a Tridentine bishop. He had to wait until 1727 for his symbol, the shamrock. His feast day of 17 March wasn't included in the Roman Breviary until 1631 and didn't appear in the Revised Roman Calendar until 1632.

Patrick had a really big secret. When he was fifteen, he tells us, he did something extraordinarily appalling that haunted him for the rest of his life. However, annoyingly, he doesn't tell us what it was. It is difficult to guess what this terrible thing could have been, given the standards of the fifth century when running amok with an axe was regarded as light entertainment. It was a lot more than accidentally killing the cat, an awful lot more. His contemporaries knew what it was because he told them, but they wouldn't or couldn't bring themselves to tell us.

Naked Irish pirates kidnapped Patrick from his home in Britain when he was sixteen. In those days, Irish pirates went on raids stark naked so that brambles and branches wouldn't get caught in their clothes and impede their swift movements. They seem to have been indifferent to anything else catching on brambles. Tough men! Patrick thought that he deserved to be hauled away by pirates because of whatever it was he had done the year before. This was the first sign of his Stockholm syndrome.[39] At that time he was indifferent to religion. The experience was traumatic for him, and marked the beginnings of his religious piety.

Patrick was sold to a slave owner near Killala in Co. Mayo. He was put to work as a shepherd. But Patrick was no Spartacus. For six years he was an abjectly submissive and obedient slave. He turned to religion in his crisis and began to pray non-stop. One night a sheep told him, apparently in a dream, that he should prepare to go home, and that a ship was waiting for him in a port 200 miles away. He set off to find a boat loaded with pagan pirates who were willing to take him home. They sailed away together. We learn a fifth-century phrase from him – to "suck someone's nipples", meaning to make friends. He tells us that he was unwilling to suck these pirates' nipples. I don't believe him because after they landed in Gaul he spent some time marauding with these pirates, providing us with yet more evidence of his Stockholm syndrome. He was enslaved again for sixty days before the Lord set him free. He returned home eventually to his parents' house in Britain.

His parents welcomed back a changed Patrick: he had become an obsessive Christian. The Celtic church with which Patrick became more and more involved was less interested in theology and abstract thought than in keeping away from women. At home he had a dream that a man

---

[39] Stockholm syndrome is a psychological phenomenon in which hostages express empathy with, and even develop positive feelings towards, their captors, usually to the point of defending them.

called Victorius brought him letters, asking him to return to Ireland to convert the native pagans to Christianity. Patrick spent the next twenty years training to be a bishop so that he could go back to Ireland to do just that, ignoring his parents' pleas for him to stay.

Patrick's many critics in the British Church, suspicious of his intentions, accused him of being motivated by greed and wanting to fleece the Irish natives, probably in revenge for his kidnapping. Not only that, he also operated without Papal authority. To counter these accusations, Patrick tells us that he actually spent his own money converting Irish pagans. Irish pagan women used to throw their jewellery onto the altar when he was saying Mass, a cultural practice that in later centuries evolved into throwing underwear onto the stage at rock concerts. He tells us that he gave back the jewellery and asked the women to control themselves. Patrick probably toured the country in a tent, like a circus, with a bodyguard of Irish princes that he paid for, again out of his own funds. He claimed divine rather than Papal authority, which theologically made him the first Protestant in Ireland.

The nomadic tribe the Visigoths had sacked Rome in 410, which caused Patrick to believe, or, more likely, fervently hope, that the end of the world was nigh. From his writing we learn that he seemed ready and willing, extremely willing, to suffer martyrdom. But, as we all know, when you want something so badly no one will give it to you.

He died of old age but we don't know when because at the time nobody cared. He may have died in or around 490, and he may be buried in Downpatrick in Co. Down.

Saints of the Irish Tradition

Irish history is crowded, unsurprisingly, with saints of the Irish tradition. In that convention, a person became a saint by converting pagans and opening churches, as opposed to a saint of, for example, the Italian tradition, who would have gained his or her sainthood by being eaten by a lion.

There are loads of saints in Irish history but sainthood had only a relatively narrow window of opportunity between the fifth and seventh centuries. After that you could forget it, unless you were exceptional. Some of the most boring people on Earth were saints precisely because they were allowed to do nothing except pray, build churches and convert the local pagans. For some, like Abbán (d. 520), it was a family business because his brother, Gobnait, was also a saint. I wonder what their parents were like? After Patrick, each county or region in Ireland liked to have its own saint. A candidate would move to a vacancy and found a church, but usually after a stint as a hermit in the local hedge.

The priests and monks liked to nominate just one person as being responsible for converting everyone. They tended not to give historical credit to the extras. Hence, Patrick converted all of us on his own, and Colum Cille converted all the Picts in Scotland in singlehanded retribution.

Saint Colum Cille (521–597) was related to the O'Neill royal dynasty of Ulster. He was tall and handsome with a ferocious temper. When he became a monk, life in the monastery adapted to its noble guest because an angel used to grind the corn for him and do his other chores when it was his turn. He was also a Latin poet, a scholar and a warrior.

His comrades, the soldiers of Ulster, used to have a favourite joke: they would say that they would only fight for their king if a certain man called Donnbo would fight with them. This was funny because Donnbo was known for never leaving his mammy's house. In one of his earlier saintly interventions, Colum Cille promised Donnbo's mammy that nothing would happen to her son if she allowed him to fight the fierce men of Leinster with Ulster's king, Fergal. Colum Cille guaranteed her, as a prospective saint, that he would bring Donnbo home to her safe and sound. Donnbo's mother reluctantly agreed, so Donnbo, King Fergal and the soldiers of Ulster marched off to fight against the men of Leinster, of whom they were actually terrified. Colum Cille, perhaps knowing something the rest of them didn't, chose not to join them on this occasion because he was needed for supervising his angel's chores back at the monastery.

The night before the battle, King Fergal asked Donnbo for a song because he had a considerable reputation as a musician. Donnbo declined because his nerves were at him but he did promise that, come what may, the next night he would sing for his king. The next day, Donnbo, Fergal and 9,000 soldiers of Ulster were slaughtered.

The night after the battle, Murchad, son of the King of Leinster, promised his armour and chariot to anyone who would bring him back a memento from the battlefield. As all the Leinster men were afraid of the dark, a Munster man volunteered to go. When he got there he found Donnbo's head singing songs to King Fergal's headless body because Donnbo was keeping his promise to his king to entertain him, come what may. The Munster man carried Donnbo's head back and set it up on a post in the corner of Murchad's house to provide entertainment. Donnbo sang wild songs and sweet music the likes of which they had never heard before. This was before television was invented.

There is no record of the conversation between Colum Cille and Donnbo's mammy when she discovered that her precious Donnbo's head had been turned into a jukebox.

Colum Cille had to leave Ireland as a penance precisely because of this kind of rash promise-making and inept interference in military affairs and battles. He also had problems with illegal copying of intellectual property. His former master, Finnian, loaned him a Psalter.[40] He copied this

---

[40] A Psalter is a book containing the Book of Psalms. Many were highly illuminated and were objects of great value.

without permission. It was not a simple oversight because this was before the invention of photocopiers. It took months, and sometimes years, to make a copy of a Psalter. But Colum Cille was a fantastic reader and copier of books. He learned Greek in order to talk with the angels because they didn't know either Irish or Latin.

Colum Cille also left Ireland because he needed to get away from his family, an often-ignored reason for the popularity of emigration out of Ireland. He founded a successful monastery on the island of Iona that became one of the most influential monastic settlements in Europe. It was so important that it was the first Irish monastery to be attacked by Vikings, ever, in 795. What an honour! Many of his kinsmen eventually followed him to Iona, becoming abbots in charge of a growing number of monasteries and establishing the Irish tradition of following family members abroad. These relations went on to establish new monasteries in Scotland.

Bridget (439–524) is the female patron saint of Ireland and our first woman bishop. When Bridget's mother became pregnant with her, her father, who was a warrior, sold Bridget's mother to a poet but retained ownership over the unborn child. The poet, in turn, sold the mother to a druid in whose house Bridget was eventually born. The druid kindly sent Bridget back to her father where she became involved with dairying. She had a form of lactose intolerance because she could only drink milk from white cows with red ears. She was also obsessed with fire and was possibly an undiagnosed pyromaniac. She wanted to commit herself to the celibate life, which was an ambition that dismayed her parents.

After many family rows, her father eventually allowed her to become a nun. She immediately established a convent in Kildare. As abbess, she was accorded the status of bishop. This was an accepted role for women until the twelfth century, when there was a collapse in feminist consciousness.

Her convent developed into a "double monastery" of monks and nuns. She invited a local would-be saint, Dál Messin Corb, to become co-bishop with her. We can only imagine the nervous tension amongst the monks with all those nuns around. The silence of the monastery night was regularly broken by the sound of the lash of a whip on flesh as the monks flogged themselves for penance, and perhaps the nuns also just to be sure.

Bridget has a reputation for being especially kind to cows and the poor. She carried out her missionary work from a chariot, performing many miracles including "resolving" an unwanted pregnancy. Sometimes she overdid it with the spells. Once, she gave a man "love water" to give to his wife who had stopped having sex with him. He put the water in his wife's food, drink and bed, as instructed by Bridget. Soon the wife couldn't keep her hands off him. She would chase him everywhere for sex. One morning she woke to find that he had fled from the bed early. She tracked him down the road to the seashore and saw him across the water on a peninsula, where he was trying to hide. She threatened to drown herself if he didn't come back. As he swam ashore, I imagine he was muttering to himself that he would never ask Bridget for help again.

Many things that Bridget made increased in size. For example, she wove the first cloth in Ireland and, when a rich landowner promised he would give her, rent free, the grazing for her cow that her handmade cloak would cover, she spread the cloak on the ground. He should have known better, given the times in which he was living. The cloak just spread and spread, as you might expect.

Saint Brendan the (Not-so-Accurate) Navigator (484–577) was born in Kerry. He is one of the most daredevil saints of the Irish tradition. He had adventuring genes because his family was descended from Niall of the Nine Hostages, who had fought the Romans and was the prime suspect in

Patrick's kidnapping. He wanted to become a soldier like his famous ancestor, but, being the eldest in his family, he was obliged to become a monk and hence a saint. Like many in Ireland, the nuns taught him. A particular nun, Ita, helped him in later life with his voyages. He learned a form of navigation from Bishop Erc, who was also a druid and was therefore familiar with astronomy and mathematics. An angel visited Brendan in a dream to reassure him that he would guide him across the ocean to the paradise of Hy-Brazil and would look after him on his voyages, bringing him, if not his entire crew, safely home again.

Before Brendan, a monk called Mernoke had sailed west off the Irish coast in search of an isolated place where he could be an undisturbed hermit because Ireland was crowded with hermits at that time. Mernoke discovered an island paradise with all the herbs, fruit trees, gold, silver and jewels that a hermit could ever need. A native on the island told Mernoke that Jesus had helped him to find that place. He spent a year and a half there and was so happy that he thought it was just half an hour. We all know what that feels like when we come home from being on holiday. He eventually sailed home and told Brendan, who became insanely jealous. Immediately deciding that he just had to go there too, Brendan chose the twelve best monks in his monastery and set sail in a small boat. This first voyage was a disaster, so he built a larger boat to try again.

Before the second attempt, Brendan fasted for forty days and forty nights. Since Moses, this was the standard unit of miraculous time in Christian thinking; nothing significant, interesting or exciting could happen to a monk, saint or prophet in less than this length of time. Ita, the nun, advised him against using leather sails on the principle that you shouldn't sail into paradise with dead animals on your masts. She also advised him to carry blue sea holly with him as a precaution against scurvy. He took his pet raven for his shoulder, not having yet discovered the parrot. Two more monks begged to go with him when the shipload of holy men was about to set sail. Brendan agreed that they could both come but prophesised that one of them would be genuinely sorry that he did. I assume something horrible happened to that monk, but sadly we have no details.

We know what happened on this voyage because an oral account was handed down verbatim until the tenth century, when it was finally written down. As Brendan would not have expected to reach land in any shorter time frame than forty days and forty nights, regardless of winds and currents, he had provisioned accordingly. Sure enough, after that period sailing, they came to a rocky island. A friendly dog guided them to a house with a table laid for dinner. They ate, drank and slept in the prepared beds. On the next island they saw sheep the size of oxen. An old man told them that it was the land of sheep – perhaps it was New Zealand if Brendan was an even worse navigator than we assume. He told them that if they kept going they would eventually arrive at the Paradise of Birds.

One time, Brendan and his crew mistook a sleeping whale for an island. They landed and lit a fire. Not surprisingly, the whale woke up with near fatal results. This is a true story because not long ago the same thing happened to a crew of Kerry fishermen. They found a shell-encrusted island where an island had never been before, landed on it and lit a fire to make a pot of tea. When the "island" woke up and plunged into the sea, they were nearly drowned. This sort of thing seems to happen to people from Kerry.

On another island Brendan met Paul the Hermit, who had been living in isolation for forty years. During that time an otter was feeding him. They had a conversation about which one of them was holier, each insisting that the other was: "You are the holiest"; "No, you are." There is no record of any discussion about which one of them was crazier.

Brendan and his crew experienced hunger, thirst and terrible hardships before they reached what is now Madeira. They sailed to the Azores and through the Sargasso Sea, where the boat nearly sank with the pull of the seaweed that grows there, before turning for Iceland where they saw volcanoes that they imagined were the gates of hell. From there, they sailed on to Newfoundland, where they became trapped by ice for the winter on a nearby island. They saw hideous monsters with cat-like heads, bronze eyes, fuzzy pelts, boar's tusks and big bellies. This was Brendan's description of a walrus. The terrified monks fled for their lives. After reaching the Bahamas, they finally landed in America at what is now Miami. The voyage had taken seven years, which probably felt like seventy. An old Irish monk, Festivus, who already had been there thirty years, greeted them when they came ashore in Florida.

Florida was filled with exotic birds and plants. A particular bird informed Brendan that once upon a time he and the rest of the birds were all angels in heaven but when their boss, Lucifer, fell out of favour, they fell too, but only into that earthly paradise and not directly into hell. This bird was now serving the Lord in a tree with the other birds. Brendan also met an angel-like Indian who told him that, while it was the Irishman's destiny to cross the mighty ocean and land in America, it was not his fate to go down in history as the person who "discovered" America. This was the price he must pay for his navigational success. Brendan sailed back home to Ireland and Christopher Columbus got the credit 1,000 years later.

In 1492[41] Columbus sailed into Galway Bay seeking Irish help on his way to discover the western passage to Asia. Columbus had learned that Brendan visited lands in this

---

[41] Many people think he came to Galway in 1497 but by then he had already discovered America so why would he still be gathering

direction. Columbus himself wrote an account of an Indian couple who had washed ashore in Galway tied to wreckage. Furthermore, hard driftwood regularly came ashore in Galway. All of these clues together reinforced Columbus's hope of finding a western passage to Asia. Columbus sailed west from Galway with a local Irishman on board. This man was possibly the third European, after Festivus and Brendan, to set foot in the New World because he was the first off Columbus's ship, the *Santa Maria*, when it landed.

Limited Saintly Opportunities

There are countless opportunities for sinning. It is understandable that so many chose the path of wickedness because, as mentioned, it has been practically impossible since the ninth century to become an official saint in the Irish tradition. Since then we've only had Cellach of Armagh (1080–1129) and Laurence O'Toole (1128–1180) in the twelfth century, and Oliver Plunkett (1629–1681) in the seventeenth. But even Plunkett found that the gate to sainthood had long been shut to the Irish, except for those willing to go to extraordinary lengths and emulate the saints of the older Italian tradition. Plunkett was hanged, drawn and quartered. However, even then he wasn't beatified until 1920, and he wasn't officially canonised until 1975 when a berth among the saints in heaven could be found for him.

Perhaps we are just not as saintly as we used to be. Matt Talbot (1856–1925) is our only current hope. While he was alive, no one realised that Matt might be a saint. The undertaker discovered, after Matt dropped dead in a Dublin street, that he had been wearing ropes and chains wound tightly around his body. It was clear he had been wearing them for

---

evidence of a land to the west? Perhaps he returned to the city several times like most contemporary tourists.

years because they were embedded in his flesh. This was a sign that Matt may become a saint.

In his early life Matt was an alcoholic but he swore off drink and swore onto pain. He got his first chain from a "professor of philosophy", Dr Hickey, who advised him to wear it as a penance. Doing bondage penance was fashionable at that time in Ireland. The chain started a series of self-punishments that included binding his limbs with ropes, sleeping on a plank with a wooden block for a pillow, eating little and giving generously to the poor. While not yet a recognised saint, Matt has achieved the status of "venerable", which is an official step on the path to full sainthood.

Sinners of the Irish Tradition

Brendan established the tradition of the travelling Irish saint. But not all Irish saints had a stomach for ocean voyages. Many preferred to keep their feet on solid ground. Andrew was one such saint. He died on pilgrimage to Florence in the ninth century and was buried in an unmarked grave in the convent grounds. The location of his body was eventually forgotten over generations. However, when a beautiful young woman died a few hundred years later, Andrew became alarmed when the nuns unwittingly tried to bury her beside him. He had to rise from his grave to show them that his bones were buried in the place where they were proposing to bury the beautiful, if dead, young woman. The nuns resolved the necrophiliac temptation by digging up Andrew's bones and placing them in an urn in their church. In gratitude for the scandal narrowly avoided, he performed miracles on demand. While alive, he was famous for his austerity, but obviously didn't fully trust himself to resist temptation, so near at hand, after death. For most Irish saints, keeping away from women, dead or alive, was a constant obsession that continued into heaven. Unless, of course, you were one of those relatively rare saints, an Irish woman.

Infamous Sinner-ettes

Thankfully, not every woman recorded in Irish history was a saint. There were a few who dedicated themselves to sin. Mary Ann Duignan (1871–1929) was one such woman. She is arguably Ireland's most successful prostitute, ever. However, how is such a proposition to be demonstrated? What is the approved measure of success: income or number of clients?

In any case, Duignan wanted to be remembered in history as "the most dangerous woman in the world". This was a significant ambition considering her relatively respectable beginnings in Co. Longford, where she was born into a family of small farmers. She endured the stifling restrictions of family life until she was eighteen, when she stole the family's savings of £60 and ran away to America. By 1892, making up for lost opportunities for sinning in her childhood, she had quickly established herself as a prostitute and extortionist in Chicago, and earned herself the gangland name "Chicago May". By 1894 she had moved her crime franchise to New York where she became a leading figure amongst the criminals of the Tenderloin District in Manhattan.

She had three advantages in the pursuit of sin. First, she looked great. She was tall and gorgeous with glorious auburn hair and blue-grey eyes. Second, she was charming and witty, and she radiated a deceptive veneer of innocence. She had perfected a "butter wouldn't melt in her mouth" attitude. Men could not resist her. Third, she had a genius for exploitation. On a typical evening, she drugged her clients before robbing them, throwing their clothes out of the window to a waiting accomplice and leaving them naked to make their embarrassed way home, if or when they regained consciousness. Sometimes she photographed them in compromising poses in which she'd artistically arranged them while they were out cold. Occasionally she got them to write her love letters that she could threaten to show to their wives. On other occasions, she invented an enraged husband of her own who she used to intimidate them. In other words, you could have a truly entertaining night at Chicago May's place.

She moved from city to city throughout North and South America, living an unsaintly life of jewelry, furs and first-class hotels. In 1897 she took a part as a chorus girl in the hit musical *The Belle of New York* as a front for her prostitution and extortion rackets. She claimed to have married a Wild West gunslinger before actually marrying James Sharpe in 1899. But she left him in 1900 and moved to London, which she made her European headquarters of sin.

Being described in police files as "the worst woman in London" delighted her. She was on her way to notoriety. In London she extorted money from aristocrats, politicians and prominent businessmen. International jewel thief and all-round bad boy Eddie Guerin became her lover and extortion partner. In 1901 they burgled the American Express offices in Paris, netting $300,000.[42] Guerin was arrested. Duignan was arrested soon after when she visited him in gaol. It must really have been love or maybe she wanted to know where he had stashed the cash. But she was back on the streets by 1905, either by getting a presidential pardon or by seducing the prison doctor and then blackmailing him; we don't know the exact escape plan that she used. That same year, Guerin escaped from the notorious Devil's Island prison colony[43] by bribing guards with funds that Duignan sent him.

---

[42] About €5.3 million in contemporary currency values.
[43] Devil's Island (Île du Diable) was a notorious island prison used to

Duignan and Guerin were reunited in London but the romance quickly turned violent. Guerin beat Duignan and threatened to throw acid in her face. What's a girl to do but shop him to the London police? But Guerin was free within a year, having beaten a French extradition warrant in court.

Duignan and her new boyfriend, Charlie Smith, tried to gun Guerin down in a London street. Despite emptying a revolver at him, she managed to hit him only in the foot. Perhaps she still loved him, unconsciously.

Following a sensational one-day trial at the Old Bailey, Duignan, flatteringly described as "the most notorious woman in Europe", was convicted of attempted murder and sentenced to fifteen years hard labour in Aylesbury Prison. There she met fellow Irish inmate and woman of historical note, Countess Constance Markievicz (1868–1927),[44] who was an Irish revolutionary, suffragette and socialist.

Duignan was released after ten years and deported to America, now having American citizenship through her marriage to James Sharpe. In any case, we Irish have always liked to send the troublemakers as far away as possible. She returned to prostitution. But her beauty and charm had diminished in gaol, so she found it much harder on the game.

While in gaol in Detroit in 1926, she was persuaded by the celebrated criminologist August Vollmer to write her life story. In her successful illustrated autobiography she described herself as "the most dangerous woman in the world", thereby achieving her life-long ambition. While

---

detain French convicts between 1852 and 1946. Henri Charrière wrote the bestselling *Papillon*, later made into a film with Dustin Hoffman, detailing his successful escape from the island on a raft made from coconuts. A surprising number of Irish people ended up there by breaking the law in a French jurisdiction. Guerin was sent there because he committed his robbery in Paris.

[44] For more on the life and death of Markievicz, see Only Men Go Out with a Bang in Chapter 1.

engaged to marry her old flame and would-be fellow assassin and lousy shot Charlie Smith, whom she had just met again after a separation of twenty years, she tragically died following surgery in 1929. She had been operated on for a gynaecological complication.

Ireland has produced its share of prostitutes whose lives were the stuff of literature. We were forced to read the life of the sourpuss and would-be saint from Dingle, Peig Sayers (1873–1958), in school when we could have been reading the autobiography of another Peig, Margaret Leeson (1727–1797), who was a high-class prostitute. Peig wrote her memoirs when she retired from the game. These memoirs made her a lot of money because many of her clients paid her not to be included.

Her brothels were the go-to places for the who's who of Dublin fashionable society. She was a noted wit. The Lord Lieutenant Charles Manners was one of her clients. One evening at the theatre, when she was asked who she had slept with last, she replied, "Manners, you blackguards." She refused to take on Lord Westmorland as a client because she said that he had treated his first wife badly by flaunting an affair. Not surprisingly, she is regarded as one of Ireland's original feminists.

The Dreaded Anatomists

Traditional Irish charm may be used to lure unsuspecting murder victims into your house. William Burke (1793–1829), born in Co. Tyrone, is one of our most accomplished murderers but is usually described as a "grave robber". This is unfair because he never robbed a grave. He killed people and handed them to the anatomists before they were buried, thereby eliminating the inconvenience of having to dig bodies up. His niche market was the provision of still-warm fresh bodies in the most efficient way possible. In contemporary business parlance, he was in supply chain management.

Burke didn't come to his anatomical innovation easily. He tried several careers before settling on body procurement as his chosen vocation. He was a servant, baker, weaver and labourer. He played in the Donegal Militia Band, where he was regarded as an accomplished flautist. He married Margaret Coleman from Ballina in Co. Mayo. They had two children together. In 1818, following a row with his father-in-law over land, as often happened in Mayo at that time, he left his wife and children and went to Scotland to work on the building of the Union Canal. When the canal was completed, he started a career as a cobbler. Then he met his new girlfriend, Helen McDougal. When they both chanced upon Margaret Hare, who ran a boarding house, she suggested that they move in with herself and her husband, William, to run the boarding house together. Burke and McDougal agreed, and Burke embarked on his penultimate career, lodging-house manager.

In 1827 an old lodger called Donald died in bed in the Hares' lodging house. He owed the Hares £4 for rent. Hare had the brainwave of selling Donald to the local surgeon, Dr Robert Knox, for dissection because, at that time, the market for corpses was buoyant.[45] Burke and Hare got £7 10s[46] for Donald, no questions asked.

---

[45] In the nineteenth century the demand for human cadavers soared with the growth of anatomy demonstrations in medical colleges. In the beginning, demand was met through the use of bodies of executed criminals. However, as demand outstripped supply and criminals couldn't get themselves executed in sufficient numbers, the shortage of corpses discouraged many medical schools from questioning their suppliers too closely. Criminal elements were attracted to this lucrative trade and body snatchers, also known as resurrectionists, resorted to grave robbing to supply the market.

[46] About €450 in contemporary currency values.

Burke and Hare realised that running a lodging house in fact left them in a prime position for bumping people off. They decided to intervene in the natural order of things rather than await the serendipitous demise of more of the guests lodging in their house. To guarantee cashflow, they smothered eleven guests in total, who were attracted by the "no hidden catches" advertising campaign launched by the Burke and Hare syndicate. Burke had a natural advantage in the body-supply business because he was charming and mild-mannered. Those who met him and lived regarded him as friendly. He won the confidence of his potential bodies down in the pub before luring them back to the lodging house.

Burke and Hare smothered five others off-site, including women and children. They smothered "Daft Jamie Wilson", a mentally retarded nineteen-year-old, thereby demonstrating that, even in the nineteenth century, they were equal opportunity murderers.

Smothering was a requirement for selling corpses into the anatomy business because it left no evidence of violence on the bodies: violence might have damaged the vital organs, thus interfering with the value of the dissections. Dr Knox's school of anatomy paid between £8 and £14 a go, depending on the specimen and condition.

Eventually, when Mary Docherty was smothered other lodgers became suspicious, or maybe even sober, on finding her body under a pile of straw. They called the police. As this was before phones, it necessitated the panicked lodgers running down the street together screaming, "Police! Police!" In return for not being prosecuted, Hare agreed to give evidence against Burke and his girlfriend, Helen McDougal. Burke was convicted while McDougal got off.

Burke was hanged in Edinburgh in front of a crowd of 20,000 spectators. The crowd shouted "Burke him! Give him no rope!" referring to his suffocation technique. Thus, a new verb entered the English lexicon – "to burke", meaning to suffocate. For example, you might say,"I am burking in this house. I'm off down the pub to see if I can meet some interesting people."

Alexander Munro, who was Dr Knox's main competition in the anatomy game in Edinburgh, publicly dissected Burke's body in front of a large excited crowd.[47] The authorities felt that it wouldn't be cricket to allow Knox to dissect his own main supply chain manager. Burke's skeleton was put on display in the University of Edinburgh's anatomical museum, where it can still be seen.

The Highway

However, the sin of killing people doesn't mean that you cannot love as the Bible commands. William Crotty (1712–1742) and his wife Mary were the Bonny and Clyde of eighteenth-century Waterford. Theirs is the story of violence, betrayal, blazing blunderbusses and love.

Crotty took up the career of highwayman when he was eighteen, after his father was evicted from their small farm. Sadly, "highwaymanry" is yet another obsolete profession. He hid out with Mary in the Comeragh Mountains in a small cave now known as "Crotty's den". He often strode around the streets of Tipperary, Kilkenny and Waterford armed to the teeth with a blunderbuss, a brace of loaded pistols and a dagger, defying any lawman to confront him. He was a dead shot with either hand. While he enjoyed a Robin Hood reputation amongst the locals, he was also capable of sudden and random outbursts of violence, usually involving

---

[47] Like public hanging, this is yet another one-time popular entertainment no longer available to us. See the section Rope for Humanity at the end of this chapter for an example of the decline in the public nature of hanging.

his blunderbuss. He was a noted dancer and liked to show up unexpectedly at wakes and patterns[48] to dance with the ladies, clinking his way around the dancefloor.

His lieutenant and number two gang member, David Norris, was arrested but released so quickly that Crotty's gang suspected that he gained his freedom by agreeing to spy on Crotty for the local magistrate, Mr Hearn. For his own protection, Norris had himself put back in gaol. But Norris's wife was upset by this, and, wanting her husband home as soon as possible, she betrayed the location of Crotty's hideout to Hearn. The magistrate surprised Crotty when he was climbing out of the den, which was accessible only by rope, and shot him in the mouth. Following an amazing example of musket gunplay, Crotty escaped. He ran directly to Mrs Norris's house for help. She welcomed him in. Having gotten him completely drunk with whiskey and disabling his many guns, she sent for Hearn, who quickly surrounded the house with a troop of soldiers. Despite being drunk and without his full complement of working firearms, a desperate gunfight ensued.

Crotty was eventually taken prisoner and hauled away to Waterford where he was put on trial. Norris was the main witness for the prosecution. When he was found guilty, Crotty asked for a stay of execution until his child was born but this unreasonable request was refused. He was hanged in Waterford on 18 March 1742 and his head was put on a spike outside the gates of the gaol.

Mary, his wife, was inconsolable, and may have drowned herself in grief or been transported to the Colonies. We don't know exactly what happened to her. I like to think she turned up in the dead of night at the Norris's with blunderbusses blazing.

---

[48] The celebration of a saint's feast day was known as a pattern.

Gentleman Pickpocket

Those who were too squeamish to smother or shoot people could pursue the sinful profession of gentleman pickpocket, like Dublin man George Barrington (1755–1804). His vocation began following a schoolyard fistfight. Sensibly, because he was badly losing, he resorted to stabbing his opponent. The headmaster was so upset that he flogged Barrington. Barrington retaliated by stealing ten guineas (£10 10s) from him and a watch from his own sister, before fleeing the school.

Before long, he joined a troupe of unsuccessful actors who encouraged him to steal to support them. This was a time when, rather than waiting tables, out-of-work actors engaged in crime to make ends meet. This was how he discovered his innate talent for pick-pocketing.

From the actors he learned how to disguise himself. His favorite camouflage was to pose as a clergyman. In 1775 in London, he was caught stealing a jeweled snuffbox from a Russian count. He talked his way out of that jam using his native Irish charm. But in 1777 he was sentenced to three years' hard labour in a hulk.[49] He was freed after a year but was soon back inside where he attempted suicide, being too much the gentleman for a hulk.

At last a mysterious posh visitor to the hulk who took pity on him had him liberated. He returned to Dublin and then moved on to Edinburgh, and back again to London to keep ahead of his reputation for crime. But, alas, he had lost his edge. As his best days were behind him, he was soon back in the courts.

---

[49] In the days of sailing ships, old or worn-out ships that had their rigging removed were called "hulks". These were sometimes used as floating prisons where prisoners would serve out their sentences or wait to be transported overseas.

In 1790 he made what his contemporaries regarded as a brilliant speech from the dock in the Old Bailey in London. Practically singlehandedly inventing the discipline of psychology for the occasion, he argued that his crimes occurred despite his own best efforts. But notwithstanding his eloquence, he was transported to New South Wales, Australia. However, while he was on board the transport ship there was a mutiny amongst the prisoners. Luckily, Barrington sided with the captain, who won in the struggle. As a reward he was pardoned in 1792.

He reinvented himself as a "respectable gentleman" and became superintendant of convicts in Parramatta[50] in 1796, and later high constable. He retired in 1800. But in a shocking development, for me anyway, he was declared insane by a commission. He died in 1804. Many disreputable authors cashed in on his fame and numerous dodgy histories were written about him.

Banking

Not all historical sinning involved sex or death. It could involve money. If for some unfathomable reason you couldn't be a prostitute, "grave robber", anatomist or "surgeon", highwayman or gentleman pickpocket, you could try banking, also known by the historical term "swindling". Even back in the nineteenth century, banking was amongst the top career choices of the degenerate.

This is the vocation John Sadlier (1813–1856) chose. Sadlier came from a wealthy Catholic family in Tipperary. He was suited for commerce because one of his ancestors was King Henry VIII's chief butler's accountant. He joined the family law firm in Dublin in 1837. Just two years later he was involved with his uncle in establishing the Tipperary

---

[50] Parramatta is now a suburb of Sydney.

Joint Stock Bank. They soon opened nine branches in Tipperary, Carlow and Kildare.[51] I have no expertise in this area as I am not a banker, but I believe that rapid expansion may be an indication of either unprecedented success or unprecedented failure.

Sadlier rapidly gained full control of the bank's funds. In 1847 he ran for election to Parliament. Through the judicious application of the Tipperary bank's funds to the electorate, he won a seat in Carlow. By 1852 the bank's funds had helped his brother James and his three first cousins to join him in Parliament, becoming what was called the "Papal Brigade". He became a minister in 1853 but was forced to resign when he was found guilty of masterminding a plot to imprison a Tipperary bank customer who had refused to vote for him in the election. "Sadlierian" became a by-word for political corruption. However, political corruption was only a prelude to his banking style.

In 1852 the Tipperary bank became insolvent after Sadlier withdrew £288,000. He had drained the bank with his brother's help to fund a series of disastrous speculations in hemp, sugar and iron, while issuing annual accounts showing that the bank was thriving.

Amongst his many roles, he was chairman of the London and County Joint Stock Bank, where he already had a massive overdraft. He now turned to this bank for more funds. He purchased the Newcastle upon Tyne bank, using the Tipperary bank drafts. He then used the Newcastle bank funds to bolster the Tipperary bank.

He sold 20,000 forged shares in the Royal Swedish Railway Company, of which he was chairman, to his cousin, who barely financially survived the resulting prompt collapse of the railway company. Sadlier also sold forged land deeds,

---

[51] This is an expansion rate to rival that of the great Anglo Irish Bank at the beginning of the twenty-first century.

spent rents from properties that he held in receivership and confiscated marriage settlements held by his solicitor's office. From all these financial gymnastics, I mean instruments,[52] he raised a total investment fund of £1.5 million, and promptly lost it all in one big disastrous speculation.

He committed suicide by drinking prussic acid.[53] Dear, oh dear. I am not a psychologist, but it seems to me that he was either on a deliberate path to self-destruction or didn't actually understand the complexities of the financial instruments and was embarrassed to admit it to his colleagues. Charles Dickens based his character Merdle in *Little Dorrit* on John Sadlier.

Sadlier's family were financially wiped out because they were liable for the bank losses. They were even politically ruined, it was that bad. And, of course, they all fell out with each other in a downward spiral of blame. Sadlier's brother James was declared an outlaw and fled to Switzerland, the home of the banking business, where he was murdered by an unknown thief who tried to steal his gold watch in 1881.

A Professional Heir

For those who couldn't sin by become a banker, highwayman, anatomist or prostitute, there was the ever-popular path of becoming an heir, either by marrying a rich woman or by being a sycophant to a rich relation. Finding a rich wife was often precarious because the object of one's plans, or her rich relations, might violently resist the proposed nuptials, especially if they hoped to inherit her money themselves. Naturally, becoming a professional heir often necessitated murder. Planning a relative's premature death

---

[52] You may, like me, not be familiar with what are called "complex financial instruments". But, as they say in the banking world, there is no need for you to understand these instruments. Just trust them.
[53] Prussic acid is better known as cyanide.

was difficult because there was no formal training available. Because anything could go wrong with one's plans to inherit a fortune, it amounted to a form of gambling. This combination of vices made becoming a professional heir one of the most challenging paths to moral ruin.

Being a gambler alone was a popular form of sinning, with records showing that betting on turkey versus goose road races could be lucrative. John MacNaghten (1722–1761) may have been a gambler and a would-be heir, but he was also, probably, the unluckiest man in Ireland, ever. With such bad luck you might have thought that he would have given up gambling, but apparently that is not the way betting works: there is always the chance your luck will change on the very next bet.

He dropped out of Trinners in 1740 after just one year, setting a pattern for later generations of students. Following a series of failed or short-term positions, including running a poor house and founding one of the first farming societies in Ireland, he decided he had better marry money. He was charming and popular so he had little difficulty in persuading Mary Daniels to marry him in 1752. He even promised her that, once married, he would change his ways and quit gambling. One evening, when returning home to their house in Dublin, some local leg-breakers accosted the devoted couple at their front door. MacNaghten had lost big and the enforcers' employers wanted their money back. Mary, who was heavily pregnant, dropped dead with shock.

Mary's brother, with the same naïveté as his sister, got MacNaghten a job as a revenue collector in Coleraine, Co. Down. This was a great job for someone with a gambling addiction. When he rapidly embezzled £800, his brother-in-law was forced to repay £2,000[54] to forfeit a bond of good conduct on MacNaghten's behaviour.

---

[54] About €88,000 and €220,000 respectively in contemporary currency values.

Short of funds, he decided to marry money again, and succeeded in seducing fifteen-year-old Mary Knox. Going against her parents' explicit wishes, she partially married him. She only read part of the marriage service. This small oversight allowed her family to have the marriage annulled, and to kick MacNaghten out.

He then paid a visit to his childless eighty-two-year-old Uncle Edmund, who was on his deathbed, to see if he could be named his heir. Edmund was so appalled at the prospect that he got up and went in pursuit of a new wife. He married a young woman, fathered two sons, got back into bed twenty years later and died at the grand old age of 102.

After many more scrapes, MacNaghten returned in despair to the pursuit of Mary Knox. He did the only thing he could. With three accomplices he ambushed her coach in an attempt to abduct her in November 1761. Five bullets – not four, three, two or even one, but five bullets – from MacNaghten's gun hit Mary, fatally wounding her where she sat in the coach. He didn't mean to shoot her, at least not before marrying her. He was also wounded.

MacNaghten would have been firing flintlock pistols or muskets. These were highly inaccurate weapons, which would have needed to be individually loaded with powder, shot and wadding, probably by his accomplices, and discharged singly into the coach. A well-trained soldier could average four shots per minute. If we assume there was a five-minute gun battle between MacNaghten and Mary's servants, with his accomplices loading at half-professional speeds, with one accomplice put out of action after two minutes and a second after four, and only MacNaghten firing, this would produce a total of twenty-two shots fired. This would give MacNaghten a hit rate on Mary of one in four. Lucky shooting!

He was arrested and promptly put on trial. He defended himself because, I imagine, he couldn't afford an attorney.

He wasn't accomplished at it because he didn't plead insanity. Instead, he made an impassioned speech that included an appeal for pardon for his accomplices. He failed on all arguments, and was found guilty.

However, he was so popular that none of the locals wanted to build the gallows. But Mary Knox's uncle agreed to build it himself. When he finally climbed onto the home-made gallows, MacNaghten jumped with such enthusiasm that the rope around his neck broke, and he landed on the ground alive and well. He could have run away or pleaded for clemency on the grounds that at last his luck had changed. But, no, he said he didn't want to be known to history as "half-hanged MacNaghten", so he climbed back up on the gallows with a new rope and jumped again. This time the rope worked.

Perhaps Mary Knox's relatives first got the moniker into circulation, but we now know him as "half-hanged MacNaghten".

Landlording

A traditional way to be a rotter in Irish history was to be an evicting landlord who threw his poor tenants onto the roadside. Better still, if you were a nineteenth-century landlord you could have made yourself a justice of the peace and impose the law yourself. Ah, what a life! However, Colonel Saunderson, an Irish landlord, describing the disadvantages of that profession, said, "If we reside on our properties, we are shot, and if we go out of range we are called absentees."

Adolphus Cooke (1792–1876) was the illegitimate son of a landlord, Robert Cooke, and an unknown servant. Becoming an eccentric landlord was a traditional career move in these circumstances. As a landlord he proved to be mad maybe because he couldn't distinguish himself as being notoriously bad. First, he joined the army because that was an established training ground for a considerable number of eccentrics. In 1835, when Robert Cooke died, his two legitimate sons having predeceased him, Adolphus Cooke inherited the estate in Cookesborough, Co. Westmeath. At last, he could give full reign to his idiosyncrasies as a landlord.

The army had taught him the virtue of discipline, so he drilled his tenants like soldiers in the mornings. He threw them off the land if they lost any of the tools that he gave them. He passionately hated children. He once gave a beggar £5[55] because he was childless, and complained bitterly that a father of twelve children was extremely "naughty".

But, as a landlord, he wasn't all bad. He loved animals, if not children and people. He believed that the animals on his estate were the reincarnations of his own relatives. When a bullock was drowning in the river, he herded the other bullocks onto the riverbank to make them observe a lesson in water safety. He fought a bull that attacked him, waving a red coat as a cape and brandishing a sword like a Spanish bullfighter. When the bull was just about to gore him to death, a maid rescued him. Naturally, being eccentric, he fired her as a reward for her bravery. She should have known better.

Cooke came to believe that the turkey cock on his estate was his reincarnated father, Robert. Therefore, this turkey had to be treated with enormous respect. He became frustrated by the disobedience of his dog Gusty, and became so exasperated that he eventually put the dog on trial in front of a jury of sycophantic tenants. Reluctantly, they found the dog guilty, and Gusty was condemned to be hanged by Cooke in the guise of a judge. But no one amongst the tenants would volunteer to carry out the sentence. A local sage called "The Bug Mee" eventually agreed to do it. He dragged poor Gusty away to the dog gallows. Minutes

---

[55] About €350 in contemporary currency values.

later he came back with Gusty still alive and wagging his tail, claiming that the turkey intervened on the dog's behalf, begging for clemency. The Bug Mee got the cushy job of looking after the turkey and Gusty for the rest of their lives.

When Cooke died, the local attorneys were delighted to discover that he had made three different wills. One will bequeathed everything to Dr Wellington Purdon, who had been subsequently disinherited for fox-hunting on the land, killing several of Cooke's own relatives in the process. Purdon sued Edward Pakenham, another claimant to Cooke's estate, arguing that Cooke was mad. However, the court found that Cooke was "not insane". They didn't find him sane; just not insane – an entirely different conclusion. Normal insanity, as then understood, usually involved killing someone. Cooke hadn't achieved that distinction.

John Rutter Carden (1811–1866) was a landlord who was generous to those tenants who blindly obeyed his will but merciless to those who didn't. In other words, he was a control freak. He was called "The Woodcock" because he was shot at so often by the local peasantry but was never hit.

On one occasion, he was waylaid by two of his tenants near Nenagh. These two were absolutely determined to actually shoot him dead at close range. He knocked one of them unconscious with his riding whip, and chased and captured the other. He hauled them both off to Nenagh Gaol, where they were hanged. The locals, who had had enough, descended on his castle with pitchforks and burning brands, establishing the standard template for future mob-inflicted house sieges in *Hammer House of Horror* films. When the rabble surrounded his castle he got on the roof with a grapeshot-filled swivel gun. Unsurprisingly, the peasants instantly panicked and fled.

In 1854 he became the High Sheriff, making himself both the law and the outlaw. He then began his career as an obsessive lover, setting exceptionally high standards for posterity in the art of stalking. Like many stalkers, he did not present an outward demeanour that suggested a struggle to conceal an immense capacity for love.

Carden fell insanely in love with Eleanor Arbuthnot, who was a posh English woman living near Clonmel, Co. Tipperary. He followed her everywhere and asked her relatives for her hand in marriage. When they rejected him, he decided that he and Eleanor should elope together. He wrote to Eleanor, laying out his plans. She refused to run away with him. In the most appropriate lady-like terms, she informed him that, while she was flattered by his attentions etcetera, he should leave her alone and cease and desist bothering her.

Naturally, because not every single word in the correspondence was actually negative or threatening, and she had, after all, used definite and indefinite articles, he decided that she really loved him but just didn't realise it. To help her to full consciousness of her repressed feelings, he decided to kidnap her while she was travelling home from church in her carriage. He knew that as soon as she was in his kidnapping arms she would realise how much she really loved him.

He convinced six servants to help him by persuading them that she did actually love him. It is more likely they were obeying him out of their long-established terror of him, which he interpreted as affection. With his servants in tow, he attacked her carriage with pistols, lengths of rope for tying her up and two bottles of chloroform just in case she temporarily forgot her real affection for him. He was meticulous in his planning. He had laid on a relay of horses to carry the happy united lovers from Tipperary to Galway, where he had a steamer waiting to take them to London. He invested over £7,000[56] in the enterprise.

Eleanor, along with her sister and their own lackeys in the carriage, fought Carden and his six servants to a standstill.

---

[56] Approximately €500,000 in contemporary currency values.

Carden was arrested and found guilty of attempted abduction. He was sentenced to two years' hard labour in Clonmel Gaol. However, his mates, the magistrates, begged him to stop stalking Eleanor. They promised to let him out of gaol early, say after an hour, if he agreed to desist in his attentions. However he refused, so he served the full two years.

When he got out he went to India for a break but returned early to recommence the stalking. He followed Eleanor to Dublin and London before being arrested again in Kingstown, now Dún Laoghaire, for plotting another kidnap. This time he had to put up securities to stay out of gaol.

Given the times he lived in, he had to write a pamphlet publically explaining his behaviour – that is, that Eleanor didn't realise that she really loved him, and if it wasn't for her interfering relatives the two of them could be blissfully happy together for ever and ever.

Neither he nor Eleanor ever married, proving to him that he was right all along – that she did in fact love him and no one else would do.

Sinning in Name

Surnames only came into general use in Ireland in the eleventh century. Before then we had forenames followed by the name of a better-known family member or a place associated with a particular person. Thus, we have Gormlaith, daughter of Flann Sinna, or Finbarr of Cork, who was a saint. Having a long name will help you be remembered in history, either as a saint or a sinner. Being called Sir William Pierce Ashe A'Court, Baron Heytesbury is better than Ed Ball, milkman. However, being called Ed Ball, milkman, international explorer, pianist, trapeze artist, Trapist monk and leader of men is a step in the right historical direction. Reginald Thomas Amesley Ball-Acton is noteworthy because he was killed at Ypres in 1916. It was rare for long-named people to be killed in the First World War because they usually remained behind the lines sipping cognac, which was one of the few roles in that war demanding extensive military experience. He must have wandered into a trench by accident while looking for his drinks cabinet.

There is an actual Ed Ball (1916–1987) in Irish history who had a longer version of his name, Edward Francis Allen Preston Ball, and an unsympathetic mother whom he just had to kill. Because Edward Francis Allen Preston Ball, or let's call him Ed, couldn't find a job, he lived at home with his separated mother in Dublin. We can only guess why his mother was separated; perhaps it was because Ed was living at home. However, in this he was quite normal for an Irish son. He found job satisfaction in unpaid walk-on parts in plays at the Gate Theatre.

On 17 February 1936 his mother, not appreciating his thespian potential, refused to give him £60 to go on a foreign tour with the Gate Theatre, so he did the only thing that he could do – he split her head open with an axe and dumped her body in the sea. After a six-day trial the following May, he was found guilty but insane, and was detained indefinitely in the Central Criminal Lunatic Asylum, where he was visited by some of his friends from the theatre. He was eventually released and went abroad as he had originally wanted.

One of my favourite names for a sinner in Irish history is Clotworthy Skeffington (1743–1805). He fell off his horse in 1757 and landed on his head. The rest, as they say, is history. The bump had unpredictable moral consequences. While on his mandatory Grand Tour of Europe, he decided to settle down in Paris, where he ran up debts of £30,000[57] through what was called fashionable living – womanising, gambling and investing in a scheme to import salt from Africa, as

---

[57] About €3 million in contemporary currency values.

you do. While he had an annual income from his estates of £5,000, he chose to avail of a French law that allowed him to go to gaol for twenty-five years in lieu of paying his debts. He settled down to life in the Hôtel de la Force gaol. He met a woman and married her in gaol in 1787. She failed to bust him out twice before finally hiring a mob of peasants to break him out in 1789, the year the French Revolution began. One advantage of the French Revolution was the ready availability of peasant mobs.

Clotworthy was back in debtors' prison in London by 1793, having separated from his gaolbird wife. His new girl-friend, Elizabeth Blackburn, moved into gaol with him. He was soon out again because his debts were deemed to be fraudulent. But he was back in again in 1796. He was eventually released when he was persuaded to place his estate in trust.

Back home in Antrim, he had to beat off a different mob of peasants who attacked his castle in 1798. You need to be careful with peasant mobs. They are notoriously difficult to control and can go either way. Indeed, that may be a reason for their waning popularity.

Murder Mystery

There are disappointingly few real-life murder mysteries in Irish history because, fortunately, the authorities were resourceful at finding suitable culprits for the crimes, innocent or guilty. However, William Bourke Kirwan (c.1814–1880?) is at the centre of a still unresolved mystery.

Kirwan studied art, becoming an accomplished miniaturist. He exhibited at the Royal Hibernian Academy between 1836 and 1846. Like many people in Irish history he was a multitasker because he also worked as a picture cleaner, anatomical illustrator and property speculator. This kind of occupational combination is familiar to us from the Celtic

Tiger era in Ireland when everyone could include property speculator in their curriculum vitae. He married Maria Crowe in 1840, and they lived together in Merrion St, Dublin. They had no children. However, William had eight children with his mistress, Maria Kenny. He divided his time evenly between living at home with Maria-the-wife and with Maria-the-mistress and the children in Sandymount.

In June 1852 Kirwin and his wife went to Howth on a painting holiday from where they made regular visits to Ireland's Eye island off the coast. He sketched while she bathed. On 6 September, when the boatman returned to pick them up, Kirwin told him that Maria-the-wife was missing. A search followed and Maria-the-wife's body was found laid out on a wet sheet at an area called Long Hole. The coroner returned a verdict of accidental drowning. It seemed that Kirwin was in the clear.

However, shortly after the verdict, Kirwin moved Maria-the-mistress and the children into his house in Merrion St. When the landlady of the holiday lodgings at Howth heard about the new domestic arrangements, she called the police, which was the principal pastime amongst seaside landladies. She told the police that she had overheard Kirwin threaten his wife while they were staying in her lodgings. Overhearing threats was the second most common hobby amongst seaside landladies.

Meanwhile, witnesses in Howth came forward to testify that they could hear screaming from Ireland's Eye on 6 September, the day Maria-the-wife died. The police yielded to the mounting indignation of the people of Howth and ordered for the body to be exhumed. An autopsy revealed that Maria-the-wife had died of asphyxiation, and not drowning, so Kirwin went on trial for murder in December 1852.

Isaac Butt (1813–1879) defended him. Kirwin's choice of attorney may have been a mistake because Butt was never motivated by money and, therefore, could not have been a real attorney. He was a distinguished lawyer but he lived in relative poverty because he had principles. He took on causes rather than lengthy litigations. His mind wasn't fully on the law because he was also a writer, pamphleteer, translator, historian and journalist, as well as a politician. He failed to take himself seriously as a barrister, scholar or popular politician. His obituary in the *Times* read, "He mocked and trifled with Fortune when she was in her most gracious mood and turned his back upon her richest gifts."

As Butt was such an unconvincing attorney anyway he might have argued for additions to the M'Naghten Rules[58] on insanity and claimed that his client, Kirwan, was insane on two novel grounds: first, that Kirwin had moved Maria-the-mistress and her eight children into the house with him and, second, that Kirwan had hired him, Butt, to defend him. However, Butt did argue that Kirwin had no motive because Maria-the-wife already knew about Maria-the-mistress. He told the court that Maria-the-wife most likely died from a fit because she was epileptic.

Despite this, Kirwin was found guilty and sentenced to death. But new evidence was produced at the last minute. It was proven to be impossible to hear screams from Ireland's Eye in Howth, so, shockingly, the witnesses must have been lying or imagining things. Furthermore, proof was offered that Maria-the-wife did in fact suffer from epileptic fits. Based on this timely overwhelming evidence of the absence of evidence against Kirwin, his sentence was commuted to life in prison. Phew! He must have been relieved.

He was eventually released in 1879, having served twenty-seven years. He was ordered to emigrate to America. He joined Maria-the-mistress and his children there, but he died soon after.

---

[58] These rules are discussed in Murder in a Time of War in Chapter 1.

However, did he do it? Those who, at the time, were convinced of Kirwan's guilt found the circumstantial case against Kirwin damning: he was Protestant and Maria-the-wife Catholic. But being innocent or guilty is legally irrelevant in the history of Irish justice. Pleading innocence is a naive defence against being hanged or sentenced to life in prison. You would do far better by pleading insanity.

Rope for Humanity

Hanging is a form of public entertainment that has gone out of fashion. In the nineteenth century, a journalist with the *Freeman's Journal*, J.B. Hall, attended a hanging so that he could bring the details to a wider audience. Even by then hangings had moved indoors, thereby depriving the citizenry of a popular free distraction, such as that provided by the execution of Robert Emmet (see Chapter 1).

Hall gives us an account of the execution of twenty-year-old Patrick Walsh in Galway Gaol. Walsh, by the laws of probability operating at executions at that time, was innocent. Not that being innocent was relevant. However, Hall seemed to think it was important to mention it, just in case anyone was curious about such an abstract legal concept.

Walsh was accused of taking part in the Letterfrack murders in which John and Martin Lydon were killed.[59] It

---

[59] The Letterfrack murders remain shrouded in mystery. From the vague reports in the *Irish Times* in 1882, it is difficult to unravel the facts. John Lydon and his son Martin were attacked at their home in April 1881. Seven or eight men were involved. The two were dragged outside and shot. John died immediately but Martin lived long enough, according to his mother, to supposedly identify one of the killers as Patrick Walsh. But, while dying after the assault, Martin Lydon swore a deposition that he couldn't identify his assassins. However, Patrick Walsh was twice put on trial. While his defence team argued that Lydon had been unable to identify his attacker,

seems that he was found guilty on the testimony of those who had actually murdered Lydon. Both the testimony and the verdict were regarded as wildly inconsistent, even for trials at that time. However, Walsh was convicted and Judge Lawson sentenced him to be hanged on the morning of 22 September 1881. A popular call for a reprieve was refused. Calls for reprieves became more popular after executions were moved inside because the public no longer saw an advantage for themselves in a hanging. Hall hoped that he wouldn't be allowed in to witness the execution for his readership, but thankfully he was.

A scaffold had been erected in the middle of the prison courtyard. A crowd could be heard praying outside the walls, or perhaps they were merely muttering that they couldn't see anything. When a bell sounded, the condemned man emerged through a door, accompanied by a priest and two warders. Walsh mounted the scaffold and the hangman tightened a leather strap across his arms. The priest recited the litany and Walsh delivered the responses with increasingly intense devotion.

Walsh forgave those who had falsely testified against him. Then the hangman strapped his knees, placed a white cap over his head, drew the rope tight around his neck and pulled the lever. Hall fainted.

When he recovered he was asked if he would like to meet the executioner for a chat. He found him inside eating

---

John Lydon's wife contributed damning hearsay evidence of Martin's dying testimony. Other witnesses, who were popularly believed to be the real culprits, changed their evidence about Patrick Walsh's dress in what seemed like an afterthought to clinch a conviction. There was definitely reasonable doubt, as having to stage two trials proves. A leading witness for the prosecution, Constable Kavanagh, was subsequently shot dead outside Letterfrack Barracks in February 1882. Walsh's brother Michael was also sentenced to death for the murder but that sentence was commuted to penal servitude.

a breakfast of bacon and eggs. On the floor beside him was a bag holding a rope. The executioner told the assembled pressmen that this rope, which was one of his own inventions, had special humanitarian properties. Before leaving for his next assignment he gave each man his card – "William Marwood, Executioner, Horncastle". He was a busy hangman.[60]

*

From looking at crime and punishment in Irish history, it seems that the only guaranteed way to avoid a rope around your neck was to be an attorney. It was more rewarding by far than sainthood, and the easiest form of sinning.

---

[60] For more on Marwood's work see The Vincible Invincibles in Chapter 1.

3

Glorious Irish Men and Women of the Battlefield: When It's Not Good to Talk

Certain people in Irish history seem to have been washed along by a tide of events dictated by good or bad luck. Luck seems to play a particularly major part in the life of a soldier. But a soldier couldn't be lucky (or unlucky) without a glorious war. Luckily for our Irish soldiers, there never seemed to be a shortage of wars they could fight in.

High Kings

Brian Boru (c.941–1014) is Ireland's best-known warrior king because he understood the value of publicity. Boru was born sometime in the middle of the tenth century. Back then the main news headline items were death notices and battle results, and not the dates of birth of people who might or might not influence the outcome of future battles. The ancient sources guess that he was born in 941.

Boru controlled the Church, which at the time was the principal author of public image. The tenth-century monastery was the spin centre of its time. Like Elvis, Brian Boru's best career move by far was his death in 1014, at the sharp end of a Viking axe. But this wasn't any ordinary head splitting, which were quite common at that time. He contrived to have his skull divided in two while he was praying, thus elevating him to the status of saintly martyr.

Boru was particularly interested in spin because he was a parvenu on the kingly scene in Ireland. Like all rising stars, he was insecure. His dynasty, the Dál Cais, had only begun with his father. Boru's older brother actually succeeded to the kinship of Cashel, and thus Munster,[61] in 951. Happily, his brother was murdered in 976, allowing Boru to take over. The first thing he did was revenge his brother's murder, thereby establishing his reputation with his own clan, who would have expected him to demonstrate outrage if he couldn't manage an actual show of grief. His prestige quickly eclipsed that of his dead brother.

Boru had a genius for dynastic marriages. At different times, he married into the leading royal families on the island. Again, fortunately for him, he was able to marry four different provincial princesses because all of his wives obligingly predeceased him. When his fourth wife died, surprisingly, he didn't marry again. Perhaps he had exhausted the supply of princesses or the remaining ones felt being married to him was too dangerous. But Boru had daughters to marry off.

One daughter married the king of the O'Neills in Ulster. Another daughter married Sitric Silkbeard, King of Dublin. Sitric was the son of one of Brian's own wives, making him both his stepson and son-in-law. The next daughter married the son of the man who murdered Boru's brother. But Boru

---

[61] In the tenth century, Ireland was divided into six centres of power. These were the five provinces of Ulster, Leinster, Connaught, Munster and Meath, which comprised parts of Leinster and Ulster. The sixth was the mainly Norse or Viking Dublin.

killed his brother's murderer in battle in 978. This probably didn't endear him to that particular son-in-law. In any case, this was a time before the discovery of family affection.

Along with his innate marital skills, Boru also had some martial abilities. He carried out the standard raids of the time that obliged him to slaughter men, women, children and animals. He also established his authority by regularly touring the country. He never allowed serial defeats in raids and battles to undermine his determination to go down in history as our greatest soldier king. Though handy with a sword or an axe, he was probably an even better administrator than a warrior. While ruling with an iron fist, or axe, he was one of the first Irish kings actually able to delegate. He broke with the Irish tradition of direct control-freak monarchy.

As Boru had lived by the axe, and administration, so he was determined to die by the careful administration of an axe. In 1014 he marched against the Vikings to his career-defining moment at the Battle of Clontarf. This manouvre was in aid of accessing the lucrative trading networks in Dublin. According to his image makers, Brian's son Murchad from his first marriage, with whom he didn't get on, took responsibility for the fight while Brian retreated to a tent to pray with his back to the open flap.

The monks, whom he hired for 20 ounces of gold to produce his myth, portrayed this battle as the ultimate showdown between evil heathen Vikings on the one side and, on the other, delightful Irish soldiers forced to kill only in defence of an unambiguously noble cause. This account was only completed in the twelfth century because the monks were slow to get the message out, probably because they had to illuminate each page with elaborate and price-less illustrations. In their version, the Vikings were assigned the role of the invincible despicable pagans, while Boru's Irish side were rightly described as being nice: certainly too courteous to be appreciated by the gauche Norsemen.

Both Murchad and his son were killed in battle, but the friendly Irish won the day. However, a stray Viking sneaked up behind Brian while he was praying. He split Brian's devout head in two because he was such an especially nasty Viking. This act exposed the Vikings for what they were: really impolite people.

However, I wouldn't be surprised to learn that this Viking was actually one of Brian's own spin monks in disguise who was stage managing the battle, because, in order to succeed in terms of public relations, Brian had to die. Thus, Brian became an instant royal martyr, saintly ruler and a tragic loss. It was probably one of the most successful image management exercises in Irish history, and a credit to the monks who did everything with just quill and parchment and without social media technology. They did such an outstanding job that I believe them.

The obituary written by the monks after the Battle of Clontarf described Brian Boru as the "over-king of the Irish of Ireland, and of the foreigners, and of the Britons, the Augustus of the whole of north-west Europe". He is also described as the Emperor of Scotland. Not bad for 20 ounces of gold.

A Model Army

What counts in Irish history as "visiting" often involved a violent reluctance on the part of the guest to leave the country when the hospitality was exhausted. This is how, for example, Oliver Cromwell qualifies to feature as a "guest" in Irish history. He was over here bashing us on our heads, meaning that he was not at home in England bashing his countrymen on theirs. What if Oliver Cromwell had fallen in love with a young Irish lass, or lad? Would things be different now? Would there be a portrait of him in every Irish home with a candle burning under it? But it seems he didn't really like us. I don't think he liked anyone.

In 1649, Oliver Cromwell brought his New Model Army[62] to Ireland. This army was the only law-abiding entity in the country at that time. The New Model Army in Dublin seems to have been – literally – a model army. When not actually killing each other, the life of the soldier was more regulated than any other in history. By the middle of the seventeenth century, most European armies had developed a compre-hensive body of law to maintain discipline and ensure justice in the army's dealing with civilian populations. This martial law was usually read out to the soldiers on a weekly basis. Obviously, many didn't pay attention. Courts-martial in Cromwell's army consisted of all the officers of the rank of ensign or higher sitting as a court. There was no quorum but officers were regularly fined or reprimanded for not attending.

Captain Sanchey, who was late into court on Wednesday, 11 February 1651, had his excuses rejected and was fined 5s.[63] that had to be paid there and then. On another occasion, 24 December 1652, Captain William Sands was fined 2s. 6d. for leaving court without permission. That fine was to be passed on to the poorest soldier under his command. Sands probably left court because he was bored or busy, since it

---

[62] The New Model Army of England was formed in 1645 by the Parliamentarians in the English Civil Wars. It was comprised of full-time professionals rather than the more usual part-time militia. Its leaders were prohibited from taking seats in Parliament, which encouraged a separation between them and the political and religious factions among the Parliamentarians. The army's generals could rely both on its internal discipline and its religious zeal to maintain a dictatorial rule. In the end it went out of control, ultimately overthrowing Parliament as well as the King, and enforcing a Commonwealth by direct military rule. The English were almost as happy as the Irish to see the end of Cromwell and his newfangled army.

[63] About €23 in contemporary currency values.

was Christmas Eve and the court was only hearing the usual cases of drinking, swearing, "drinking lewd healths"[64] and uttering scurrilous speeches; predictable punishments were death, whippings and, perhaps the worst, wearing a sign around your neck that read "Drinking Health", or in our terms, making toasts.

Common offences that came before the courts-martial included cursing, which was punishable by a fine; communicating with the enemy or surrendering a town, castle or fort without cause, which were punishable by death; striking an officer or drawing a sword on an officer, which were both punishable by death; mutinous assemblies – death; murder, theft and robbery (to a value above 12d.), rape, "unnaturall abuses" – death; failing to report for duty fully armed – severe reprimand; selling, losing, pawning or gambling away your weapons were punishable by imprisonment or by a sentence at the discretion of the court; extorting food or money from the locals, or stealing a plough horse, livestock or other goods from the locals – death; wandering away or straggling behind the column – death; wandering over a mile away from camp without permission – death; drawing a sword without an order – death; abusing or frightening the landlord of a pub or hostel – death; burning a house or barn – death; spoiling crops or ships that might be of use to the army – death; charging the enemy and retreating "before they come to handy-strokes" was punishable by death to every tenth man with the rest being demoted; failing to report discontented mutinous types amongst the ranks or failing to prevent "private fights" – death; drunkenness, disorder in army quarters or defrauding soldiers of

---

[64] Nowadays these are called drinking toasts. While it is now common practice to use a toast to praise someone, back then they were often opportunities to make vulgar comments in public on unpopular officers, and their wives and daughters.

pay led to the perpetrator being cashiered or thrown out of the army, which was the worst imaginable outcome for those many officers with no imaginations; and embezzling victuals or ammunition – death.

The courts-martial had a pleasing range of penalties. Riding the wooden horse was a punishment designed to be extremely uncomfortable on the nether regions. The wooden horse consisted of a plank positioned on its side and supported by a frame. The edge of the plank could be rounded or sharpened, depending on how kind the person supervising the punishment was. The plank was just high enough that the feet of the punished could not touch the ground. Weights could be tied to the heels to increase discomfort. Sometimes the soldier also had to wear cans around his neck, especially in offences involving drink. A soldier could reasonably predict if he was likely to be sentenced to the wooden horse. The sensible defendant would appear in court having padded his trousers in preparation. However, we know the Cromwellians were perverse puritans, so it is probable that when a soldier arrived in court with a voluminous arse, he would be given an alternative punishment such as having his heels tied to his neck for an hour.

Another punishment was to run the gauntlet, which involved running between two lines of soldiers from your own company who would beat you with cudgels. It was always wise to try to be on good terms with your comrades in the hope that they wouldn't hit you too hard. Of course, you might not want to brain your comrade when it was his turn because you never knew the day when you would be running the gauntlet yourself. Sometimes, for added interest, you might be made run the gauntlet with your hands tied behind your back.

A popular punishment was to wear a sign around your neck in a public place, detailing your offence. Unfortunately, the signage usually came with a combination of other punishments. You might be tied to the gallows with a noose around your neck, standing on tiptoe for a few hours to prevent strangulation. You might have cold water poured down your sleeves for being drunk. This happened to Edward Sparrow on 3 January 1652. He had a quart of cold water poured down each sleeve after a notable drinking session. I imagine Edward wasn't appealing the sentence because he got off relatively lightly. For swearing you might have had your tongue bored through with a red-hot iron, after it was pulled out with a pliers.

There were also sentences in the form of fines, dismissal from the army, death, demotion, whippings of varying numbers of lashes, and having to publicly confess your guilt to the offended party.

From the transcripts of the courts-martial we have a record of the punishments meted out. However, we know nothing of the defendants other than their names and their alleged offences and punishments. My favorite penalty is the death sentence where it could be applied to anyone who broke out of prison while awaiting execution. Also, murder and manslaughter were both capital offences, punishable by death. This is what Lieutenant Colonel Primiron Rochfort discovered when he was found not guilty of the murder of a man called Turner after mounting a fantastic defence. The court eventually decided Turner died from blows to his head after the fact so Primiron was found guilty of manslaughter. Before he could high-five his legal team, Primiron was immediately sentenced to death for the lesser offence. Sadly, no one is called Primiron any more.

So it's clear that the life of a soldier, and some of those who came into contact with him, was not always a bed of roses. Sometimes flora other than roses was involved. For example, John Holland, who was found guilty of stealing onions from Francis Welden's garden, was ordered to be whipped through his regiment the following Wednesday with a "rope of onions or other garden stuffe" about his neck. His happiness with the punishment was short-lived because he also received thirty lashes. William McNally was ordered to return a stolen cow to Art Toole. But Humphrey Morley was tied neck and heels for stealing a pair of silk stockings. Maybe he had worn them and laddered them, so he couldn't return them.

Francis Quince was found guilty of conveying away Nathaniel Winsley, a soldier, and gaoled until such a time as he could produce Winsley and his horse and arms, or produce anyone else with a horse and arms to take his place. On the same day, Murtogh Cullen and his wife were tried for harbouring Donogh O'Derg and his wife. They were found guilty by a vote of the court and sentenced to death. But the court showed leniency and allowed the couple to draw lots to see who would hang and who should go free. (Imagine, sometimes officers, like the aforementioned Sands, didn't attend court or left early. What were they thinking?) Murtogh won the lottery. However, his wife was pregnant so she got a reprieve until the child was born. Then she was hanged.

Major Elliot was found guilty of keeping oats from his men. He was also found guilty of neglect of his duty of provisioning his troops, and not calling the quartermaster's attention to the same. He was found guilty of detaining his soldiers' pay; guilty of giving them passes to go to England without the commander's leave; guilty of selling Lieutenant Brumwell's horse to another soldier; and guilty of detaining his men's cloths. While he was found not guilty in a matter involving a cow, the court noted that he didn't seem to tolerate cursing or mutinous mutterings amongst the soldiers. Two days later he was sentenced to death. No, not really. I am only joking. Because he was an officer, he was dismissed from the army rather than executed.

John Rice, found guilty of theft, was to be hanged because he had been condemned for theft before. Obviously, he wasn't an officer. His accomplices Philip Boggis and Charles Baker were to be whipped from the castle gate to the gallows and to receive forty lashes. Jane Backwell was sentenced to be whipped from the gallows to her own house, and there to get thirty-nine lashes. I assume, because she was a woman, she was entitled to one less lash than the men.

John Walker confessed to a charge and was sentenced to be taken to the gallows with a rope round his neck, where he was made stand on tiptoe to contemplate the twenty lashes he would receive that evening. This is an early example of psychological torture. Thomas Seaton was imprisoned for being up at an "unseasonable" time of night: a particularly heinous crime. I am sure Cromwell must have wondered what the world was coming to when four hundred weight of cheese was stolen. We don't know if the thief was ever caught.

However, the entire country breathed a collective sigh of relief when the New Model Army finally went back to England in 1653, allowing us to get back to our normal lawlessness. Whatever his other atrocities, I blame Cromwell for bringing the law to Ireland.

Battle Dresses

It is impossible to know how many Irish women served as soldiers in the past because those who did disguised themselves as men. You might think that surely everyone could tell the men from the women. But if I had been an officer commanding a platoon of giggling curvy soldiers, regularly checking their face powder rather than their gunpowder, I would repress my concerns as long as they showed a bit of gumption in a fray. Besides, men in those days wore more face powder than the women, and their wigs were even bigger and blonder.

We do know of one Irish woman who was a brave soldier. Christian Davies (c.1667–1739), from Dublin, had her life story published posthumously in 1740 as *The Life and Adventures of Mrs Christian Davies*. The book was attributed to Daniel Defoe but it may not have been him because he was dead at the time of publication.

Following a failed youthful relationship, Davies moved in with her aunt who was an innkeeper. She inherited the inn in 1688 when she was twenty-one. She then fell madly in love with the waiter, Richard Welsh. They married and had three children together. In 1692 Welsh vanished. Davies was frantic because she really loved her waiter. She discovered that he had been press-ganged into the British Army for the Nine Years' War (1688–1697), which was also known as the War of the Grand Alliance, the War of the Palatine Succession or the War of the League of Augsburg. The army were aware that many potential soldiers, either male or female, were not attracted to the idea of standing in neat rows waiting politely for the opposing side to take their turn to shoot at their brightly coloured uniforms. This is why they introduced the more persuasive recruitment device of press-ganging. "The press", or hitting the potential recruit over the head after getting him drunk in a tavern, and then dragging him away unconscious to the ranks, was the favoured technique of the navy, but it did occasionally happen in the army.

In order to find her husband, Davies could have dressed as a man and hung around the local tavern waiting to be pressed. Instead, having suitably disguised herself in trousers, she travelled to the nearest most active part of the Nine Years' War in search of her missing husband.

Davies enlisted in a company of foot soldiers that was fighting in Flanders. She was wounded at Landen in 1693. While recovering from her wounds, she courted the daughter of a local burgher to enhance her cover. She was so convincing that she was involved in a duel over the fair maiden. She returned to Dublin without finding her beloved Richard when peace broke out in 1697.

Happily, war broke out again in 1701 in the form of the War of the Spanish Succession, which was a great opportunity for fighting soldiers because it involved almost every country in Europe and lasted for thirteen years. It was fought over subtle balances of power in Europe which would not have been of concern to anyone on the ground doing the fighting or looking for their husbands.

Back in trousers, Davis rejoined the army in 1702 and fought her way around Europe. In 1704 she was wounded in the hip at Schellenberg in Liechtenstein. Medicine was not so sophisticated back then that the operating army "surgeon" was qualified enough to notice that she wasn't a man while treating her hip wound.

She recovered and fought in the Battle of Blenheim in August 1704, in which she at last – oh, happy day – found her Richard. He had not been as loyal as his devoted wife. He had taken up with a Dutch woman, despairing of ever seeing Christian again after just twelve years apart. Davies sliced off the Dutch girlfriend's nose and got her husband back.

She fought on with Richard until 1706 when part of her skull was blown away. "Surgery" had advanced since her previous operation because, this time, her gender was revealed. Feminists would undoubtedly argue it was because the surgeon found brain matter in her skull. She was dismissed from the service but continued as a camp follower to be with her husband. She carried food, water and orders through the lines as the cannon balls whizzed around her cracked head. Richard was killed at the Battle of Malplaquet in 1709. Christian was devastated. She immediately married Hugh Jones but he was killed at the siege of St Venant within a year.

She retired from the military life in 1712. She visited Queen Anne in London, who awarded her a pension of a shilling a day for life for her services. Davies returned to Dublin to open a pie and beer house, which was a brilliant idea that we would welcome even today. Between her pension and pie sales she was comfortably off and content, but she married an alcoholic soldier who squandered all of her money. She became less and less "respectable" for a female soldier with a hole in her head and hip. When she died she was given a three-volley salute over her grave.

A Late Developer

You can become a soldier by accident, especially when war breaks out around you. Today, age will usually excuse you from service but this wasn't the case in the past. Tragically, nowadays, many people will spend their entire lives in office jobs without ever realising that they have a talent for fighting.

Ambrose Higgins (1720–1801), arguably Ireland's most successful person ever, became a military sensation relatively late in life. His is also a story of incongruous paternal love, extremely well hidden but definitely present in the end, thus proving that even soldiers have emotions.

Ambrose Higgins was born in Meath in 1720. He was the son of minor gentry who, in the fashion typical of most minor gentry, had fallen on hard times. He joined the British Army for the practical purpose of having a career, but, because promotion was slower than he liked or thought he deserved, and there were no worthwhile fights, he resigned his commission and emigrated to Spain.

Spain was then, as now, a popular destination for Irish emigrants. Higgins was to be educated by an uncle who was a Jesuit. But he didn't like the religious life and settled instead in Cadiz as a bank clerk. Five years later, his younger brother William left Spain to become the president of Asunción.[65] Higgins thought he had lost his mind, so he followed him to talk him into coming back. He failed and ended up staying in South America working as a peddler before setting up a business in Lima in Peru.

When he was forty he returned to Spain to try to get an official government appointment in South America. While he was ambitious for glory and fame, the only job he was offered was as a draughtsman to John Garland, a fellow Irishman who was an engineer. He took the post because he had lost money in speculative business and was in debt. He sailed to Buenos Aires in 1763, and set out on the long trek across the Argentine Pampas, arriving in Mendoza in June at the beginning of winter. While crossing the Cordillera he almost froze to death in the snow. In fact, one of his three porters did die. This experience gave him a business idea.

He persuaded the Captain General of Santiago de Chile to allow him to build a series of travel shelters across the Andes. Higgins proposed brick structures with sloping roofs to allow the snow to slide off. The mule drivers who regularly crossed the mountains agreed to provide the materials free of charge. Thus, he is credited with introducing the postal system between Argentina and Chile. At last Higgins had come to the positive attention of the authorities.

Higgins, who was suffering badly from the cold, retired to Spain in 1766 but returned to South America with a commission to write a report on Chile. In the middle of his report writing there was a major uprising of the Araucanian Indians in southern Chile. At forty-nine years of age he was made a captain of dragoons, and with his mounted infantry he impressively subdued the rebels. Higgins, suddenly discovering that he was a brilliant soldier, went on the offensive.

---

[65] Asunción was later renamed Paraguay.

However, he was generous and humane in victory. He invited 200 Indian chiefs, the Captain General of Santiago de Chile, the Bishop of Conceptión, who was one of the most powerful churchmen in South America, and numerous officials to conferences with Indians that he organised. He advocated trade with the Indians, and resisted suggestions that they be annihilated or deliberately turned into alcoholics like many of their North American counterparts.

In 1773 he was invited to Lima to meet the Viceroy, Manuel de Amat. Higgins instantly liked Amat, and Amat liked Higgins. By 1789, Amat had promoted him to the rank of field marshal. During this period he had an ongoing feud with the Bishop of Conceptión. The Bishop liked to pompously progress through Indian territory to show off both himself and his high office to the Indians. Higgins offered to provide him with an armed escort. But the Bishop refused. When the Bishop was inevitably captured, his own Indian retinue offered to play a game of hockey: if they won, the Bishop would be released; if they lost, he would be killed. They lost. But they immediately suggested that they play the best of three, to which their opponents sportingly agreed. Disappointingly for Higgins, when the Bishop's Indians won the next two games, the Bishop was released.

On 28 January 1787, Higgins was appointed governor, president and captain general of Chile, and effectively ran the country for the next eight years. The laws that he introduced on taking office prohibited pigs roaming the streets, put a stop to people doing their washing in rivers upstream of other people and banned throwing the clothes of those who died of infectious diseases into the streets. He ordered that men had to be faithful to their wives, and refrain from brawling, carrying arms and swearing in public. Beggars had to join the army within three days or leave the city; holy-week penitents couldn't flog themselves in public. He changed his name to O'Higgins, and rebuilt the city of

Osorno in southern Chile. On 26 May 1788 O'Higgins was given the title Marqués de Osorno.

He sent his nephew, Demetrio, to Ireland to attain a fake genealogy showing his descent from Sean O'Higgins, Baron of Ballingarry, thereby making him one of the first celebrities to trace his ancestry in Ireland, fake or otherwise. This document was sent to the Spanish court, entitling him to become Don Ambrosio O'Higgins, Barón de Vallenar – the Spanish translation of Ballingarry, I assume. The Creole landowners, who were the biggest snobs on the planet at that time, hated the *parvenu*.

O'Higgins promoted free trade and abolished slave labour, which had been in force since 1544. Through a strategy of road and town building, he opened up the country. He introduced new taxes and started a fishing industry. When he invited four Indian chiefs to celebrate the accession of Charles VI to the throne of Spain, he outraged the local colonial landed gentry. They really did hate him. However, the ordinary people regarded him as a reformer and a hero. In 1795 the Prime Minister of Spain, Manuel de Godoy, appointed him to the most important post in the Spanish Empire: viceroy of Peru.

O'Higgins was concerned with his countrymen's comforts. In his imagination he was hospitable to visitors to his palace but in reality he wasn't. In 1795, when the explorer George Vancouver visited, he was appalled by the filth and dirt in the palace. It must have been bad if an eighteenth-century explorer noticed it. Vancouver observed that the dust was so thick in his apartment that it needed a shovel rather than a broom to remove it.

O'Higgins was progressive politically for the time and place; emotionally he wasn't. He had an overly developed parental attitude to all those under his care, with the exception of his actual son. Though psychology had not yet been invented, I think we can safely conclude he over-compensated in the care of his subjects because of his well-disguised guilt over his neglect of his own son. As with many men in Irish history, O'Higgins was extremely emotional but went to extraordinary lengths to disguise the fact that he had any feelings. The effort resulted in his developing a red complexion that, combined with his small stature, resulted in the Indians giving him the nickname *El Camarón* (The Shrimp).

In 1772, when O'Higgins met the young Isabel Riquelme, who was a colonial with some Indian blood, the fifty-two-year-old lieutenant colonel of dragoons fell madly in love. She was fourteen and beautiful. He wasn't. He was short, red-faced, fat and severe looking, with no sense of humour. He also had a long pointed nose and large bushy eyebrows. He promised to seek permission from the Spanish King to marry her because any official needed royal permission to marry a colonial. He never actually married her. Five years later he succeeded in persuading her to have sex with him. I cannot imagine what he said. She conceived a child, Bernardo, who was born on the feast of Saint Bernard. O'Higgins then promptly left her when he realised that his usually stony heart was getting in the way of his ambition.

Bernardo O'Higgins was born when his old man was fifty-seven. There is an inevitable set of desperate acts of idiocy that the young children of old men must perform in order to try to gain the attention of someone who just wants to sleep in front of the fire with the newspaper over his head. Bernardo did all these before he would go on to serve with distinction in the wars of independence from Spain, earning him the title "Liberator of Chile".

However, first he was given to foster parents. When he had just learned to recognise them as his parents, he was taken away as a four-year-old by a detachment of dragoons sent by his father, Don Ambrosio. They galloped into town, kidnapped Bernardo and took him to an estate, where he would be looked after by a friend of Don Ambrosio, Don Albano. He would try to keep Bernardo from the attention of the authorities, since the child was the illegitimate result of a relationship with a Creole woman that had not been given royal permission.

In 1788, when Don Ambrosio was the ruler of the whole country as the captain general of the King of Spain in Chile, he visited the young Bernardo. Soon after this, Bernardo was sent to a special school for the education of the sons of Indian chiefs. After two years he was sent to the Royal College of San Carlos in Lima, in Peru. When he was sixteen, when Don Ambrosio became viceroy of Peru, Bernardo was sent to Spain to get him even further out of the way.

As viceroy, Don Ambrosio ruled over a population of one million. He ruled from a throne-like seat with a red velvet canopy in his audience chamber. But Lima itself was a cesspit. He issued laws of good government and started a road-building plan. Though dour and outwardly and inwardly humourless, he enjoyed the title "The Great Viceroy". The colonial Creole landed gentry continued to hate him. He hated Lima. The eighty-year-old pined for the fresh air of Chile.

He learned from spies that the Venezuelan revolutionary Francisco de Miranda was plotting revolution in London against the Spanish Crown. He also learned that Bernardo was one of Miranda's followers. In fact, this was Don Ambrosio's own fault because Bernardo had wanted to join the British Navy but was barred because he was illegitimate. Bernardo had written to his father begging him for help so he could join the navy, but he got no response. What choice had he but to fall in with the charismatic revolutionaries? He was extraordinarily charismatic himself.

Bernardo's annual allowance of £300 from his father was normally stolen each year by those assigned to look after him. They forwarded about £1 to Bernardo from the fund. Thus, Bernardo was reduced to poverty. He did write frequently to his father to let him know how he was. Since Bernardo had enormous affection for his father, he only complained when his circumstances were unusually dire. Otherwise, he was of a cheerful and optimistic disposition, unlike his old man.

At one point Bernardo was so poor that he wrote to tell his father that he couldn't leave his room because he had no proper clothes to wear outside. He couldn't attend classes because he had no coat to wear. He even sold his piano. But, still, his father did nothing. Bernardo wrote that he was actually so poor that he had resorted to cutting his own hair, did his own sewing and mending, and wore the same suit for four years straight. He also wrote to tell his father that he didn't want to beg from his few Irish friends because this would embarrass his father, obviously not realising that being a revolutionary against his father's own government was slightly more embarrassing.

Naturally, Don Ambrosio's bitter Creole enemies informed the authorities in Madrid about Bernardo's revolutionary leanings. Don Ambrosio was forced into retirement when he was eighty-one because of the scandal. He was replaced by his archrival, the Margués de Avilés.

Don Ambrosio was so enraged with Bernardo over his forced early retirement that he became even redder, gave himself a brain hemorrhage and was carried to his deathbed. He asked his old friend Tomás Delfin to help him make his last will and testament. He wanted to cut Bernardo off completely but Delfin begged him to reconsider. Don Ambrosio refused. After days of pleading, he finally relented. On 14 March 1801 he drew up his will, officially recognising Bernardo as his son for the first time. He also left Bernardo, who was still in the same unwashed suit, an estate in Chile. He died four days later.

Because he was illegitimate, Bernardo could never get recognition for his father's aristocratic titles. Throughout his life he maintained an obsessive regard for his old man. In his turn, Bernardo went on to become an accidental soldier, and the liberator of Chile from Spanish rule. I suspect his father would have been proud but would never have admitted it.

An Army Marches on Butter

War is fantastic if you are a butter merchant in Cork because you can sell your butter to an entire army of customers. War is bad when it ends suddenly and you are left with a butter mountain. This is what happened to Jeremiah O'Leary in 1815 after Napoleon's dramatic defeat at the Battle of Waterloo. The British forces needed a lot of butter for their wars with France.

When the war ended, Jeremiah's son, the young, naive and inexperienced Daniel Florence O'Leary (c.1802–1854), joined the crowd of penniless, de-mobbed, battle-hardened soldiers who were thronging Dublin. This mix of unemployed veterans and newly impoverished youths like O'Leary desperately needed a new conflict. Fortunately, a cause presented itself in the form of Generalissimo Simon Bolivar's liberation of South America from Spanish colonial rule. This war promised lavish pay, rapid promotion and the distinctively attractive uniforms usually favoured by South American revolutionary forces.

O'Leary would have been told that he needed to act quickly because the war in Venezuela was practically won, and his biggest danger would be to miss this once-in-a-lifetime opportunity, or annual opportunity at least. Most of the Irish recruits were badly provisioned and had little food. In one instance, within a month of arriving at Margarita Island off the coast of Venezuela, 250 died of typhus. The rest were eventually placed under the command of General Rafael José Urdaneta y Faría, who was described by his contemporaries as being a slave to women and cigars. He was not a competent general, even by the standards that pertained amongst the rebels. He was in the habit of going into battle with two of his mistresses. When not actually fighting, he lay all day in a hammock with his other mistresses.

The Irish recruits dwindled through sickness and death. Some joined the rebels in Colombia. O'Leary was lucky to survive the initial hazards. Auspiciously for him, O'Leary avoided Urdaneta and was posted to the Dragoons of the Guard of General José Antonio Anzoátequí. He was subsequently involved in all of the campaigns that led to the freeing from Spanish rule of Colombia in 1819, Venezuela in 1821, Ecuador in 1822, Peru in 1824 and Upper Peru, afterwards known as Bolivia in honour of Bolivar, in 1825.

Like Don Ambrosio O'Higgins before him, O'Leary discovered that he was a naturally dashing cavalry officer. At the Battle of Pontano de Vargos he received a stylish saber wound to the face, and was reported killed. His death was even published in the Cork newspapers. Promotion came as fast as the recruiting agents had promised. Unfortunately, the war ended in 1826 when the Spanish admitted that they were beaten and withdrew from South America. If it had only kept going for just one more year, O'Leary may even have become a generalissimo like Bolivar.

Count Your Enemies

Fighting wasn't the only route to the top of the South American social order for Irish men and women. You could copulate your way to the summit of society. This is what Eliza Lynch (1834–1886) from Cork did. When she met Fransisco Solano Lopez in Paris in 1854, they became lovers. Lopez was the son of the dictator of Paraguay and was leading an extravagant diplomatic mission to Europe. Lynch followed Lopez to Asunción, Paraguay. The elegant house he gave her became the centre of a cosmopolitan scene and the focus of gossip. They had six children together.

When Lopez succeeded his father as dictator in 1862, Lynch became the driving force behind the introduction of European culture and fashion. At that time in polite Paraguayan society it was a fashion essential to have dedicated enemies, and Lynch was extremely *au courant*: she had fifty society lady enemies. But these ladies now found that they had to suck up to her for both political success and well-being.

A definitive diagnosis of insanity amongst despots remains notoriously evasive for psychiatric medicine, even now. Lopez may have been actually insane, though it is hard to distinguish the subtle differences between your common or garden sane dictator and an actual insane one.

Brazil, Argentina and Uruguay allied against Lopez in the War of the Triple Alliance, 1864–1870, in which 90 per cent of the men and 50 per cent of the women of Paraguay died. Lynch has been blamed for the war, but, as with the insanity issue, opinion remains divided. Insane or not, Lopez, along with Eliza, their children and a few die-hard loyalists, had to flee into the surrounding jungle, as you do, when Brazilian troops occupied Asunción. When the family was eventually hunted down, Lopez and his oldest son, Fransisco, were killed in front of Lynch. At the time she was wearing a ballgown that had become ragged from the journey through the foliage, and a pair of silk slippers unsuited to the terrain. She had to dig their graves with her bare hands.

By 1870 she had managed to acquire about one-third of the land of Paraguay in her own name. But the new government declared her an outlaw, and confiscated her property. It was rumoured that Lopez had hidden a vast treasure siphoned from the people with Lynch's help. She was deported back to Europe but not before the fifty outraged society ladies demanded that she be put on trial and shot for her crimes against propriety, as she was not married to Lopez. Shooting your defeated enemy with a firing squad was positively avant-garde in the best South American social circles. When the Government invited her back, Lynch became suspicious that they only wanted to force her to reveal the location of the treasure. It remains lost to this day.

Lynch did eventually return in October 1875. The peasants greeted her warmly. You can rely on peasants to have fickle memories. But the fifty outraged ladies were still fuming. She left for Buenos Aires where she wrote a passionate defence of her career as Lopez's mistress. When she died in Paris in 1886 she was buried in Père Lachaise Cemetery. Her body was exhumed in 1961 and returned to Asunción by the then Paraguayan dictator General Alfredo Stroessner, who may also have been insane. Who knows? He declared her a national hero. She is either an evil genius or a national icon, or maybe they are the same thing. Nevertheless, she was yet another shining example of the opportunities enjoyed by the Irish in the historical development of South America.

War: The Last Resort of a Ham Actor

When all else fails, you can become a soldier and then fail at that. This is what Richard Barry (1769–1793), 7th Earl of Barrymore, did. When he was young he was interested in racehorses, gambling and practical jokes. But these professional interests were nothing compared to his obsession with amateur dramatics. We all know someone whose life has been destroyed by part-time thespians. They start by dabbling in Ibsen before moving on to overdose on hardcore late Beckett material, like *Breath*, and expect to see family and friends in the audience at every performance.

Barry was a friend of the Prince of Wales, the future George IV, who nicknamed him "Hellgate" on account of his recklessness. He squandered his family fortune building and running a private theatre for his own shows. To avoid his debts he became a member of Parliament. He was so clueless that he didn't even marry money. Instead he married the daughter of a sedan chairman, an eighteenth-century taxi driver.

Having exhausted all possible ways to support his dramas, he became a soldier. Just as his new career began, he was killed instantly when a musket exploded while he was undertaking what seemed the safest job in the army of the Napoleonic Wars – escorting French prisoners of war in the peaceful scenic countryside of Kent, England.

His brother, Henry, succeeded him as Earl of Barrymore. Henry must have wished an exploding gun blew his brother's head off years before he became involved in amateur dramatics. King George IV called Henry "Cripplegate" because he was lame. Another brother, Augustus, who was a gambling clergyman, he called "Newgate" after the debtors' prison. Their sister, Carolina, he called "Billingsgate" because of her foul language. Billingsgate was a fish market that was established in London at the end of the seventeenth century. The women who sold fish had a notorious reputation for foul language. That king was extraordinarily witty and clearly had a lot on his mind during those difficult times.

Our Waterloo

It took an Irish soldier, Arthur Wellesley (1769–1852), also known as the Duke of Wellington, to finally defeat Napoleon at the Battle of Waterloo in 1815, and bring the Napoleonic Wars – which had been fought on and off since 1803, and were themselves a continuation of the French Revolutionary Wars from 1789 – to a definite end. Win or lose, we have to like Napoleon better than Wellesley, even if the latter was Irish. But Wellesley always denied being Irish. He was born in Dublin, but famously argued that being born in a stable doesn't make you a horse. But being born in a stable doesn't necessarily make you a horse – you might be an ass. His contemporaries regarded the fact that he could compose such a *bon mot*, or have it composed for him, as proof of his Irishness. Typically, once he defeated Napoleon, the English laid claim to him.

Wellesley was thick in school, which was no handicap for a young Irish gentleman wishing to enter the army. He also became a member of Parliament, again no burden, before embarking with the Duke of York on an allied campaign that planned but ultimately failed to invade Revolutionary France from the Netherlands. The campaign was an internationally recognised fiasco at a time when the standards for such things were extremely low. Not just any debacle would qualify; incompetence above and beyond normal duty was required. His brother was governor general of Bengal in India, so Wellesley took himself out there. Surviving contact with the enemy guaranteed him promotion, though his critics attributed his success to nepotism. But he did have a dramatic success in 1804[66] that earned him a knighthood, and a lot of prize money to boot.

Wellesley competently ground out results without flair. Napoleon and his marshals were brilliant and entertaining to watch but perhaps ultimately fragile. What Wellesley lacked in brainpower he made up for in organisation. During his command of the Peninsular[67] campaign he paid particular

---

[66] An outnumbered Indian and British force under the command of Wellesley defeated the Maratha Imperial Army at the Battle of Assaye in 1803. This battle was part of the Second Anglo-Maratha War fought between the Maratha Empire and the British East India Company. The battle was Wellesley's first major victory. This success, combined with others, ultimately led to the defeat of the Maratha Empire in 1804, which in turn led to the British becoming the dominant power in India.

[67] During the wider Napoleonic Wars, the Peninsular War was the

attention to logistics, military intelligence and harsh, rather than effective or thoughtful, discipline. Most of his soldiers were Irish but he didn't think much of them. Wellesley won in Spain because the French had to withdraw to other theatres of the war: Napoleon's army was freezing in Russia. Wellesley emerged from the Peninsular campaign as a duke, and with a grant of £400,000[68] from Parliament.

By 1814, the now 1st Duke of Wellington had reached France in time for the French surrender. But Napoleon escaped from where he was in exile on the island of Elba, and was soon back in power for a new 100-day reign. Wellington was put in command of the Anglo-Dutch forces and, along with Marshal Blücher, was to defend Brussels from a French invasion. Wellington's army met Napoleon's forces at Waterloo on 18 June 1815. Wellington held them up until the arrival of Blücher's Prussians, which forced the French to flee. Paris fell within three weeks, and Napoleon was forced back into exile, this time on the island of St Helena.

Wellington became prime minister of Britain in 1828, making him the most successful Irishman in Britain, ever. His government was unpopular and collapsed in 1830 because he was implacably opposed to any kind of parliamentary reforms. But the fact that he became prime minister is more important than his being competent in the role, right? His opposition to reform caused his house in London to be twice attacked by mobs waving pitchforks and burning brands.

He held the post of leader of the House of Lords three times between 1828 and 1846, twice as prime minister and once as foreign secretary. During his final period in that

---

name given to the conflict which was fought on the Iberian Peninsula (Spain and Portugal) from 1807 to 1814, between France and Spain against Britain and Portugal, and then France against Spain, Britain and Portugal.

[68] Approximately €16.5 million in contemporary currency values.

office he asked for the military command of Ireland in 1843, but his colleagues studiously ignored him. By this stage in his life, everyone was assiduously ignoring him. He had grown deaf, probably from the sound of cannon balls whizzing close past his head. Imagine, not one of them hit him. How unlucky is that?

Meanwhile, back on St Helena, where Napoleon was trying to enjoy his forced retirement, an Irish surgeon, or perhaps "surgeon", Barry Edward O'Meara (1786?–1836) was looking after his health. Was he a real surgeon? Napoleon thought so but there are no records of him attending either Trinity College or the Royal College of Surgeons. However there were private medical schools in Dublin at that time so, for Napoleon's sake, let's hope he went to one of those. Not that there was much on the syllabus in any case. But it is agreeable to have a qualified doctor.

O'Meara had been an army surgeon but was dismissed from service for participating in a duel. Technically, I suppose dueling is against the Hippocratic oath if looked at in an holistic medical context. He joined the navy, where there was a woollier interpretation of the oath, and rose to the rank of full surgeon, probably because he had all his limbs. He was serving on board HMS *Bellorophon* when Napoleon surrendered to her captain Frederick Maitland on 15 July 1815.

O'Meara impressed Napoleon with his knowledge of languages. It was practical for a ship's surgeon to recognise the language in which his patients were screaming as he sawed off their limbs. Because of this, and because Napoleon's own doctor refused to accompany him into exile on St Helena, Napoleon asked for O'Meara to attend him. Napoleon's own army surgeon, the brilliant Dominique Larrey, a surgeon without quotation marks who is usually considered to be the father of modern military surgery, left Napoleon to dedicate himself to civilian medicine. With

Larrey thus unavailable, O'Meara was made confidential physician to Napoleon. This appointment was ironic because he reported every detail of Napoleon's health and state of mind he could back to the British authorities. He was an incredible gossip for a confidential doctor. O'Meara fed Napoleon gossip from all over the island, and also reported on Napoleon to the British Admiralty. He treated Napoleon for insomnia, swelling of the legs and pain in the liver. We know this because he told everyone.

The island's governor, Sir Hudson Lowe, realised as early as October 1816 that O'Meara was spying on everyone on St Helena. Lowe fell out with both Napoleon and O'Meara. He ordered O'Meara to stop spying. But Napoleon would only have O'Meara as his doctor. Eventually, O'Meara was ordered off the island. In total, five Irish surgeons attended Napoleon for the rest of his life while he was in exile.

O'Meara wrote to the Admiralty suggesting that Lowe might assassinate Napoleon. Because of this letter, O'Meara was dismissed from the navy in 1818. Naturally, he began a pamphlet war against Lowe. These pamphlets were popular and ran through five editions, and were also published in French. Lowe began libel proceedings against O'Meara, to the delight of his attorney. But this promisingly lengthy litigation had to be dropped due to legal technicalities. Not, however, before O'Meara was reduced to penury, forcing him to marry the fabulously rich widow Theodosia Beauchamp. This outcome forces me to reluctantly concede that the law isn't all bad where it encourages romance.

O'Meara moved back to Ireland. In 1836 he died from erysipelas of the head, a now obsolete disease, which he contracted at a Daniel O'Connell (1775–1847)[69] rally.

---

[69] Daniel O'Connell, who is often referred to as "The Liberator" or "The Emancipator", was an Irish political leader in the first half of the nineteenth century.

Off to Sunny Spain

On those peaceful moments when there wasn't a fight going on at home in Ireland, it was always nice to have one abroad that you could go to. Thus the Spanish Civil War of 1936–1939 was an ideal opportunity for Irish soldiers to go down in someone else's history.

The Spanish Civil War was broadly a conflict between nationalistic fascists and international-minded republicans supported by communists. Irish soldiers had to work out what side they might best fit into. Exasperatingly, the war produced too many political shades of grey rather than the simple black and white favoured by the typical Irish crusader. Why do the Spanish have to have such complicated fights?

The Irish who supported the Spanish nationalists were led by Eoin O'Duffy (1890–1944), while the communists and republicans were led by Francis Richard (Frank) Ryan (1902–1944).

Duffy added the "O" to his name during the Irish War of Independence when he commanded the Monaghan Brigade IRA with distinction between 1919 and 1921. Following independence, in February 1922 he became chief-of-staff of the National Army. In September 1922 he became commissioner of the Civic Guard, the unarmed national police force which eventually became An Garda Síochána. By 1925 he had an established reputation as a gifted organiser, the kind of person whom anyone starting a fascist organisation would turn to for logistical help. He was also something of a pamphleteer because he wrote articles for *Iris an Gharda* (*The Garda Review*). He was popular, though feared, among his Garda colleagues.

He promoted a Gaelic identity as he interpreted it, which included, apart from adding "O"s to your name, promoting native strains of Irish dogs in the Irish Native Breeds Society, which was a form of dog eugenics consistent with his fascism.

O'Duffy became a fascist when he learned that fascists were implacable enemies of communism, and he had a pathological fear of communists. He used the special branch of his police to undermine communist elements wherever he could imagine them: amongst republicans, Fianna Fáil party members, members of the Irish Native Breeds Society, liberals and actual communists. He travelled widely because he led Garda pilgrimages to religious shrines all over Europe.

These excursions brought him into contact with European fascists. O'Duffy became enchanted by the glamour of fascism, particularly its penchant for uniforms. In 1932 he became involved with the Army Comrades Association (ACA). The main purpose of the ACA was to provide physical protection for conservative political groups from potential attack by left-wing organisations.

The following year, because he was steadily becoming extreme, he lost his job as police commissioner. By 1933 he was the leader of the ACA. Members of the ACA later became known as "The Blueshirts" because of their blue fascist uniforms. They would become the largest non-governing fascist party in the world. In fairness to O'Duffy, he did introduce gaudiness to what was a relatively colourless Ireland in the 1930s.

This was a confusing time for Irish fascists. O'Duffy changed the name of the ACA several times in six months before most of the political parties protected by that organisation merged to become Fine Gael. He was forced to resign as president of Fine Gael in 1934, following an inevitable split. He continued to preside over a declining Blueshirt movement, now outside Fine Gael, until 1935, when another split amongst the Blueshirts gave rise to a sub-group called the National Corporate Party (NCP) led by O'Duffy. These changed their blue shirts to green in 1936.

Tactically, the Irish fascists prioritised forming organisations, wearing uniforms and staging splits to counter the threat of Irish communism, which at its highest level barely existed outside of O'Duffy's imagination. In the mid-1930s there were less than 100 card-carrying Communist Party of Ireland members. Ironically, the growth of the Blueshirts enhanced the attractions of communism for many of these recruits. In other words, O'Duffy was more responsible for the growth of communism in Ireland than any other influence. But fortunately for O'Duffy Spain was alive with communists. A fascist campaign from Ireland was just what was needed to wipe them out.

In August 1936 O'Duffy began to organise an Irish Christian crusade to fight the republicans in Spain. Despite the mandatory splits, he raised an Irish Brigade for the Nationalist side under General Franco on the simple basis that they were fighting evil communists. In traditional Irish fashion, he promised Franco that tens of thousands of volunteers would turn up, but only about 700 turned up on the day. O'Duffy had kept with the Irish revolutionary tradition of promising big and delivering small. It seems Franco was a student of Irish revolutions and knew what to expect.

O'Duffy took his volunteers to Spain in 1936. Those who were still conscious after six months wanted to go home. The experience was like an extended stag weekend on the Costa del Sol – some were sick from the heat, some were dead and the rest were utterly demoralised.

O'Duffy developed a reputation for drinking too much in Spain, like many thousands of Irish tourists after him, contributing to the ineffectiveness of his brigade. Some commentators thought that, such was his incompetence, he may have even been siding with the republicans. A contemporary Irish-Spanish commentator, Ian Gibson, wrote that when O'Duffy's brigade mistakenly shot fellow nationalists it didn't impress Franco, who was obviously a perfectionist.

The brigade members who survived left Spain feeling profoundly Catholic and nostalgic for rich butter on a delicious boiled Irish spud. O'Duffy wrote an account of the campaign, *Crusade in Spain*, in 1938. His NCP faded away and into Irish history. Some of his fascist veterans of the Spanish campaign enlisted in 1940 with the Allied forces to fight against German fascism, which just proves that their grasp of the politics was shaky. Maybe it was the German uniforms they didn't like.

On the Republican side, the Irish left-wing volunteers were presented with a confusing array of squabbling factions in Spain. Their leader, Frank Ryan, had been a member of the IRA who engaged in street confrontations with O'Duffy's Blueshirts. However, by 1934 he had split from the IRA to form the Republican Congress that opposed Franco's coup in Spain in 1936. The Spanish left-wing Government supported the raising of an International Brigade that attracted 45,000 foreign recruits to the side of the republicans, including Ryan's Irish recruits. As a first step in their crusade these recruits had to make their way to London. From Victoria Station they were supposed to travel by train and ferry to Paris in discrete groups in order not to call attention to themselves. The Irish, in groups of forty or more, occupied the bars on the trains and ferries, drinking and loudly singing rebel songs. From Paris they crossed into Spain in groups of about a dozen, and joined up with their countrymen in the English-speaking Battalion XV, which was the British Battalion. In the British Battalion a variety of communists are republicans were united under the rationale of an English-speaking command. The international communists naively imagined that both the language and a shared transnational ideology would bind them together against their common enemy, international fascism. But such innocence reveals just one of the reasons why communism failed as a world political force.

The Irish communists found themselves under the competent command of Captain Nathan, who had vast military experience. However, some of that experience had been gained as a Black and Tan[70] during the Irish War of Independence, where he had been personally involved in the killing of two Sinn Féin men in Limerick. This news item quickly went round the Irish ranks. According to Ryan, the British Communist Party was run by Black and Tans who "made a bags of everything".

Because the communists were exceptionally democratic, and loved conferences, conventions, committees and sub-committees, several meetings were organised, resulting in Nathan being promoted off the front line, where he could have saved lives, and up the ranks, where he couldn't. Captain Nathan defended himself by arguing that he had volunteered to the International Brigades as a Jew committed to the fight against international fascism. But the Irish communists hated their British officers more than the fascists they were fighting.

The Spanish communists, who were real communists, quickly learned that the Irish communists were so uncomfortable with both the anti-religious culture of Spanish communism and the British command that there were regular drunken punch-ups amongst the International Brigades. No self-respecting Irish communist would shoot a nun, a sentiment they shared with the Irish fascists. In any event, the hundred or so Irish communists managed to undermine the ideological coherence of the entire British Battalion.

---

[70] The Black and Tans were a makeshift paramilitary unit, composed largely of British veterans of the First World War, who were employed by the British authorities to suppress the Irish Republican Army (IRA) during the Irish War of Independence. The moniker arose from the colour of the improvised uniforms worn by its members. Although originally established to target the IRA, the Black and Tans became notorious for their attacks on the Irish civilian population.

Ryan requested that the Irish in the British Battalion be transferred to the American communists in the Lincoln Battalion. But the American communists, who weren't real communists either, didn't want them. They didn't need what they considered to be a bunch of drunks fighting amongst each other. In the end, about thirty Irish joined the Lincolns while the rest stayed with the British. One of the reasons that the Spanish republicans eventually lost the war was because of their Irish-like tendency to form splits. There were so many splits on the republican side that it is not practical to document them all. Ryan seems to have become the leader of a break-away Lincoln faction.

Jim Prendergast, reporting for the *Irish Democrat* communist party paper, wrote that one of the Irish fighting at Jarama, Dan Boyle from Belfast, was slightly upset to read in the morning paper that that he had been killed in action the night before. Dan generously distributed his cigarettes to his friends on the possibility that he might not get to finish them later. However the paper was correct with the story, if not with the date, because he was killed that evening.

Ryan fought O'Duffy's Brigade at Jarama. He was wounded in 1937 and was sent back to Ireland to recuperate. By March 1938 he was back in Spain. He was wounded again, captured and sentenced to death. But an international campaign for clemency got his sentence commuted. Two German military intelligence acquaintances had him released from gaol and brought to Berlin in July 1940 during the Second World War. He attempted to travel home by German submarine with Séan Russell (1893–1940)[71] in August, but when Russell died at sea the submarine turned back to Germany where Ryan stayed until his death in 1944.

---

[71] Séan Russell was the leader of a faction following a post-1922 split within the IRA.

I Spy

Maureen (Paddy) O'Sullivan (1918–?), from Dublin, became an undercover agent in the Second World War at a time when they would take anyone who could speak French and hadn't enough sense to be terrified. Her mother died when she was an infant. Her father wasn't able to look after her because up until recently Irish fathers weren't able to look after children on their own. After several years of failed effort, he sent her to Belgium to live with an aunt.

In school in Belgium she became fluent in French, Dutch and Flemish, and had a working knowledge of German, which were the ideal qualifications for a secret agent. In January 1939 she began training in London to be a nurse. When the Second World War started she could have returned to her father and spent the conflict safely in Dublin. Unlike the rest of the world, we didn't have the Second World War in Ireland; we had the Emergency, which was boring because nothing happened – absolutely nothing. Not surprisingly, Paddy chose to remain in dangerous London. It was better to have a bomb land on your head than to die slowly of boredom.

In July 1941 she joined the Women's Auxiliary Air Force (WAAF). By 1943 she was accepted for Special Overseas Executive (SOE) training because she spoke French. The SOE had been set up by Prime Minister Winston Churchill to co-ordinate all subversive actions against the Germans overseas. Paddy attended instruction in subversion in Winterford, Surrey, where her trainers described her as being pleasant, purposeful, independent and able to manage people, but having little or no practical or mechanical sense. They also said she was accident prone. This judgement was proven true when she got to France.

She was next sent to subversion finishing school in Scotland where, from the reports, it appeared the training was having an effect on her combat instincts. She was definitely changing. Her trainers now described her as stubborn and undisciplined with an uncontrollable temper and no team spirit: think Private Pyle in the toilet scene in the film *Full Metal Jacket*.

Paddy then transferred to wireless training school in London where her discipline was a problem. But she was popular with her classmates even if she couldn't turn on a radio, let alone change a valve.

In March 1944 she was finally sent on a mission. She was dropped by parachute into a field in France with two radio sets and twenty-two containers of arms to distribute to the beret-wearing, striped jumper-clad British and French chaps waiting in the hedges below. She landed on the flat of her back, winding herself badly and knocking herself out. She woke up with a cow licking her face. I wonder how the Germans lost that war.

Surprisingly, the resistance commander on the ground, Major Teddy Meyer, was not impressed with this entry, nor with the fact that her training didn't include learning to ride a bike, an omission he detected when he instructed her to hop up on a bike like a good chap and do the rounds checking the radio sets that were hidden in various locations, which she couldn't fix anyway even if she was able to cycle there. As bicycles were the only form of resistance transport, she had to learn on the job.

Soon she was adept at cycling and even mastered radio maintenance. She developed her cover as a Belgian girl searching for her missing husband. She didn't blow up bridges or slit the throats of sentries, but she did adapt quickly as a radio operator.

One day a German soldier stopped her while she was cycling along with a radio in a suitcase strapped to her bike. He demanded that she open her case. Before she could, a helpful German officer approached the attractive fraülein to enquire if he could be of assistance. Paddy told the officer that her mother was German and that she was Flemish, and she would love to go on a date with him. The suitcase was forgotten amid all the eyelash batting. Now I know why the Germans lost the war. Women batted their eyelashes in the 1940s – I have seen the films – and they smoked many ciga-rettes while doing so.

Six months later Paddy returned to London, where her exploits were published in the *Daily Mail* and *Sunday Express*, making her one of the first female SOE officers to receive publicity. Public acclaim is terrible for the spying business. Her superior spies were understandably upset.

In June 1945 she was sent to Calcutta in India, where they imagined she wouldn't be widely known, as an agent with the French. Her story again appeared in the local press. In September 1945 she was back in London receiving a Most Excellent Order of the British Empire medal (MBE). Paddy disappeared from history around 1950. Perhaps she went deep undercover.

*

In the past the outbreak of war was usually celebrated with a street party. Wars aren't the cause of celebrations anymore. Even tourists tend to avoid them. War, what is it good for? Well, a career in the army actually – and a chance to go down in history.

4

The Sporting Irish:
From Wrestling to Chess

What sporting ambitions can Ireland's fat children have? The tug-of-war ceased to be an Olympic event in 1920. Contemporary Olympic Games discriminate against the sedentary. There are just a few sports left in which the fat can excel.

In the past, a fat child who didn't have the face for chess could have listened to sports commentators on the radio. For decades in the twentieth century, Irish childhood Sundays were spent in the following way. Accompanied by your parents, siblings and perhaps a surviving grandparent, you would climb into the back of a Ford Cortina, probably green, to be driven to a sand dune by the sea or any other godforsaken spot. A collective of Cortinas would park within hailing distance of each other and the occupants would get out, leaving all the doors open. Your father would prepare himself for the coming ordeal by tying a knotted handkerchief around his head, while your mother spread a Foxford rug on the damp ground beside the car. Your mother would then hand around the tea and ham sandwiches to the adults, and the Fanta and banana sandwiches to the children. Naturally, it was either raining or freezing or both, but memory has the power to add sunshine and blue skies to our worst recollections because otherwise we would all go mad.

Your father would close his eyes in meditation on the rug beside the open car door and listen to a GAA (Gaelic Athletic Association) match on the car radio, which would be turned up to maximum volume. Michael O'Hehir (1920–1996) would narrate the events of the match, while you sat in the epicentre of the commentary coming from all the car radios simultaneously. Ah, the good old days.

I loathed them. I liked the banana sandwiches but I hated Michael O'Hehir. On those Sundays I wished that I were dead. Then I wished that Michael O'Hehir was dead instead. But I was too young to appreciate his special gift. He had the unique ability as a sports commentator to make the world appear to move faster, which was something the bored adults appreciated. Balls would fly like meteors from one bronchial player to the next. The most sluggish overweight fullbacks in the history of football would run on varicose-veined legs as fleet as Apollos.

O'Hehir was born Michael James Hehir in Glasnevin in Dublin. He added an "O" to his name later because it is easier to get on in the GAA with it. In his final year in school, he began to broadcast commentaries on GAA games, having entered a broadcasting trial when he was eighteen. He went to UCD[72] to become an engineering student, but, in traditional fashion, he used his time in engineering to concentrate on higher things.[73] He left in first year to become a broadcaster.

---

[72] University College Dublin is the largest university in Ireland. While Trinity College is known as Trinners, surprisingly UCD has no diminutive form.

[73] See the example of Percy French in The Non-Applications of

From 1938 his commentaries helped boost the popularity of Gaelic games across the country. He had an ability to add drama to the most banal passages of play, which constituted the majority of the action. He quickly became the most recognised voice in Ireland. In the 1940s and 1950s people gathered around radios in kitchens and pubs just to hear his voice. Even missionaries in Africa paused in their beating of African children in schools to gather around longwave radios to imbibe his nostalgic accent from Ireland.

From 1945 he began to comment on horse racing. He was able to make the slowest horses appear unimaginably speedy, and every race seem to have an extraordinarily close finish, even when there was half a mile between the horses. He was offered the job of commentating at the Aintree Grand National by the BBC, which he did for twenty-five races. His big break came in 1967 when most of the field fell, allowing a 100-1 shot, Fionavon, to climb out of the heap of horses and jockeys and win by a mile to the sound of O'Hehir's apocalyptically excited commentary. He also read racing tips for the Hospitals Trust,[74] sponsored by Vaseline hair tonic. There is no data available on how many heart attacks he may have induced in his listeners.

In 1961 he set up Radio Telefís Éireann's (RTÉ) sports department, where he was head until 1972. He provided the commentary on Roger Casement's (1864–1916) reburial in

---

Engineering in Chapter 7 for a guide on how best to spend your time as an engineering student.

[74] The Irish Hospitals' Sweepstake was a lottery established in 1930 to finance hospitals. One of the organisers was Richard Duggan, who was a bookmaker. This sweepstake was popular in Britain and America. The winner was determined on the outcome of several horse races, including the Irish Grand National. Because the Adelaide Hospital's governors disapproved of gambling, that was the only hospital not to accept money from the Hospitals Trust, which distributed the profits.

Glasnevin Cemetery in 1965. I imagine he made the cortège appear to move like a Grand Prix race. He was popular in America, dating from his famous broadcast of an All-Ireland football final from the Polo Grounds in New York in 1947. Subsequently, he provided a five-hour emotional commentary at John F. Kennedy's funeral in Washington. He was offered jobs in America based on his Kennedy commentary, but sadly he declined, choosing to remain in Ireland for the rest of his life.

He broadcast ninety-nine All-Ireland finals during his career. On the eve of the one hundredth, he suffered a stroke, having been responsible for countless strokes up and down the country over the years amongst over-excited fathers listening to their car radios. He was able to make two flies crawling up a wall sound like the ultimate struggle of life and death. He made GAA games, and thereby the players, seem interesting. Something I am not able to do.

Throwing Your Weight Around

A traditional Irish approach to athletics was to not develop one's potential. Not training at all, avoiding exercise or movement as much as possible, smoking or being paid by advertisers to smoke, drinking and developing a generally contemptuous attitude to fitness could achieve this. It was essential to rely only on one's natural attributes. Being big was a major advantage. You are either big or you are not, and small people know that stretching exercises will only achieve so much. In the past, if you were big you might have been inclined to throw things. Big Irish people liked to throw stuff at the Olympics. Wrestling[75] and throwing stuff, including your opponent, were popular athletic distractions.

---

[75] There are three mainstream traditional forms of wrestling: Cumberland, Freestyle and Greco-Roman. In Cumberland wrestling,

Edmond Barrett (1877–1932) is the only Irish man to win both an All-Ireland GAA hurling medal and an Olympic gold medal. Barrett, from Kerry, worked in a quarry to build up his muscles before emigrating to London in 1902 where he joined the police, amongst whom wrestling was popular at that time: that is, wrestling each other and not the public in general.

Barrett won an All-Ireland Senior Hurling Championship medal with the London Emmets, who beat the Cork-based Redmonds in the 1901 GAA final, which was actually played in 1903. In 1901, for the purposes of hurling only, Britain was designated a fifth province of Ireland. The winners of the British Championship would meet the Irish provincial winner to decide the overall All-Ireland title. This was the only time a hurling final was won by a team outside of Ireland. In 1908, Barrett won the British heavyweight free-style wrestling title. He was then included in the Olympic team for shot put, javelin, wrestling, tug-of-war and free-style discus. The latter is an event where you are allowed to throw the discus any way you like but, for spectator safety, not where you like because this was a time before nets. At the London 1908 Olympics, Barrett won a gold medal in the tug-of-war, and a bronze in the heavyweight freestyle wrestling. He was knocked out of the first round of the

---

both contestants start with their arms locked around each other, their chins resting on the right shoulder of the other. You lose if you lose your grip or if any part of your body except your feet touches the ground. Freestyle wrestling is also called catch-as-catch-can because it allows the wrestler to catch hold of his opponent anywhere he can. No holds are barred. It is derived from a number of traditional styles, including English folk and Irish collar-and-elbow wrestling. Freestyle wresters win by their opponent's submission or pinning. Greco-Roman doesn't allow holding below the waist and wrestlers in this style win through throws, pin falls or points scored during three two-minute rounds.

Greco-Roman wrestling. In the first round of the shot put he was in excellent form. He threw a lifetime best to put him in fifth place going into the second round. However, one of his competitors cannily dropped his shot onto Barrett's foot, forcing him to retire.

The "Irish Whales" were a collection of Irish athletes who were adept at being large. One of these Whales was Con Walsh (1881–1961), who was 6 feet, 4 inches tall, weighed 15 stones and had enormous physical strength. A fellow Whale advised him to take up step-dancing lessons to improve his agility in hammer throwing. This was as far as his formal training went.

He represented Canada in the London 1908 Olympics, where he won a bronze medal in the hammer behind fellow Irish Whales John L. Flanagan (1873–1938) and Matt McGrath (1875–1941), who were both representing America. This was the only time in history when Irishmen made a clean sweep of Olympic medals in an event. Flanagan, from Limerick, became the first man ever to win three successive Olympic gold medals in a track and field competition. McGrath, from Tipperary, was eccentric because he did believe in training. He won silver in 1908, giving rise to a two-week community drinking session in Nenagh. At the 1908 Games, McGrath threatened to hospitalise the American team flag carrier if he dipped the flag as he passed the royal box. This gave rise to the tradition that the American flag is never dipped at an Olympic ceremony. He won gold in the hammer at the 1912 Olympics.

Pat O'Callaghan (1905–1991), from Cork, was also big but not a member of the Whales. He developed an interest in the hammer while studying medicine in Dublin. At home during his summer holidays, he made his own hammer using a cannon ball from Macroom Castle, as you do. Practice led to the Olympic Games in Amsterdam in 1928 where, as a complete unknown, he won the gold medal. In 1932, he successfully defended his Olympic title in Los Angeles, winning the gold with a final throw of 176 feet, 11 inches, becoming the only Irish person to successfully defend an Olympic gold medal. After an accident with a hammer in which a child was killed, he went to America to pursue professional wrestling. Sam Goldwyn offered him the role of Tarzan in the Hollywood blockbuster – a role that needed no acting abilities because even Cheetah the chimp managed – but he turned it down. The role went to Johnny Weissmuller, the former Olympic champion swimmer. O'Callaghan returned to Ireland.

If not throwing them yourself, it was handy to be able to jump out of the way of javelins, hammers and discs. Tim Aherne (1885–1968), from Limerick, represented Britain in the 1908 Olympics in the long jump, the standing long jump and high hurdles. He entered the hop, skip and jump event against a strong field of nineteen competitors, including hot favourite Eric Larsen from Norway. In second place before the final round, he hopped, skipped and jumped to an Olympic gold and a world record of 48 feet, 11.25 inches. He was the only athlete representing Britain to win a gold medal in a field event until they could find one of their own, Lynn Davies, to win the long jump in 1964. Tim's younger brother Dan beat his world record in New York in May 1911 with a hop, skip and jump of 50 feet, 11 inches.

Large Irish people didn't have to go to the Olympics to throw things. They could do it on our roads. William Bennett (1877–1967) was a champion road bowler, which is a sport still popular in Cork and Armagh. Before the bowling organisation Bol Chumann na hÉireann was founded in 1954, there were no formal recognised rules. Basically, it was anarchy in the road bowling world. There was no official national champion until 1963. But "Bennett the Bowler" is credited with five championships. His main rival during his heyday was "Red" Crowley. Bennett is believed to have been the first to loft a 28-ounce bowl over the 91-foot viaduct on the Cork to Bandon road. Be careful if you are ever driving that way because bowlers are still trying to emulate his great achievement.

Breaking through the Glass Jaw

We now know that exercise is actually good for us. While the sport of wrestling has declined in popularity, our interest in boxing remains constant. We always enjoy a good fight, even when we are not in it.

William Dempsey, the American heavyweight boxing champion of the 1920s, fought as Jack Dempsey as a tribute to the lesser known Irish-born world middleweight champion of the 1880s. The original Jack Dempsey (1862–1895), from Kildare, boxed under both the London Prize Ring Rules – with bare knuckles or tight leather gloves and a round ending when a boxer hit the ground – and the Queensberry Rules,[76] using padded gloves and with fixed three-minute rounds. Several of Dempsey's early fights in New York were interrupted by the arrival of the police. These were declared no contests. By 1886 he had thumped his way to undisputed middleweight champion of the world, beating Jack Fogarty, George Le Blanche and George Fulljames, amongst others, along the way.

Throughout the 1880s he was the second most famous athlete in America behind the boxer John L. Sullivan.[77]

---

[76] This enlightened boxing code was published in 1867 as "The Queensberry Rules for the Sport of Boxing". There are twelve Queensberry Rules. John Douglas, 9th Marquess of Queensberry, publicly endorsed the code, thereby giving it his name. This is the same Queensberry who was sued for libel by Oscar Wilde (1854–1900), whose family are detailed in Family Ties in Chapter 6. By 1889 the Queensberry Rules had come into use in America.

[77] John L. (Lawrence) Sullivan, also known as the Boston Strong Boy,

However, Dempsey was handsome, personable, well mannered and relatively urbane. You could invite him round for tea, which you couldn't do with John L. because the latter's only social accomplishment was beating people up. Still, Dempsey would probably have preferred to drink all of your available booze rather than the tea. Women loved him. He was a technically gifted boxer and remained cool under pressure. He out-boxed his opponents when he could but also slugged it out if he had to. He enjoyed the moniker "Nonpareil", which meant that he was unique.

From 1884 to 1887 he remained unbeaten in fifty-two fights. On 13 December 1887, he fought Johnny Regan on the Long Island coast. After eight rounds, the rising tide engulfed the ring, forcing a halt to the contest. The opponents, together with their entourages and supporters, travelled twenty-five miles by tugboat to another venue on higher ground. Regan's spiked shoes had already opened a gash on Dempsey's shin at the first venue. Regan had been observed sharpening those spikes before the fight. In the new venue, when it began to snow, Regan kept hitting the ground to try to slow the match because, according to the London Prize Ring Rules, a round ended when a contestant was down. But Dempsey managed to knock him out in the forty-fifth round before the venue was snowed out.

Dempsey was defeated only three times in sixty-eight contests. He was the first modern middleweight world champion. He is probably the greatest Irish-born boxer and pound-for-pound fighter, ever. He died from tuberculosis before the booze could kill him in 1895.

---

was the last heavyweight champion of bare-knuckle boxing under the London Prize Ring Rules and the first heavyweight champion of gloved boxing under the Queensberry Rules. He was the first American sports hero to become a national celebrity and the first American athlete to earn over one million dollars.

James "Lugs" Branigan (1910–1986) was a boxer and a policeman who originated the *Dirty Harry* approach to Dublin's street crime. He became an apprentice fitter at the Great Southern Railways when he was fourteen but he hated the experience. He was regularly bullied and beaten by his colleagues because he was so wimpy. He joined the Garda Síochána in 1931, barely meeting the chest measurement requirements. To beef himself up, he took up weight training, rowing and boxing. He quickly became a physical fitness fanatic.

In the 1930s he started training every morning at 5.00 a.m. He regularly fought in Garda Boxing Club bouts. He fought at cruiserweight, light heavyweight and finally heavyweight class between 1936 and 1939. He lost as many fights as he won. He was a dogged rather than a skilful boxer. In 1936, after many beatings along the way, he eventually won the Leinster heavyweight title.

At a boxing tournament in 1938 in Berlin in Germany he was knocked down nine times by a vastly superior opponent, staggering back to his feet each time before he could be counted out. His was the original *Rocky* performance. The crowd, which included Göring and Goebbels,[78] went wild. While he was not anti-Semitic, he did keep a scrapbook of

---

[78] Hermann Göring was a leading member of Adolf Hitler's Nazi Party. He was commander-in-chief of the air force from 1935 until the final days of the Second World War in 1945. In 1941 Hitler designated him as his successor and deputy in all his offices. Göring commited suicide after being sentenced to death by the Nuremberg Trials, which were a series of military tribunals held by the victorious Allied Forces to prosecute the leaders of Hitler's Third Reich.

Joseph Goebbels, who had a doctorate in literature, was the Nazi Minister of Propaganda from 1933 to 1945. He was probably Hitler's most devoted follower. As a one-time failed novelist he ultimately exercised total control over the German media, arts and all public communications. Goebbels had his six children killed before both he

Hitler's life and times and shared the Nazi obsession with physical fitness. A Garda doctor told him, perhaps too late, that the kind of beating he took in Berlin could lead to brain damage. He retired and became a boxing referee. He refereed more than 16,000 fights.

From 1936 he was a Garda on the beat in the Kevin St "A" district. He cycled his beat and specialised in preempting potential trouble by causing the trouble himself. He earned a reputation for dispensing instant justice with his fists on Dublin's mean streets. He was an efficient public servant because his normal practice was to spare the courts the time, and the paperwork, by beating up a considerable proportion of those he caught breaking the law. A 1940s Dublin criminal gave him the nickname "Lugs" because of his big ears, but he beat up anyone he overheard calling him that. Approaching the likely troublemakers, he would pull on a pair of tight-fitting black leather gloves while muttering something about the thugs "making his day".

He liked to have the first arrest of each New Year in the station, so he would usually have a few criminals who he caught earlier lined up so he could charge them when the clock struck midnight. To control the violent excesses of Dublin Teddy Boys in 1957, he was obliged to attend the film *Rock Around the Clock* at least sixty times. He hated the film.

He often defended young offenders or tried to get them jobs to keep them out of trouble. One mother of a family of offenders said, "Mr Branigan always got a cup of tea in this house before he lagged (beat) one of me boys." He sorted out marriage problems by beating up husbands who beat up their wives. He also served as a state bodyguard to visiting dignitaries, including Elizabeth Taylor, Cliff Richard and the second greatest footballer ever, George

---

and his wife committed suicide in Hitler's bunker in Berlin at the end of the Second World War.

Best (1946–2005).[79] He was promoted to sergeant, and given a van called "Branno five" to help round up criminals. When he retired, he received a canteen of cutlery and a set of Waterford glass from Dublin's prostitutes, who he liked to call "pavement hostesses".

He carried many scars from knives and bottles, and was once bitten on his backside when sitting on a suspect to subdue him. In court he referred to the biter as being "worse than the Balubas. At least they cook you first." While the Balubas are one of the Bantu peoples of Central Africa, the name appealed to popular Dublin imagination as a term to describe any so-called primitive peoples, including themselves. At that time Dubliners would have relied exclusively on *Tarzan* films for their ethnographic understanding of native Africans. The term "Baluba" was also used with reference to someone who had done something foolish, like allowing themselves to be apprehended by Branigan.

Stephen "Crusher" Casey (1908–1987), from Sneem in Kerry, was a world freestyle wrestling champion, a rower and a tug-of-war champion. He had natural talent because his father had been a sparring partner of the legendary John L. Sullivan, and a rower in a team of Sneem rowers in New York sponsored by the Vanderbilts.[80] Casey emigrated to London in 1933 where he began work as a hotel porter. He

---

[79] It is traditional in football circles to claim that Edson Arantes do Nascimento, better known by his nickname Pelé, is the best footballer ever, but naturally fans will persist in debating these matters forever.

[80] Collectively, the Vanderbilts are the seventh wealthiest family in history. Their fortune was established by Cornelius Vanderbilt, who left school aged eleven and went on to build a railroad and shipping empire. Cornelius's son and heir William Henry extended the family fortune to become the richest man in the world by the time of his death in 1877. The family's prominence lasted until the late twentieth century when most of their many mansions were torn down. Other Vanderbilt homes have been sold or turned into museums.

twice threw a wrestler out of the ring who had unwisely issued a challenge to all-comers in the audience.

After 201 European professional victories he moved to America to wrestle there. In sixteen months of wrestling in America, during which he had 316 victories, he finally defeated Louis Thesz for the undisputed world title in 1938.

Crusher Casey had a famous rivalry with another Irish wrestler, Dan O' Mahoney (1912–1950), whose ring name was Danno Mahony. Danno was from Ballydehob in Cork. He established his reputation for extreme strength when he lifted a car belonging to the school inspector out of a drain when he was twelve years old. When Danno and Crusher fought each other in Dublin in 1938 in front of a crowd of 16,000 people there was no winner. Danno had invented a wrestling move called "the Irish whip" that Crusher Casey actually used to defeat him later that same year at Mallow, Co. Cork in the twentieth round in front of just 3,500 witnesses. The crowd was small because the Bishop of Ross had declared that dutiful Catholics should not attend wrestling on a Sunday.

Crusher Casey reputedly had the most powerful hands and he also invented his own move, "the Killarney flip". In four fights against Crusher Casey, Danno never managed to win. There is a statue of Danno in Ballydehob village.

Crusher Casey turned to boxing. In 1940, under his new identity as "The Sneem Machine", he challenged Joe Louis, the then world heavyweight boxing champion, to a fight for a purse of $50,000 that he put up himself. Louis wisely refused the challenge. The Sneem Machine's brother, Jim Casey (1912–2000), won the Texas, Canadian, Southern United States and Pacific Coast heavyweight wrestling titles, but neither brother would agree to fight the other. There is a statue of Crusher, aka The Sneem Machine, in Sneem village.

Jack Doyle (1913–1978), from Cork, was a boxer, singer and playboy, which is a rare combination of talents, even in Irish history. While working as a docker and a farm labourer, he read a boxing instruction manual called *How to Box*, which inspired him to become a pugilist. He wasn't deterred by the fact that he was never technically impressive. He had a glass jaw and a lethal right hand, which meant that most of his fights never went on longer than two rounds, because he would either knock out his opponent or be promptly knocked out himself. Furthermore, he reasonably ignored his fitness, which wouldn't be needed over a mere two rounds. But he also neglected to develop any defensive techniques, which would have been useful. He boxed under the names "The Gorgeous Gael", "The Body Beautiful" and "The King of Clout", but not under the names "The Jaw of Glass" or "The Tub of Lard".

Doyle began his boxing career with ten straight knock-outs, that is, he knocked out ten of his opponents. He then quickly became addicted to alcohol and women. During a particular boxing match against the undistinguished Jack Pettifer in either late 1932 or early 1933, one of his few fights to go beyond two rounds, he was so exhausted from his social life that he had to be revived with brandy between rounds. He managed to barely win that one. In 1933 he fought for the British heavyweight title. However, by then he was suffering badly with venereal disease (VD).

In an effort to even his odds, he decided to concentrate on damaging the below-the-belt anatomy of his opponent. He was disqualified, banned and fined. His Irish support-ers loved him and were happy to believe his disqualification was a British conspiracy. No one in Ireland could imagine that Doyle actually had VD; it was not a recognised disease in Ireland at that stage because no one in Ireland had sex. Serendipitously, the disqualification allowed him to pursue his singing ambitions.

Doyle starred in several local films and travelled to Hollywood in 1934 where he landed the lead in two films,

McGlusky the Sea Rover (1934) and *Navy Spy* (1937). There he married the actress Judith Allen in 1935. They performed together in concerts. However, his fans in Ireland had cooled on him because he had married a divorcee, which was a state of being also not recognised in Ireland at that time. In Hollywood his friends Errol Flynn and Clark Gable did recognise both divorce and VD. He divorced Allen and re-entered the ring in Britain in 1937, after preparing with three wins and one loss in Madison Square Gardens in New York.

He was far ahead in his first British fight following his film career. But when he punched his dazed opponent as he was sitting on the bottom rope, he was disqualified again. In another fight, as he advanced to finish off his bewildered opponent with a haymaker right, he missed and fell through the ropes and into the press seats, knocking himself out. His gallant opponent gave him an opportunity for revenge in another fight. This time Doyle put his semi-conscious adversary on the canvas twice before closing in for the coup de grâce. As he rushed in, he fell onto the end of his challenger's fist, knocking himself out again. He was then beaten in Dalymount Park in Dublin in the first round of a Heavyweight Championship of Ireland exhibition fight against an untrained blacksmith.

Doyle earned a vast amount of money from his boxing, singing and films. At one time he kept a mansion at Ascot in Britain, with bodyguards, servants, chauffeurs and a singing teacher. He had an affair with the car heiress Delphine Dodge, her fifteen-year-old daughter and her sister-in-law. The Dodge men had to both threaten him at gunpoint and pay him £10,000 to keep him away from the Dodge women. An actress, Betty Strathmore, took poison in front of him in a hotel room, so desperate was her love for him. She wasn't famous enough for us to know if she survived. He married the actress Maria "Movita" Castaneda, who appeared in the 1939 film *Mutiny on the Bounty*. They toured together until divorcing in 1945. He also had an affair with the actress Diana Dors.

After this, he had a period of homelessness when he slept in a van on Henrietta St in Dublin. In desperation, he became a wrestler. He lost his first fight to his friend Michael "Butty" Sugrue (1924–1977).

Butty, from Kerry, had joined Duffy's Circus, as you should, as "Ireland's strongest man", which involved him dragging a cart filled with ten men around the big top with a rope clenched between his teeth. Butty became a successful wrestler, and used his winnings to open a chain of popular Irish pubs in London. For publicity, he persuaded one of his barmen to spend sixty-one days in a coffin buried in the garden of one of his pubs. He challenged his friend Jack Doyle to a wrestling match in Killorglin in Kerry in 1953 to help resurrect Doyle's wrestling career. Unfortunately, Doyle lost in the first round, ruining the entertainment for the crowd and his own comeback. Butty also promoted a fight at Croke Park in 1972 between Muhammad Ali and Al "Blue" Lewis, which was also a disaster for him. It was badly organised and only a small crowd turned up, despite Butty's promise that any profits would go to "the mentally handicapped children of Ireland".

Butty often paid an impoverished Doyle to sing in his London pubs. But Doyle's singing career took a knock when Butty died while carrying a refrigerator up the stairs in one of his pubs in Shepherd's Bush in London. Doyle spent most of the rest of his life in relative poverty and homelessness. In 1972 he returned to Cork, where a huge crowd turned out for his own cabaret act. In 1978 they turned out again for his funeral.

If you couldn't sing, act, or box clean, you could get exercise by becoming a famously dirty boxer like James Elliott (1838–1883). Elliott was born in Westmeath but emigrated to America when he was an infant. He specialised in being a dirty fighter, which is not surprising considering he started his boxing career as a member of an Irish street gang. He had a destructive right hand combined with a capacity to withstand terrible punishment from superior boxers. Unlike Doyle, he didn't have a glass jaw. He had a concrete one. He also had a devastating head butt, eye gouge and bite. In 1861 he knocked out Nobby Clarke in ten rounds as a heavy-weight boxer. He then fought Hen Winkle. That fight was declared a draw after ninety-nine rounds. As prizefight-ing was illegal in America, you could win if your opponent was arrested on his way to the fight. After getting several potential challengers arrested, Elliott was himself eventu-ally arrested and sentenced to two years in Trenton State Penitentiary.

When Elliott got out of gaol in 1865 he went into the protection racket business to support his drink and gambling interests. In 1866 he was with General John O'Neill in his invasion of Canada.[81] By 1867 he beat Bill Davis in a nine-round fight to take the heavyweight title of America. In 1868 he defended his title against Charles Gallagher. After twenty-three rounds, Gallagher's seconds refused to allow their man back into the fight because of all the gouging, biting and butting from Elliott.

Elliott found it increasingly difficult to find opponents because of his reputation, so he drifted back into crime. In 1872 he was convicted of the highway assault and robbery of the popular Negro minstrel Hugh Dougherty, who almost died from the attack. Elliott got eighteen years in gaol. After eight years he was released, partly due to his going blind.

He was back in the ring in 1879 to challenge the reigning American champion John J. Dwyer. Blind and out of shape, he was badly beaten after twelve rounds. So he dipped his

---

[81] See Beneath the Green Waves in Chapter 5 for details of the Fenian invasion of Canada.

gloves in turpentine and attempted to gouge out Dwyer's eyes in the thirteenth round to even the odds. Dwyer's seconds managed to wash out his eyes. Dwyer had to knock Elliott out in the fourteenth round to retain his own sight.

Elliott's next fight was against the great John L. Sullivan under the Queensberry Rules, which didn't suit him. He was flattened in the third round. In March 1883 Elliott was shot dead over a gambling row as he left a saloon in Chicago.

Not all prizefighters were dirty. There were a few honourable ones. Michael McCoole's (1837–1886) popularity soared after he refused to hit his opponent, Joe Coburn from Co. Armagh, when he was down on one knee, something which he was allowed to do. He turned his back to give Coburn a chance to get up. Coburn won the fight by hitting McCoole behind the ear. Nice! There were other things a clean fighter could do. If you were being bitten, for example, you could rely on your supporters to rush in and rescue you. That was allowed.

Sometimes the audience was more of a hindrance than a help. Jack McAuliffe (c.1866–1937) was knocked out only once in his entire boxing career when the father of a man he had just beaten hit him with a chair. Though knocked out that time, he was never declared beaten over seventy-five fights, one of which went on for sixty-four rounds.

Some people imagine that boxers end up in the sport because they have limited opportunities in other areas. But Isaac Weir (1867–1908) could have been a jockey, a pianist, a dancer or a comic singer. His father had wanted him to become a priest. Instead, Weir ran away to Manchester in 1885 where he won several minor boxing matches. The following year he went to America to become a featherweight bare-knuckle boxing champion. He holds the record for participating in the longest world title contest in any weight division when the police stopped his fight against Englishman Frank Murphy in the eightieth round. Weir was never the undisputed world featherweight champion because of the unwillingness of the American boxing authorities to recognise world title fights that did not include an American.

The Dreaded Pedestrianists

Even if our ancestors didn't value physical fitness as much as we do, they still managed to move quicker than us. We know from the archive of black and white silent films of athletic events from the end of the nineteenth century that people ran faster than we do now, and they jumped faster, if not higher – all without the aid of exotic performance-enhancing drugs. However someone must have been on drugs, if only for the sake of science.

Being a runner was outrageous enough without using drugs to add to the stigma. A professional runner was one of the lowest forms of sporting life at the beginning of the twentieth century. Perhaps the greatest anxiety a parent could have had at that time was that their child would become a professional runner, commonly known as a "pedestrianist". The brief relief that your little angel wasn't going to become an attorney or a poet could be instantly destroyed by this unhoped-for career choice. Picture the tableau of the distraught home where the mother sobs inconsolably into her apron at the kitchen table, while the father, clutching a shotgun in one hand, points to the door with the other, indicating that his would-be pedestrianist son should get out and never return.

Beauchamp Rochfort Day (1881–1946?) was a pedestrianist. In Day's case we don't know the details of why or how he was the victim of such a fate. Perhaps his mother was threatened with having to become a boxer, attorney or prostitute, so he chose to sacrifice his own honour to save her from having to go on those games. We will never know. What we do know is that he was fast.

Day, from Dún Laoghaire, Co. Dublin, first demonstrated his weakness for running when he won the 100 yards in 10.2 seconds in a school sports event. In 1900 he won a 440 yards race in 49.4 seconds, which was half a second quicker than the American Olympic champion at the time, Maxey Long. The race official couldn't believe his eyes. The time was officially amended to 50.8 seconds so that it became a new Irish record but nothing more dramatic. However, a racing promoter, the pimp of late nineteenth-century life, was present at that race. He persuaded Day to turn professional.

From 1902 to 1906, Day travelled the world openly as a pedestrianist. At that time, runners often raced under assumed names, probably to reduce the personal shame. Gambling syndicates sponsored them. A syndicate demanded that their runners should race strategically, which meant finishing in a pre-agreed order. Bookies had learned from bitter experience that it was easier to get people to obey orders than horses or greyhounds. Day had an ongoing rivalry with the Australian pedestrianist Arthur Postle, who was known as "The Crimson Flash". In April 1907 in Perth, Day bet every penny he had on himself, and set a new world record in the 450 yards of 47.8 seconds. In America he won $3,000[82] for running 100 yards in 10 seconds flat. Sport historians regard Day as our greatest Irish sprinter ever.

A Horse of the Same Colour

Horse racing, or racing anything, is one of the oldest and most popular sports in Ireland. In the past, if you were of a plump build you could have tried tug-of-war. If you were skinny you could have become a jockey. Michael Dawson (1865–1926) weighed in at just 5 stone, 7 pounds and was one of the most sought-after jockeys in the country.

---

[82] Approximately €65,000 in contemporary currency values.

If you were fat and couldn't competitively ride your own horse in an actual race, you could own one. For that, you just needed money. Richard "Boss" Croker (1841–1922), from Cork, was one of those rich people who had money and nothing else. When Boss was five, before he earned his nickname, his father, Eyre Croker, took his family to live in America. Eyre became a horse doctor.[83]

Boss wasn't a noted student. But he did distinguish himself with his fists in the school yard, and then in the boxing ring. The Tammany Hall Organization[84] that controlled the Democratic Party in New York needed people like Boss to help maintain political order. In 1865 he became a hired thug for Jimmy O'Brien, who was a ward boss.[85] He became an alderman in 1868 and a coroner in 1873, which gave him an official income of $25,000 per annum. As the Hall was mostly an Irish political organisation, there just had to be a split. In the split, Boss sided with the Young Democracy faction, which was led by the notoriously corrupt "Honest" John Kelly against the even more corrupt William H. Tweed. Kelly eventually succeeded in becoming the lead man after Tweed's surprise conviction.

---

[83] See footnote on "doctoring" in Chapter 1. Quotation marks are not needed in the horse doctoring profession because "horse doctor" and horse doctor is the same thing in the imagination of a nervous sick horse.

[84] The "Hall", which served as the Tammany Society's headquarters, was built in 1830 on East 14th St in New York. Tammany Hall became the centre for the Democratic Party's control of most of the New York City elections. It played a major role in dominating New York politics by helping immigrants, most notably the influx of Irish after the Famine, to rise up in American politics. Many became ward bosses.

[85] The Tammany Hall ward boss served as the local vote gatherer and provider of patronage. Effectively, they were enforcers of party policy. Tammany Hall became synonymous with wide-spread political corruption, most notably under William H. "Boss" Tweed.

Boss Croker held just one other official post, that of city chamberlain from 1889 to 1890, but he unofficially controlled the city's Democratic Party, manipulating all city offices for seventeen years. Under his influence there were property and planning frauds, protection rackets, prostitution and saloon bars. He amassed about $8 million of personal wealth.[86] He was probably the most corrupt person in the world at that time. However, in 1894 his "career" stalled when a reforming candidate became mayor. This marked the end of his political life. By 1903 he had emigrated to Europe to start anew as a respectable person.

He saw horse racing as a means by which he could pursue respectability from his English base. However, being a famous thug, even a fabulously rich one, didn't help his cause. But horses became his passion. They didn't care about his pedigree because only their own equine bloodlines mattered to them. Against advice, he raced imported American horses that did badly. He split with his trainer and acquired new horses. He decided to have these horses trained at Newmarket in England, which would have helped his quest for respectability: if his horses could be respectable so could he by association. However, the Jockey Club refused his request for a licence because he wasn't a gentleman. In a rage he moved to Ireland where he had another falling out, this time with his Irish horse trainer. But money can address some problems. He bought a fast horse called Orby. By 1907 Orby became the first Irish-trained horse to win the Derby. King Edward VII refused to greet Boss in the winner's enclosure after the race. However, this royal snub did help him to become a national hero back in Ireland.

Orby romped home first in the Irish Derby in 1907 to make Boss a freeman, if not a gentleman, of Dublin in 1908.

---

[86] The lowest estimate of contemporary values is about €160 million.

Orby's half-sister Rhodora won the English 1,000 Guineas race for him. Boss then had an ungentlemanly idea that he hoped would make him instantly socially acceptable. He insisted on incestuously mating the two champions in an effort to produce a super-horse. The two respectable horses must have been horrified, but what could they do?

The birth of a hideously deformed foal killed Rhodora. Despite this eugenics setback, Boss won two Irish Oaks races and was the leading owner in Ireland in 1911. However, notwithstanding the exciting genetic engineering experiments, he was becoming bored in Ireland. His death ended the boredom. He left $5 million to his second wife, Bula Benton Edmunson, who was fifty years younger than him. There are no reports of Edmunson being bored after her husband's death.

If you couldn't be a skinny jockey or a fat owner you could have been a trainer. But it was necessary to find a great horse to make you look talented. Arkle (1957–1970) was just such a horse. He was the greatest Irish steeplechaser ever. Tom Dreaper (1898–1975) is best remembered in Irish history for being the trainer of Arkle. Arkle won the Cheltenham Gold Cup three times in a row, the Irish Grand National, the Hennessey Gold Cup twice, the Whitbread Gold Cup and the Leopardstown Chase. From twenty-eight starts, or races, he won twenty-four prior to being injured in the King George VI Chase at Kempton Park, England. Despite breaking his leg, he finished second in that race.

This legend of Irish horse racing began life in 1956 when his mother, Bright Cherry, visited his father, Archive, for a night, or at least a few minutes of love, known in smutty horse circles as an equine quickie and to polite horse people as a cover. Archive had failed to win a single race in his career. However, his father, Nearco, who was Italian, was unbeaten in Italy, where we must allow that perhaps the horses were slower. His mother, Booklaw, won several classics. Archive's fee was 48 guineas[87] for a cover – he was a cheap gigolo – a fee that had to be paid even if the horses only wanted to talk. However, despite his lack of success on the track, Archive had been doing reasonably as a stud-horse, siring five future winners. By coincidence, after the romance with Bright Cherry, his offspring started winning races, driving up the price of a date with him. But as Boss Croker knew and many others have found out since, horse breeding is not scientific. It is closer to breeding people. As it took Arkle five years to mature and demonstrate his quali-ties, Bright Cherry and Archive were never to repeat their moment of passion. By then it was too late – poor Archive had been bumped off by his owners.

Arkle was born at 3.30 a.m. on 19 April 1957 at Ballymacoll Stud, Co. Meath, which at one time belonged to Boss Croker. He almost broke a leg when he was just a few months old. When he was exactly a year and a day old, he almost lost an entire leg when he jumped a hedge containing a strand of barbed wire. As he struggled to free himself, the wire dug deep into his flesh and opened a flap of flesh a foot long to reveal his off-fore cannon bone. Forty stitches were required to reattach the flesh.

Understandably, male horses don't like to risk jumping prickly fences because of their low-hanging sensitive parts. However, to help them overcome this worry, their consider-ate trainers cut off the vulnerable parts. Arkle had his cut off in the autumn of 1958. He was then sold at Goff's Ballsbridge

---

[87] Guineas were gold coins minted between 1663 and 1813. The name came from the Guinea region in West Africa where much of the gold used to make the coins originated. The value of a guinea was officially fixed at £1.s. (21s.) in 1816 or £1.05 in modern decimalised currency. Although no longer circulated, guineas are still used for pricing race horses, where the purchaser pays in guineas while the seller receives payment in an equal number of pounds with the difference traditionally going to the auctioneer as commission.

Auction in 1960 for 1,150 guineas. The Duchess of Westminster, Anne Sullivan, from Cork, bought him. When Arkle turned up for training in his new home, Greenogue in Co. Dublin, he got stuck with the new stable boy since he was the last choice of everyone in the yard. As is the way with many great horses, he looked too scrawny to impress.

Arkle's first race was at Mullingar on 9 December 1961 with Mark Hely-Hutchinson on board. Hely-Hutchinson, the second son of Lord Donoughmore, was an amateur jockey and Guinness employee. He was the only jockey in history never to win a race on Arkle; he finished third. Seventeen days later, Arkle and Hely-Hutchinson ran at Leopardstown in another Bumper[88] race. They finished fourth.

Arkle had his fifth birthday on 1 January 1962 because racehorses all celebrate their birthdays on 1 January. The life of a professional racehorse is tough. He got neither cake nor cards. But Arkle was made of stern stuff. He hid his tears and, undeterred, he won his first race on 20 January at Navan – a hurdle race for novices over a distance of three miles. He started at 20 to 1 with Liam McLoughlin on board and just flew past the opposition. From then on his regular jockey was Pat Taaffe (1930–1992), who rode him in twenty-six races.

Like all great athletes, Arkle had a classic rivalry with a contemporary, in his case an Irish-bred horse called Mill House. Although Irish, Mill House was regarded as English in horsey circles because he had emigrated. Arkle lost in his first race against Mill House at Newbury in the Hennessey Gold Cup in 1963. However, he won his first Cheltenham

---

[88] Shorter races without obstacles for novice horses that have not yet run over obstacles are usually referred to as Bumpers. National Hunt races are usually over obstacles. Steeplechasing, or chases, are over fences that are a minimum of 4.5 feet high. Hurdling takes place over hurdles that are a minimum of 3.5 feet high.

race in 1963, the Honeybourne Chase. But Mill House went one better, winning the Cheltenham Gold Cup. They met again the following year at Cheltenham to contest the Gold Cup.

The 1964 Cheltenham Gold Cup was one of the greatest horse races in history. The Irish crowds were for Arkle. The English supported Mill House. Only four horses ran in the race. Arkle won by five lengths and Dominic Behan[89] wrote the song "Arkle" to commemorate this famous victory. For his victory in the Irish Grand National that followed, the handicappers had to change the rules to get horses into the race against Arkle, who was made carry an unprecedented 26 pounds more than the next best horse, Flying Wild.

In 1966, Arkle broke a pedal bone in the King George VI Chase at Kempton Park. Despite the injury, he finished second to Dormant, who, though not ironically named, had no broken legs. That was the end of his racing career. On Sunday, 31 May 1970 a vet ended the life of Ireland's greatest ever athlete with a jab of a needle. He was just thirteen.

For those in history who thought that horses were too moody, jockeys too skinny and they were not rich enough to be owners, there was always greyhound racing. Dogs are cheaper and don't need riders, and you could bet on them and lose all your money the same as with horses.

Gordon-Bennett

Motor sports are great because they allow competitors to sit down while getting exercise. John Colohan (1862–1932), from Dublin, was a physician and pioneering motorist so he must have known that cars are good for us. He gave up all his medical practices in 1903 when he took up motoring,

---

[89] See Family Ties in Chapter 6 for details on Dominic Behan and his writing brothers.

which became his full-time career. He studied motor engineering in Germany, and learned to drive in France. The
Light Locomotive Bill was passed in 1896 in Britain and
Ireland, raising the speed limit from 4 to 14 miles per hour.
By 1903, this was raised again to a fantastic hair-raising 20
miles per hour. Inspired by the new speed limit, Colohan
purchased a 3.5-horsepower Benz Velo Comfortable, and is
credited with being Ireland's first car owner.

In 1899 Colohan won a wager by driving 135 miles from
Dublin to Galway in twelve hours. Obviously, with a time
like that, this was before the invention of traffic congestion,
in this case, at Kinegad. That time could be achieved only
because there was one car on the road. In 1901 he acquired
a 7-horsepower Daimler, and then a 24-horsepower one that
he souped-up to a massive 30 horsepower, making it probably the most powerful car in Ireland. He was known as the
"mad doctor" because naturally only lunatics drove horseless carriages back then.

He became a founding member of the (Royal) Irish
Automobile Club (RIAC) that organised the 1903 Gordon-
Bennett race, which was the greatest international sporting
event held in the country at that time. According to the
race rules, a car could represent a country if the manufac-
tured parts originated in that country. The driver could be
from anywhere. The nationality of the winning car parts
determined the venue for the next year, or else it could be
held in France. A car made from British parts won in 1902.
However, the race was held in Ireland the following year
because of widespread hysteria in Britain against the horseless carriage. The lawyers, for once acting in the public
interest, found that the by-laws didn't apply in Ireland
so racers would be allowed to exceed 20 miles per hour.
Support for the race was sought and secured from 120 MPs,
30 county councils, 450 hotels, 13 parish priests, and the

Bishop of Kildare and Leighlin. Colohan's RIAC were the official organisers.

The circuit was a figure of eight formed by roads in Kildare, running from Ballyshannon Crossroads to Kilcullen via Athy, and across the Curragh to Kildare Town and back. Three circuits were to be completed, making the course 368 miles and 765 yards in length. The council fixed potholes, straightened bends and even laid a new stretch of road near Portlaoise for the race, so great was their enthusiasm. Hedges were cut, flags erected and an estimated 2,000–7,000 police were deployed. On 2 July the road was closed from 6.00 a.m., all side roads were blocked and all animals were confined to fields. Spectators were ordered to stay behind hedges with their livestock. Compensation of a half-crown per hen was offered for any hens that were knocked down and killed. The grief-stricken owners of deceased hens were allowed to keep the corpses. During the practice runs, local hen owners placed their fowls on the road and waited to get rich. This is one of the few occasions in history when we know why the chicken crossed the road: because it was pushed. Annoyingly, the hens quickly became adept at avoiding speeding cars so surprisingly few were run over.

The French brought twenty cars to the race on their own ferry, which was anchored in Dublin Bay. Cars poured in in single digits from Britain and Germany. The Bishop sent out an encyclical warning of the dangers of combining alcohol and race watching, urging his parishioners to restrain themselves until after the race. Twelve racers from France, Germany, America and Britain (including Ireland) started the race. A few of the competitors actually began with their handbrakes on, which stalled their engines. Seven cars turned over or ran into hedges. Charles Jarrott crashed his Napier at 60 miles per hour on a straight road. Dr Kennedy, who cycled to the crash site to administer aid, attended to both him and his mechanic.

But Kennedy was shoved aside by Lambert Hepenstal Ormsby (1849–1923), who was a self-regarding surgeon originally from New Zealand. He was full of himself because in 1877 he had invented a pocket ether inhaler, which became widely used in anaesthesia worldwide. This notable invention came after his marriage to Anastasia. None of the spectators lurking behind the hedges during the Gordon-Bennett race joked about this, though no doubt they badly wanted to, because everyone was terrified of him. He helped found the National Children's Hospital in 1887, and was president of the Royal College of Surgeons when the crash happened. Camille Jenatzy, who was a Belgian driving a 60-horsepower Mercedes with German parts, won the race in 10 hours, 18 minutes and 1 second. Jenatzy went berserk when he won and may have needed a whiff from Ormsby's inhaler to calm him down.

Stanley Woods (1903–1993), from Dublin, was a confectioner and motorbike racer. Stanley's father was a sales representative for a confectioner. Stanley persuaded his father to allow him to leave school and take up employment driving his father around the country on his sales route in the sidecar of a motorcycle. Sadly, fathers wouldn't agree to such crazy ideas nowadays, but Stanley's father did. From this beginning, Woods became one of the most famous and consistent motorbike racers in Europe. In his first Isle of Man TT race[90] in 1924 he caused a sensation by finishing fifth, despite his bike catching fire on the second lap and having no brakes, a circumstance which can actually be helpful in

---

[90] The International Tourist Trophy (TT) race for motorcycles is held annually on the Isle of Man. The first race was held in May 1907 and was called the International Auto-Cycle Tourist Trophy. The event was organised by the Auto-Cycle Club for road-legal touring motorcycles with exhaust silencers, saddles, pedals and mud-guards. The course was 10 laps of 15 miles and 1,470 yards.

a time trial. In 1925 he won the Junior TT race and in 1926 he won the Senior TT race in a record time, with brakes.[91] In eighteen years of competition, he won ten Isle of Man TT races.

In 1921 he completed the Banbridge "50" with a holly branch replacing his smashed handlebars, and subsequently rode home with the branch to Dublin. He dominated road racing in the 1930s. For a few years in that decade he had his own confectionary factory, manufacturing "TT toffee". In 1957, aged 54, he set a TT course record of 86 miles per hour. At the age of 87 he completed a lap of the TT course at an average speed of over 80 miles per hour.

Fellow Irishman Joey Dunlop (1952–2000) ultimately smashed Wood's TT records. Dunlop won a total of twenty-six TTs. He also won three TT races in one week, three times. His fastest ever lap was 123.87 miles per hour on the TT Mountain Circuit.

The East German Example

Historically, it appears that more Irish women partook in warfare than in sport.[92] It seems that women would rather fight than take exercise. It is widely believed, at least by me, that the East German post-Second World War sporting authorities dealt with the reluctance of their women to participate in track and field by getting the men to pretend that they were women and compete in the ladies Olympic events.[93] From years of sociological studies we now know

---

[91] The junior race was for bikes with a 350 cubic centimetres (cc) engine size and the senior race was for 500cc bikes.

[92] See Battle Dresses in Chapter 3.

[93] Dora Ratjen took part in the women's high jump in the 1936 Berlin Olympics. As she was later revealed to be Heinrich Ratjen, her fourth place finish seems disappointing. In mitigation, Heinrich had been brought up by his parents as a girl. Just to complicate matters,

that an ability to bore is fairly evenly distributed across the genders. It was an important landmark in the history of Irish women's struggle for equality that they were allowed to be as boring as men in whatever field they liked. This is essentially why they had to be given access to the world of golf. But there will always be a few golf clubs that resist letting them in. How boring is that? Golf has attracted its share of boring women. Rhona Adair (1878–1961) was one such. Adair, like many Irish children, was a golf orphan, having been born into a household of golfers. Her father was a founding member of the Golfing Union of Ireland.

If you believe golf is boring, then you will think Adair was really boring because she began playing golf when she was eight. She became an amateur international player so her home was stuffed with useless prizes. She even played "Old" Tom Morris in a challenge match at St Andrews in Scotland in 1899, losing by just one hole. Morris, who was the pioneer of professional golf, was actually born in St Andrews, maybe even in a golf course bunker. In 1900 Adair won the long-driving contest (173 yards) at Royal Lytham and St Anne's Ladies Open. The year 1903 was Adair's last competitive one. Inevitably, she became lady captain at Royal Portrush Club in Co. Antrim.

Mabel Cahill (1863–c.1905), from Kilkenny, moved to New York in 1889. She must have been able to play tennis because by 1890 she entered the US Open Tennis Championships. Ellen Roosevelt, sister of the future President Franklin D., knocked her out. The following year she was back. She beat

the East Germans may have been using actual women athletes but turning them into men. For example, East German Heidi Krieger won the 1986 European women's shotput championship. Heidi officially became Andreas Krieger after a sex-change operation in 1997. But he claimed he had been given so many steroids by his coaches without his knowledge that he had begun to develop male characteristics.

Grace Roosevelt on the way to the final, in which she beat Grace's sister Ellen to become the only Irish woman ever to win the US Open. She was praised for her "manly style", which has to make you wonder if we Irish were ahead of the East Germans. Along with Emma Leavitt Morgan, she also won the manly ladies doubles against the Roosevelt sisters that year.

In 1892 she successfully defended her singles title, beating sixteen-year-old Bessie Moore in five sets. Women used to play five sets back then. I suppose no modern woman could grunt her way through a full five sets and no contemporary audience endure the racket. She defended her doubles title with Adeline McKinley, and won the national mixed doubles title with Clarence Hobart. She was the first player to win all three titles in the same year.

Cahill wrote a novel called *Her Playthings, Men* in 1890. She also wrote two articles for the *Ladies' Home Journal* called "The Art of Playing Good Tennis" and the essential "Arranging a Tennis Tournament". She disappeared from history around 1905. She may have died a manly death back in Ireland.

Amelia Earhart pioneered the tradition of women aviators vanishing into the clouds never to be seen again. But we had our own aviatress in Sophie Evans (1896–1939). Evans took up flying, partly because she had inherited insanity from her father, Jackie Pierce-Evans. He had married the housekeeper, as you do. Soon after Sophie's birth he was charged with killing her mother, the ex-housekeeper. Perhaps she had begun to neglect the ironing. Crazy or not, he successfully played the insanity card in court,[94] and was locked up forever rather than facing the death penalty. Her grandfather in Newcastle West then raised Evans. He sent her to school in Dublin.

---

[94] See Murder in a Time of War in Chapter 1 for another example of this common Irish legal defence.

Evans met and married an English army officer in 1920 who had a farm in Kenya in East Africa. She took a degree in agriculture in preparation for a life on the farm. She wrote a book of lyric poetry in 1925, as you do when you live on a farm, called *East African Nights*. However, her actual nights were more prosaic because the marriage broke down and she fled from Kenya to London to become an athlete. She excelled at the high jump and the javelin. In 1923 she set a world record of 4 feet, 10.5 inches for the high jump, and a world record of 173 feet, 2 inches for the Greek two-arm javelin throw, whatever that is, in 1924. She successfully lobbied to have women included in three events in track and field in the 1928 Amsterdam Olympic Games, where she represented England as a judge.

By 1925 Evans had become the first female member of the London Light Aeroplane Club. The International Commission for Air Navigation had banned women holding commercial licences, probably on the basis that it was unladylike to be killed. Evans offered herself as a guinea pig, and, as a result of her efforts, from May 1926 the ban on women's licences was rescinded.

She set several important aviation landmarks. She was the first woman pilot to loop-the-loop, and was the first to make a parachute jump. She also set a women's altitude record of 16,000 feet. She toured Ireland, Scotland and England promoting women's flying. On one day she travelled 1,300 miles and touched down 79 times in 13 hours. In February 1928 she undertook the first solo flight by a woman from South Africa to England. Along the way she endured sunstroke and had to be escorted into Rome by Mussolini's air force. When she landed in London she stepped out of her plane wearing a silk dress, fur coat and straw hat, claiming it was so easy for a woman to fly across Africa she could do so wearing a Parisian dress while powdering her nose along the way. The press, who didn't like her, called her "Lady Hell-of-a-din".

She became a commercial pilot with the Dutch airline KLM, and regularly flew the London to Amsterdam route. In 1929 she crashed a plane in Ohio, necessitating the insertion of steel plates into her skull. This resulted in a personality change, with her father's eccentricities coming even more to the fore. One of her many husbands said of her that she had flown away in the clouds. But this was before the introduction of insanity checks on pilots so I am not sure if she continued flying. She returned to Ireland for a few years in the 1930s, where she became increasingly unstable, poverty-stricken and alcoholic. If she was still flying in that condition her passengers wouldn't have needed the distractions of in-flight entertainment. She died in 1939 when she fell off a bus. She was commemorated by an Irish postage stamp in 1998.

Some women were early pioneers of using their sporting interests to endorse a commercial brand. Nannie Power O'Donoghue (1843–1940), from Dublin, became a passionate horsewoman at fifteen. She became the leading horse authority for women in her time. She wrote the successful *Ladies on Horseback* in 1881 and *Riding for Ladies* in 1887, which were practical guides covering dress, tackle, hats, seat and horse care. These were a huge international success and helped the sale of her romantic novels.

In 1868 she published her debut romance, *The Knave of Clubs*. In 1877 she produced a book of poems, *Spring Leaves*, with one poem inspired by the suicide of her sister, who had been seduced and promptly jilted. *Unfairly Won*, which appeared in 1882, was a melodramatic romp with a spirited heroine written in what was described as "a masculine tone". The 1884 hit, *A Beggar on Horseback*, was an amusing study of provincial society habits that sold 23,000 copies. The heroine, Bet, dies after her Fenian lover is killed by one of his own men.

Anyone for Tennis?

Thomas Vere St Leger Goold (1853–1909) won the first Irish Lawn Tennis Open Championship in 1878, beating C.D. Barry 8-6, 8-6 for the £20 prize. The same year, he got as far as the Wimbledon final but lost in straight sets – 6-4, 6-2, 6-2 – to Reverend John Thorneycroft Hartley, who had to race home to Yorkshire in between the semi-final and final to deliver his church sermon to his waiting congregation.

In August 1907, Goold and his French wife murdered a Danish woman, Emma Levin, in Monte Carlo. It seems she called at a bad time while they were having a squabble. They cut her up and put her in a suitcase. Then they put the case on the express train to Marseilles. Goold and his wife were convicted. He died a year later in Devil's Island prison colony. He is the only Wimbledon finalist ever to be convicted of murder.

Sedentary Sports for All

If you couldn't run, jump, throw things or people, or if you could barely move, you could have become a chess[95] master. Jack Vard (1926–1998) could have been a contender in chess; instead he chose wrestling. In the 1937 Irish Championships of the Dublin Chess Club, ten-year-old Vard achieved the distinction, still unsurpassed, of being the only Irish person to draw two consecutive matches with two Russian masters: Alexander Alekhine, who was ranked in the world top ten, and the relatively unknown Kilkonoski. That was as near as we ever came to world domination in chess.

---

[95] Is chess a sport? It was an exhibition event at the Sydney Olympics in 2000. Many countries, including some you would have actually heard of, officially recognise it as a sport, so who am I to quibble? I sweat every time I play chess, if that counts for anything.

James Parke (1881–1946) might also have done something for Irish chess. He played for the Clones team in Co. Monaghan when he was nine, but then quit to concentrate on rugby. This may have been a rash decision because he won only twenty caps for Ireland. Revealing a tendency to quit, he quit rugby to play tennis. He won the Irish Doubles Championship five times, the men's singles European Championship just once, and only a silver medal in the 1908 London Olympics, which was a particularly successful Olympics for Britain with so many Irish athletes on their team. He played in the Davis Cup and won just a single Wimbledon mixed doubles title in 1914. In 1913 *American Lawn Tennis* magazine described him as one of the top five players in the world: not *the* top player, mind you, but in the first five. But he quit tennis in 1914 for the army when the First World War broke out. And he quit that in 1918 when peace broke out.

*

If Samuel Beckett (1906–1989) had been just a little better at sports he may not have become a writer. He was a promising athlete. At school he competed successfully in cricket, rugby, boxing and swimming. He represented Trinners in golf, cricket, chess and motor racing, proving that, even if you like books, you can still get out of the house now and again for exercise. Whatever about this writing business, what a loss to Irish sport – he could have been a famous racing-car driver.

5

The Unsinkable Irish: Explorers and Mariners on the Green Oceans

As an island people, we have an intimate relationship with the sea. The oceans have provided many Irish men and women with their identities as well as their livelihoods. Ireland has produced many admirals and vice-admirals for the British Navy when we weren't allowed to have our own. In our history of seafaring there are numberless officers, captains, pirates, fishermen and fisherwomen, ship's "surgeons", hydrographers, cartographers, botanists, biologists, adventurers, polar explorers, boat builders and ship designers. Unlike many professions, piracy has always been an equal opportunity occupation in Ireland. Buccaneering[96] has attracted notable female recruits. These women had to commence their careers by disguising themselves as boys through the simple ruse of cutting off their hair and wearing trousers. This was a small sacrifice to get a foot on the pirate ladder.

---

[96] Technically, buccaneers were pirates of the West Indies during the seventeenth century, but the name has come to describe all pirates, even Irish ones.

Dressing for all Weathers

Grace O'Malley (c.1530–c.1603) pretended to be a boy to get to sea. She was the only legitimate child of Dubhdarra O'Malley, Lord of Murrish, Co. Mayo. While Dubhdarra had a natural son, Domhnall the Pipe O'Malley, he desperately wanted a legitimate son but had to make the most of the handicap of having only a daughter. Ideally he would have wanted to marry her off to an influential man, but Grace had other ideas.

When her father refused to take her on a voyage to Spain when she was a child, she cut off her hair to pass herself off as a boy and went with him. This is how she got her nickname "Grainne Mhaol", meaning "Grace the Bald". She loved card games, which also earned her the nickname "Grainne na gCearbhach" or "Grace of the Gamblers".

O'Malley did like men, a lot. She married Domhnall O'Flaherty in about 1546. They had two sons and a daughter together. Domhnall liked to fight, a lot. While hunting, he was ambushed and killed by the Joyces, a clan who had long been on his comprehensive list of enemies. Having run Domhnall through, they believed that they could then take his castle because only a mere woman, O'Malley, defended it. But she beat off their attack.

Now in charge of the clan, O'Malley moved her headquarters to Clare Island, which she made the centre of her pirate activities. She soon had a new boyfriend – a sailor who had been shipwrecked on the island. He may have thought he was the luckiest castaway in history but that thought wouldn't have lasted long. One of O'Malley's many other enemy clans, the MacMahons, killed him just to upset her. She got revenge by killing them in turn in an ambush on Cahir Island. She seized the MacMahon castle of Doona, earning a new nickname, "Dark Lady of Doona". In fairness, this alias showed a greater poetic flair on the part of the busy

local nicknaming committee than exemplified by the previous "Grace the Bald".

She then married Richard Burke in around 1566. They had
a son, "Tibbot of the Ships". O'Malley sailed with Burke to
secure her reputation of being the "most feared pirate on the
west coast". I have no idea who the most feared pirate on
the east coast might have been. I don't even know how they
measured fear indicators back then. Did someone literally
risk life and limb going from castle to castle with a clip-
board? But she definitely wore the trousers, if not the hair, in
that relationship.

The authorities unsuccessfully laid siege to her castle in
1574. The Lord Deputy, Sir Henry Sidney, with his son Sir
Philip Sidney, was given a tour of Galway Bay on her pirate
ships. She even charged them for the tour, kicking off the
tourist industry in the West of Ireland. To spread a little fear
on the east coast, she sailed to Howth in Dublin, kidnapping
and ransoming back the son of the Lord of Howth.

In 1576, one of her many local rivals, Gerald Fitzgerald,
captured O'Malley off the coast of Limerick and imprisoned
her for eighteen months in his dingy castle dungeon before
transferring her to the English in Dublin. She was released
when she promised she would reform. Back in the west, she
refused to support a Fitzgerald rebellion against the English.
The eighteen months in Fitzgerald's dungeon could have
had some impact on her decision. He might have thought
of that before locking her up, but this was a time when we
know for certain that people changed their alliances more
often than their underwear.

O'Malley worked her way back into the confidence of
the English to the extent that, by October 1582, she and
her husband, Richard Burke, were the celebrity couple at
a gathering of the who-was-who of Connaught. That was
the apotheosis of her buccaneering career. Nicholas Malby,
the provincial governor, really liked her, a lot. When tax

collectors turned up looking for arrears, she got them drunk and gave them 300 cows to keep them happy while she sweet-talked Malby into cancelling her debts, which he did. Malby died in 1584 and his replacement, Sir Richard Bingham, didn't like her at all. Her husband Richard also died that year, unexpectedly of natural causes.

O'Malley quickly got into trouble by helping members of the Burke clan, her in-laws, to escape after they had a fight with Bingham's forces. Bingham sent his brother, Captain John Bingham, to arrest her in June 1584. He did not treat her nicely. He tied her up with a coarse rope and hauled her off to his brother who threatened to hang her. However, when her stepson, Richard Burke, offered his own son as an exchange hostage for her, she was free again. Then, in July, Bingham's men murdered her son Murtagh.

Rebellion broke out but, once more, she didn't join. Instead, she fled to Ulster. When peace was restored, she returned to Connaught and offered her son Tibbot of the Ships as a hostage to Bingham as a guarantee of her good conduct. But her belligerent in-laws, the Burkes, rebelled again in 1589 when they killed John Browne, the sheriff of Mayo, leading to rebellion in Mayo and North Galway. O'Malley supported the Burkes and used her ships to ferry in Scottish mercenaries. However, Richard Burke agreed beneficial terms for himself in 1590, leaving the others, including O'Malley, to fight on. She plundered the Aran Islands. There must have been something worth plundering there back then because there isn't now; she probably took everything that was worth taking. She then came to terms with Bingham.

In 1591 she fought Scottish marauders, probably the mercenaries she had recruited. Mercenaries were always a bit of a double-edged sword, especially if they hadn't been paid, which they hadn't been in this instance. But by now Bingham was sinking O'Malley's ships with his own fleet. Bingham arrested both Tibbot of the Ships and her natural brother "Domhnall the Pipe" and announced that he was going to hang them. O'Malley was so upset that she travelled to London to get an audience with Elizabeth I, who was also bald but not as part of a disguise, and plead for their lives. In September 1593 she was summoned to Greenwich Castle where she persuaded Elizabeth to investigate Bingham's bad behaviour. Some accounts of this meeting tell us that O'Malley spent most of the time trying to prove that she was actually more posh than Elizabeth. Bingham wisely released his two prisoners. But their feud continued.

As O'Malley got older, her judgement for an advantageous alliance faded. We must also assume that her hair grew back at some stage. In 1594, when the countrywide rebellion against English rule led by the O'Neill clan broke out, she sided against the rebels. They rewarded her choice by invading her lands and devastating them. While pillage was something that every landowner could expect every dozen or so years, she never regained her former glory. She continued to try to be a pirate but with ever-declining success – it was a young woman's career. When she died, she was buried on her pirate headquarters, Clare Island.

Like Grace O'Malley, Anne Bonny (1698?–1782) disguised herself as a boy to become a pirate and meet like-minded potential partners. As the illegitimate daughter of a Cork attorney, her father dressed her as a boy from her infancy. It was disgraceful enough for him that his child was illegitimate without the extra stigma of her being a girl. He took her to Charles Town (now Charleston), South Carolina where he acquired a substantial plantation, I assume from practising lengthy litigations in Cork.

Bonny established her reputation early, as the daughter of an Irish attorney, by stabbing her English maid to death. She wasn't imprisoned for the crime because her father was an attorney and the victim was just the maid after all. In 1718, when she married a poor sailor named James Bonny, her father threw her out of the house. The pair moved to the Bahamas. There she met the pirate leader Calico Jack. She immediately threw over her new husband and eloped with Jack. Dressed as a man, she raided the coasts of Cuba and Hispaniola.

In 1720, Jack's gang of buccaneers was captured while raiding in a stolen sloop. They were all hanged except for Bonny and another female pirate, Mary Read, who was also disguised as a man. The women claimed clemency on the grounds of being pregnant. Read died in gaol, while Bonny's father got her released after she gave birth to Calico Jack's second son. She returned to Charles Town to lead a quiet life. She married a local man, and they had eight children together. She died peacefully in bed aged eighty-four.

Night Raid

Technology has made the world a smaller place. That is a bad thing. No longer can we just sail away over the horizon and into the unknown because, with Global Positioning System (GPS) technology, we can always tell where we are to within 7.9 to 12 inches; worse, we can always be found. We could easily find our friends, neighbours and relatives if pirates kidnapped them, which wasn't the case in the seventeenth century.

Just before dawn in June 1631, an elite Turkish troop of pirates from Algiers, led by Captain Murat Rais, stormed the village of Baltimore in West Cork. William Harris and a tiny force of survivors fired muskets and loudly beat a drum, producing the impression in the darkness that a large rescue force was coming down the hill to defend the village. Hearing this racket, the Turkish Janissaries retreated to their boat. However, they had succeeded in capturing over a hundred of the villagers and carrying them off into slavery in North Africa.

Those who had managed to wake up and run to safety in the dark discovered in the dull dawn light that their families, friends, enemies and neighbours alike had vanished without trace. The raid was opportune for a minority in Baltimore who had been fed up with their mothers, spouses or children, and had been contemplating a change. For the majority, it was devastating. They had to live on in the village never knowing what happened to their families. Only two of those who were taken ever saw their homes in Baltimore again.

According to one count, 107 people from the village were stuffed into the pirate ship to be taken into slavery in Algiers. The official report into the raid claimed there were 109 captives, of whom 89 were women and children. William Gunter's wife and seven sons were taken. John Harris lost his wife, mother and three children. Robert Chimor's wife and four children vanished. John Hackett, a fisherman from Dungarvan, had been seized by the Turks and forced to pilot them into Baltimore. He was tried and hanged by the authorities within eight months of the raid. He was the approved scapegoat for official neglect and corruption further up the social ladder. Those higher-ups couldn't be hanged because they were too posh and had access to attorneys. In other words, it was natural justice.

By 18 February 1634, forty of the captives had either died or converted to Islam in a process known as "turning Turk". Back home in Baltimore, conversion to Islam was regarded as an existential change on a par with being dead. One woman, we don't know her name, had been ransomed early through the intermediary Mr Job Frogmartino from Livorno in Italy. The average ransom demanded was £200 per person. This was equivalent to about ten years' pay, which those left behind in Baltimore would have found difficult to raise, most especially those who had lost eight family members, like William Gunter.

However, for those of an optimistic nature who were taken into slavery, it was possible to have a positive outlook on the raid. Algiers had a better climate than Baltimore, Islamic medicine was far more advanced than its European counterpart, and the diet was more varied and healthy. There were also many opportunities for marriage, and professional advancement in light house work and harem duties for co-operative slaves. What was there to complain about compared to wet and windy West Cork? In Algiers there were brothels, military coups, taverns, plagues, festivals and earthquakes to distract a slave from the daily routine. There was nothing like that in Baltimore, except maybe the plagues.

In 1645, fourteen years after the raid, Englishman Edmond Cason[97] was sent as an envoy to Algiers to try to redeem the Baltimore slaves. By then, the volume of European slaves taken had reached embarrassing proportions. Cason sailed in the *Honour* with a load of cash. However, a storm drove his ship into Gibraltar Bay where it caught fire and was captured. Most of the ransom money was taken. But Cason was tenacious. He was the kind of person you would like to be rescuing you. He was the equivalent of the elite special forces today. He transferred to the *Diamond* with the small amount of money that the raiders missed. However, the *Diamond* was wrecked at Cadiz, and the rest of the money was lost. Maybe Cason wasn't the ideal rescuer after all.

The following year, fifteen years after the Baltimore raid, Cason sailed again for Algeria to free the English and Irish slaves, this time on the *Charles*. I wonder if the crew was nervous. But back then crews must have always been nervous because ships frequently sank.

---

[97] Cromwell's Parliament had passed an Act resolving to redeem captives in 1640. Cason was chosen to lead the mission. He wrote a book about his experiences in 1647 – *Relation of the Redemption of Captives in Algiers and Tunis, With a List of Captives Redeemed and Prices.*

Cason arrived safely in Algiers, which probably surprised him as much as the to-be-rescued slaves. The Pasha, or local high-ranking official of the Turkish Empire, reasonably claimed that he couldn't hand over the slaves because they didn't belong to him; having been sold on, they belonged to their new owners. However, the Pasha had helpful records of the sale prices so the new owners could be fairly compensated.

The haggling, so beloved by the locals, commenced in earnest. It was like trying to buy 500 carpets in one go. Cason eventually agreed to pay only cost price for each slave. But, naturally, the slave owners exaggerated both their cost prices and expenses incurred in running repairs and improvements. Cason agreed a reduction in the levy on the bulk purchase price of the slaves. Understandably, there was also a form of Value Added Tax on the sale of slaves because they were a luxury item. For example, he had to pay export duties of $31 per slave, attractively down from $50. To add to Cason's complicated calculations, prices were quoted in several currencies.

Cason reconciled himself to the fact that slaves serving in the Turkish fleet, children being raised in local households and older boys who had converted to Islam and moved to Alexandria and further east would not be included in the group purchase. Many owners wanted to hang on to their slaves, valuing them higher than the purchase price. Some probably even liked their slaves, an affection that was reciprocated in many instances.

The slaves for purchase were usually women-and-children combinations, or buy-one-get-a-child-free packages that cost Carson £50 each. These could have been sold on in the market for £100,[98] so the Algerians were being reasonable. Skilled slaves such as coopers, carpenters and surgeons

---

[98] Approximately €11,000 in contemporary currency values.

cost £32 each plus port charges of 61s. 6d. per head, making them about £35 each. Cason wanted to negotiate a one-price-fits-all rate but the owners rejected this, arguing the merits of individual slaves belonging to them.

By simple arithmetic, Carson worked out that he had only enough funds to redeem 250 of the total of 650 slaves on offer. Therefore, he had to choose who would go and who would stay behind. He had orders to prioritise his selection based on class, and to rescue as many posh ones as possible. But Cason was unusually egalitarian for the times. He tried to ignore that order. Instead, he selected those whom he thought he "should have for cloth". It is not clear what this phrase means but it may be that whoever had clothes to travel in would be prioritised. In all, he rescued 264, two of whom were from Baltimore: Joane Broadbrook and Ellen Hawkins, who I assume were the best dressed of the eligible Baltimore slaves. Joane had two children and was pregnant when she was captured, but there is no record of any of her children returning with her.

We also have no record of what kind of a reception the two women received back in Baltimore after a fifteen-year absence. At fundraising events that were organised to raise money for ransoms, ex-Algiers slaves were put on show and were obliged to wear chains that were usually heavier than the real things. Perhaps Joane and Ellen had to clink their way round Cork for the next fifteen years. I am confident that they must have often regretted going home.

Dying to See the World

Thomas Legge (d.1808) reached parts of the world that no other traveller had been to in his lifetime. He was the son of a ship owner but he refused to follow his father into the business. Instead, he ran away to sea on someone else's boat when he was sixteen.

He sailed on the *Swallow* to Madras in India in 1775. There he promptly deserted ship and set off as a beggar to explore India. In six years of wandering, supported only by charity, he travelled to the Sindh region, and crossed the Indian desert and Rajasthan province. He retired from begging in favour of a career casting cannon for regional despots. He spent the following twenty years casting cannon all over India, Afghanistan, Badakhshan and Uzbekistan.

He was the first European, perhaps since Alexander the Great, to travel in those parts of the world. During his extensive journeys, Legge learned Indian culture and myth, languages, alchemy, healing and divination using sheep's bones. He claimed to have found the Garden of Eden in the Hindu Kush. The garden was in a cave guarded by an angel with flaming wings. It contained the expected fruit trees along with unexpected heaps of gold and silver, which in his beggar's imagination must have meant eternal happiness. I wonder why he didn't stay. Clearly Eden bored all three people that we know were there – not a propitious advertisement for heaven.

Legge eventually returned to Jaipur, where he married a politically influential woman of Portuguese descent. Her family got him the command of a battalion in the local Maharaja's army, despite his having no experience of military matters beyond making cannons. This lack of experience quickly proved inconvenient because, in his first contact with an enemy, he was shot through the thigh and skewered with a pike. Despite his knowledge of healing, his wounds failed to mend, so he moved into a deserted Mohammedan tomb to spend the remainder of his life as a living corpse. He became a Muslim Sufi ascetic, or fakir, living on alms. He lasted several months in the mausoleum before putting it to its intended use by dying.

Exceptionally Stupid Wars

At those times in history when we didn't have our own navy, we sometimes started new navies for other countries. This is what William Brown (1777–1857) did. Brown is arguably our most successful Irish sailor, ever, because he became admiral-in-chief of the Argentine Navy.

In 1780 he was a midshipman in the British Navy before transferring to the merchant marine, and then serving on a privateer[99] in the West Indies. By 1806 he had made enough money from his life as an official pirate to settle in Buenos Aires as a trader in fruit and hides. At that time, the Spanish were blockading trade out of the River Plate, which is a large estuary between Argentina and Uruguay. In 1814, Brown was invited by the Argentine Government to take charge of a rebel naval squadron to contest control of sea trade with the Spanish. Probably bored with fruit and animal hides, he agreed.

He organised a fleet of nineteen ships into a naval force that paid unusual attention to the welfare of ordinary seamen. He defeated a superior Spanish force in March 1814. Later in the year, when he beat the Spanish again, their control of the coast collapsed. The war ended. But Brown was obviously enjoying fighting more than trading skins, so he continued to raid Spanish targets until he was captured by the British in Barbados in 1816 for breach of international trade rules – rules established by the British Navy. The

---

[99] A privateer was a privately owned ship authorised by a government to attack foreign shipping. It was a convenient and cost-effective way of mobilising forces without having to spend always scarce public money. It also allowed a country to avoid officially committing resources to a conflict, thereby facilitating deniability when something inevitably went wrong. Prize money from captured cargo and vessels was distributed amongst the owners, officers and crew. This was how Brown became rich.

people who owned his ships were understandably anxious about his continuing to fight in them. They wanted him stopped while their ships were still intact.

Illness and lengthy but, unusually, successful litigation kept him away from Argentina until 1818. On his return, instead of receiving a hero's welcome, he was first cashiered for disobeying orders, then reinstated and finally forced into early retirement. He was so disappointed with the attitude of the Argentine authorities that he tried to kill himself. The attempt failed and it took him years to recover.

He returned to the fruit and skins business, swearing to have nothing to do with the Argentine Navy ever again. Until the next time they asked him for a favour.

In 1825 the Government gave him back his command because war had broken out with the vastly superior Brazilian Navy. Brown accepted and quickly took the fight to the Brazilians. In 1827 he won a series of victories in the Battle of Juncal. By 1828 there was peace with Brazil. Brown was one of two Argentinean delegates to actually sign the peace treaty.

He retired again but his retirement was interrupted by civil war in 1828. He retired once more in 1829, in disgust at the Government. This time he swore he would have nothing to do with them ever, ever again. This time he really meant it, during peace time anyway.

In 1841 he came out of retirement to take charge of the navy in a war against Uruguay, which he described as "a stupid war". That conflict must have been exceptionally bad by the standards of South American wars at the time. He was winning the stupid war until French and British fleets interfered in 1841, capturing his squadron and bringing the obtuse war to an end. Despite, or maybe because of, his being at sea for long periods, his wife had nine children.

Fortunately, the British Navy was always happy to take any Irish with a desire to live at sea. As luck would have it, Britain's allies kept defecting so there were countless opportunities for stupid wars. Dubliner James Spratt (1771–1853) joined the merchant navy before transferring to the Royal Navy[100] in 1796 as a first-class volunteer in time for the notable naval battles of the Napoleonic Wars. He was on HMS *Bellona* at the Battle of Copenhagen, when Horatio Nelson led the main attack on 2 April 1802 on board HMS *Elephant*. The ship's gun exploded, killing the entire gun crew except Spratt; he wasn't even scratched.

He transferred to HMS *Defiance* and fought at Trafalgar on 21 October 1805. During that battle, Captain Durham of the *Defiance* decided to board the French *Agile*. In naval warfare, "boarding" is the relatively genteel term for the invasion of one ship by the savage sailors of another, often wielding clubs, axes, swords, pistols or anything that could inflict a fatal wound. But the wind had slackened and he couldn't bring the *Defiance* alongside. Spratt volunteered to swim across with a boarding party. He dived into the sea, probably with a cutlass between his teeth, calling on his hearty shipmates to follow. None of them did, so he popped up on his own beside the *Agile*. He boarded at the stern ports and singlehandedly fought his way to the poop deck,[101] as you do. He was set upon by three French grenadiers.[102] He

---

[100] In the seventeenth century there was a failed attempt to register all seamen of the British commercial fleets as a potential source of manpower for the naval warfare branch of the British forces, the Royal Navy. While transfers from the merchant to the Royal Navy were often voluntary, they were sometimes forced (pressed) in times of military need. King George V bestowed the official title "Merchant Navy" on British merchant shipping after the First World War.

[101] The term "poop deck" comes from French and refers to the deck formed by the roof of a cabin built in the rear of a ship. As this is where a boarding force or party might expect to find the captain, it is traditionally the site of the most impressive swordplay in pirate films.

[102] The term "grenadier" also derives from French, from the word

disabled two of them and broke the neck of the third. By now some of his shipmates had actually fought their way on board beside him. He saved the life of a French officer, as you should do, and took a musket ball in the leg, as you shouldn't, just before the *Agile* struck her colours and surrendered.

Back on board the *Defiance*, Spratt refused to allow the surgeon to amputate his leg, and was taken to the naval hospital at Gibraltar. There the "surgeons" reset his leg but it wouldn't knit together properly because he was thrashing around the hospital bed with a fever. They came up with the idea of setting his leg in a wooden case in order to allow it time to mend. A few days later, he began to complain of a gnawing sensation in his leg that was inside the box. When it was opened the surgeons discovered that hundreds of enormous maggots had eaten three inches off his leg.

For his actions at Trafalgar, he was promoted to lieutenant and awarded £50.[103] He recovered from his experience with the voracious maggots. While this was before the invention of counselling, it was also before the invention of post-traumatic stress disorder. In effect, people happily didn't know when they had been driven mad by an occurrence. He retired to a signal station in Devon. There he invented a "homograph", a signaling device that was the basis for the later semaphore system. The Society of Arts awarded him a medal for this invention.

Spratt was a remarkable swimmer. During his service with the navy he saved the lives of nine men who had fallen overboard, not all at the same time. In 1831 he swam fourteen miles for a bet with his different length legs. His son, Thomas Abel Brimage Spratt, who was surely destined to

---

"grenade", because this force originated in the seventeenth century for the purpose of throwing grenades.

[103] Approximately €2,000 in contemporary currency values.

become historically notable with such a name, became a vice-admiral, hydrographer, archaeologist and author.

Life on Ice

William Coppin (1805–1895) was a successful sailor, ship-builder and marine inventor who, amongst many other accomplishments, built one of the first ever ships to use an Archimedean screw propeller.[104] He also salvaged over 140 sunken ships after his own shipyard burnt down in 1846. Coppin and his wife, Dora, had two sons and four daughters. In 1849 their third child, Louisa, known affectionately as "Little Weesy", died when she was five years old. Soon after her burial, she appeared to her family as a "ball of bluish light", prophesying the, as yet undiscovered, location of Sir John Franklin's vanished 1845 polar expedition. The fate of that lost expedition, which had set out to chart the Northwest Passage sea route, became one of the most gripping mysteries of the nineteenth century. There was enormous public interest in the disappearance of Franklin, his entire crew and his two ships *Terror* and *Erebus*.

Coppin told Lady Franklin about Little Weesy's occult message in May 1850. Four hundred and thirty Liverpool merchants and bankers petitioned the Admiralty to look where Little Weesy suggested. A search in 1859, in the *Fox*, a yacht owned by Lady Franklin, found remains on King William Island, just where dead Little Weesy had indicated they would be.

---

[104] Sailing ships were driven by wind power. When wind gave way to steam power, there was competition between the paddle design and the now familiar three-bladed screw propeller or Archimedean propeller. A tug-of-war was arranged in 1845 between the propeller-driven *Rattler* and the paddle-powered *Alector* to decide the matter. The *Rattler* decisively won, making the propeller the ubiquitous means of propelling boats through water today.

Francis Leopold McClintock (1819–1907), of the *Fox*, was originally from Co. Louth. He went on four polar expeditions, all of which were in search of Franklin's missing ships. If initially he had resorted to occult instructions, he would not have had an excuse to return three times and become a polar authority in the process. Finally, on his fourth attempt, he found human and material remains. Naturally he denied using paranormal advice, as we all do. He claimed that the local Inuit guided him. He might have asked them on his first trip. He subsequently wrote a bestselling book about his experiences in the Arctic. He eventually achieved the rank of admiral in 1884.

McClintock experimented with photography and collected a vast number of zoological and fossil specimens, many of which can be seen in the Natural History Museum in Dublin. This is my preferred Irish museum. It contains a huge number of stuffed animals, including the last wildcat in Ireland complete with the bullet hole in its head where the curator shot him for his collection. We should be grateful that, in the nineteenth century, zoologists who were concerned about possible extinctions shot and stuffed everything that moved, wiggled, swung from trees or slithered along the ground, all for our future enjoyment and edification.

There were more Irish connections with the Franklin mystery. McClintock found a document under a cairn on King William Island that told the fate of the doomed expedition. Francis Rawdon Moira Crozier (1796–1848), from Co. Down, was the author of the document. Crozier, who was second in command of the Franklin expedition, wrote about how they were forced to abandon the ships when the ice trapped them in 1846. Franklin died in 1847, leaving Crozier in charge. As rations ran short, Crozier took the weakening crew of 105 men south on 26 April 1848. That is the last known record of them – they all died sometime after that date. Modern forensic tests on the skeletal remains show that vitamin deficiency and lead poisoning from canned food contributed to the deaths. Early cans, patented by inventor Nicolas Appert, were sealed with lead soldering, which caused lead poisoning. Many believe that Crozier was one of the last of the expedition to die. Maybe Little Weesy told them.

On his first search mission, McClintock became iced in but made a 760-mile journey by sled. Over the years, he developed entirely new methods of sledding from his Arctic experiences, and was a rare authority on freezing Arctic conditions. He became an inspiration to those famous explorers who came after him, especially Captain Robert Scott. Roald Amundsen, who was Scott's contemporary in exploration, eventually learned the advantages of using dogs rather than people to pull sleds. This breakthrough, which he learned from the Inuit, famously helped him to beat Scott to the South Pole by just five weeks in 1911. Scott, being British, preferred to inflict the cruelty of sled-pulling on his men and himself, rather than on blameless dogs, a decision that contributed to his freezing to death on his way back from the Pole in 1912.

Ernest Shackleton (1874–1922), from Kildare, was commissioned as a lieutenant in the Royal Naval Reserve in 1901. However, as he had already grown bored with the routine of sailing, he volunteered for Captain Robert Scott's National Antarctic Expedition on the *Discovery* in 1901–1904. Boredom was the principal motivation behind much exploration. But Shackleton was also desperate to impress the Royal Geographical Society (RGS). He was appointed third officer on the *Discovery*, and sailed away to the frozen Antarctic in 1901.

Shackleton was at ease with all ranks, and comfortable with command. Scott wasn't. Scott didn't like Shackleton because he was jealous of his natural charm and leadership qualities. Everyone else loved the saintly Shackleton.

In November 1902, together with Scott and Edward Wilson, Shackleton reached a southern latitude of 82° 28'. This was the furthest distance south that anyone had ever attained. Their dress was supplemented by woollen underpants and several pairs of socks on their hands and feet, and they dragged all of their supplies themselves on sleds, as advised by McClintock. At that time Europeans hadn't a clue about the cold in the polar regions. Nowadays, even I could get to the poles in the standard all-over thermal suit with heated underpants, and packets of high-energy toothpaste-like food in my pockets. Back then, the explorers had to stop every mile or two to brew up more tea. To Scott's great relief, Shackleton became ill and was sent home in 1903. Many Irish people are suspicious of Scott's good fortune and wonder what he might have put in the tea because we know Scott was worried that Shackleton might have proven to be the better explorer.

The following year, Shackleton realised a dream by being elected secretary to the RGS. In 1907 he sailed back to the Antarctic, this time on the *Nimrod*, with his own exploration party. On this expedition, a team reached the summit of Mount Erebus, the second highest volcano in Antartica, and another party reached the Magnetic South Pole. Shackleton made an attempt on the South Pole; he reached latitude 88° 32', which was just 97 miles short. When he eventually got home in 1909, he was given a hero's welcome and treated as an Englishman. This is typical of what happens to successful Irishmen. He was awarded a knighthood and given a medal by the RGS. Parliament gave him £20,000[105] towards his costs. This works out at slightly over £1 per mile in expenses. He wrote the popular *The Heart of the Antarctic* in 1909, and went on the lecture circuit in Europe and America to raise funds for his next expedition.

---

[105] Approximately €1.5 million in contemporary currency values.

In 1914 he sailed again for the Antarctic with a plan to cross the continent, something not actually achieved until 1958. His ship, the *Endurance*, became trapped in ice in January 1915, and by the following November it had been crushed and sunk between large floes. Shackleton and his crew camped out for months on a drifting ice floe before launching their three lifeboats for Elephant Island. From there Shackleton sailed to South Georgia Island, 800 miles away, in the largest of their three tiny boats. After seventeen days sailing with little water, he landed on the west side of the island, forcing him to make a 36-hour crossing of the frozen mountains with Frank Worsley and fellow Irishman Tom Crean (1877–1938), who was famous for his endurance. For this mountain climb they had only one rope and no proper food or gear, just the standard damp woollen underpants and socks. They drove brass screws into their boots to act as crampons. After three attempts, Shackleton succeeded in reuniting his entire crew who had been left behind at various places along the way. However, he did manage to lose Mrs Chippy, the ship's cat, and all the sledging dogs.

In 1921 he was on his way back again to the Antarctic on the *Quest*. On South Georgia Island he died of a massive heart attack. He was awarded the honorary title Doctor of Law from Glasgow University, a Polar Medal with three clasps, the French Légion d'honneur, the Crown of Italy, the Russian Order of Saint Anne, the Royal Crown of Prussia and the Chilean Order of Merit. There are two mountains named in his honour, as well as an ice shelf and an inlet. There is a statue to him outside the RGS.

While Ernest Shackleton was freezing his arse off in the Antarctic, his younger brother Francis Shackleton (1876–1941), more commonly known as Frank, was interested in the sparkle of a different kind of ice, namely the Irish Crown Jewels in Dublin Castle. Frank was a bit of a dandy, and a friend to aristocrats and society snobs. He was a close friend of Sir Arthur Edward Vicars, Ulster knight of arms and knight attendant of the Order of Saint Patrick, usually known as the Irish Crown Jewels.

Vicars got Frank a job as Dublin herald in his office in Dublin Castle, which housed the safe where the jewels were kept. Soon after, the Irish Crown Jewels vanished along with other jewels and some private family jewellery. The haul was estimated to be worth £5,000[106] if broken up and sold on the black market. Frank quickly became the prime suspect, as he was known to be living far beyond his means. Edward VII, who visited Dublin Castle in 1907, demanded that everyone in the office of arms resign. Frank resigned and co-operated fully with the commission of enquiry that was set up, but he was never charged. In 1920, in his will, Vicars named Frank as "the real culprit and thief."

By 1910, with debts of £85,000, the equivalent of seventeen Irish Crown Jewels, Frank was declared bankrupt. He fled to Portuguese West Africa where he was arrested in 1912 on charges of fraud. He served fifteen months hard labour, and when he was released his brother Ernest got him a job in an office in London. Frank eventually opened an antique shop, as you do. In 1927 a Parisian jeweller offered to sell the apparently original Crown Jewels back to the Irish Government who, being completely broke at that time, refused to buy them. The jewels were never found. However, the box in which they had been kept was recovered. It was anonymously posted back to Dublin Castle without an explanatory note.

Beneath the Green Waves

In an attempt to conquer the depths of the sea, Clareman John Holland (1841–1914) invented the modern submarine.

---

[106] About €400,000 in contemporary currency values.

He attended the Christian Brothers School in Limerick where he showed a remarkable aptitude for science. In 1858 he actually joined the Christian Brothers, and subsequently taught in a number of schools around Ireland. But in 1873 he received a dispensation from his vows on the grounds of ill health.

In the context of nineteenth-century celibate Christian Brothers, illness was often a euphemism for either being insane or having an interest in women. Many of us know, from first-hand experience of their pedagogical style, that insanity would not normally interfere with the teaching career of a Christian Brother. Therefore, I am assuming he suffered the latter disorder and fell in love with a woman. My hypothesis is supported by the fact that he eventually married Margaret Foley, who was a woman.

After he left the Christian Brothers he sailed to America. In New Jersey he got a job teaching science in a Christian Brothers school. Apparently, during his time as a teacher in Ireland, he had already invented the term "submarine". All he needed now was the contraption itself to go with it.

In February 1875 he offered his patent to the US Navy, but they rejected his idea as the "fantastic scheme of a civilian landsman". Experimenting on heavy machines like submarines can be dangerous. He broke a leg and, in November 1875, concussed himself while carrying out experiments.

Holland then offered his submarine to the Fenian Brotherhood,[107] arguing that Britain's control of the seas was the key to its power, and thus the greatest obstacle to Irish independence. Holland reasoned that if the Fenians could sneak up on the British Navy in his submarine and sink lots of ships, they could negotiate from a position of strength. With remarkable prescience, the Fenians agreed to use their

---

[107] See footnote 28. The Fenian Brotherhood was an Irish organisation founded in America in 1858 to support Irish republican activities.

"skirmishing fund" to finance Holland's experiments. With these resources he was able to give up teaching to concentrate all his efforts on building his boat.

Holland was the first person to design a modern submarine using an internal combustion engine as the power source when the submarine was on the surface of the water, and electric battery power when it was submerged. In 1878 he produced the *Holland I*, also known as the *Fenian Ram*, which was a one-man 14-foot craft. That one man inside soon discovered that defective riveting made it unseaworthy when submerged for long periods.

In 1881 Holland produced a more advanced 31-foot boat with a crew of three. I wonder who he persuaded to test his experimental submarines. I have a picture of him in my mind recruiting winos on the dockside with the promise of the finest clarets in return for the simple task of taking his prototype submarines beneath the waves. He launched a third vessel in 1882, which weighed 19 tonnes. This model developed engine trouble. Because it failed to comply with New York Harbour Board's shipping laws, being a completely new kind of boat, it was banned from the port. How was a genius supposed to succeed when surrounded by such mindless bureaucrats?

By 1883 the three submarines had cost the Fenians $60,000[108] and the leaders were worried about the ever-mounting costs of experimentation without a single British ship sunk. They took possession of the submarine but didn't know how to use it. Naturally, Holland wouldn't show them without being paid. There followed a standoff where the Fenians had the boat but Holland knew how to operate it. I don't know why the Fenians didn't enquire amongst the dockside winos for a captain. Following some unseemly

---

[108] Approximately €800,000 in contemporary currency values.

rows, they went their separate ways – a split amongst the Fenian submariners, if you like.

The Fenian Brotherhood had wanted to use Holland's submarine to regain ground against the British that was lost by their invasion of Canada in 1866 under the supreme command of Thomas Sweeny (1820–1892). Capturing Canada was a win-win for the Fenians. They could either run it as their own country or swap it back to the British for Ireland. Sweeny was responsible for drawing up the invasion plans. He developed a three-prong attack from Vermont, New York and Illinois into Ontario. The invading army would secure railways, canals and the seats of government in London, Ontario; Ottawa; and Montreal.

While Sweeny had masterminded the invasion, another Irishman, John O'Neill (1834–1878), led the actual assault. On 31 May 1866, 800 Fenians invaded Canada. They crossed the Niagara River at Buffalo, New York, and occupied Fort Erie. Two days later they defeated Canadian forces at Ridgeway and beat off the attack of the Queen's Own Rifles, an inexperienced student militia. However, after reinforcements failed to arrive, O'Neill retreated.

By the time 20,000 Canadian militia marched on Fort Erie, 700 of the Fenians had already escaped safely back over the border to a hero's welcome home. Sixteen Canadian students were killed and seventy-four wounded; eight Fenians were killed, twenty wounded and one hundred and seventeen taken prisoner. Following a brief detention for breaching US neutrality laws, the Fenians were released. Sweeny had insufficient men, supplies and artillery at his disposal; following Irish revolutionary best practice established earlier in the century by Robert Emmet,[109] he overestimated the number of his own supporters; he underestimated the

---

[109] See A Poet in a Bomb Factory in Chapter 1 for details of Emmet's rebellion.

number of Canadian militia; he was misguided that most Canadians would welcome "liberation" by the Fenians; and the British Consulate in Washington seemed to know more about the finer details of the invasion plans than he did.

How different would the world be now if the Fenians had captured Canada? Perhaps the Fenian invasion of Canada would have succeeded if the submarine had been perfected in time to support them. Against this view is the military impracticality of using submarines in prairie warfare. But what do I know? I am not a military genius.

In New York, Holland built the *Zalinski*, a submarine funded by Edmund Zalinski, who was a Polish-born American soldier and engineer, best known for his invention of the pneumatic torpedo gun. He then formed the John P. Holland Torpedo Boat Company that built the *Plunger* for the US Navy, who had seemingly changed their minds about his credentials. But the engineers of the US Navy didn't trust him. They ignored Holland's experienced advice and significantly interfered with the design of the *Plunger*. Holland had the satisfaction of seeing the navy with a boat that wouldn't manoeuvre and had to be scrapped. I imagine that he had one of the most satisfying "I told you so" meetings of the nineteenth century with the US Navy after that. Holland launched his own boat, the *Holland VI*, in 1897. This boat was 53 feet long and could hold a crew of six. It performed well in tests. It had a speed of 9 knots and could dive to 60 feet; it was armed with a torpedo launcher and an underwater cannon fired by compressed air. These amazing design innovations were driven by Holland's hatred of the English. Imagine what Edison could have achieved if he had been motivated by Holland's single-minded loathing.

The US Navy bought the *Holland VI* in 1900 for $150,000[110] and called it the USS *Holland*. This boat became the prototype

---

[110] Approximately €2.2 million in contemporary currency values.

for all future submarines. Holland was commissioned to build six more. However, his company sold his plans to the British Navy in 1901 to raise money for research. He was a bit upset. He had calmed down by 1910 when the Emperor of Japan decorated him for his work with the Japanese Navy.

Holland died in 1914 on the eve of the First World War, the conflict that would see his invention make its first real impact in naval warfare. However, it wasn't until the Second World War that the submarine became one of the most lethal and effective weapons in the German Navy, fulfilling Holland's prediction that it could threaten the naval power of Britain practically on its own.

That Sinking Feeling

It is only karmically right that, since an Irishman invented the submarine, another Irishman created the depth charge used for sinking it. Walter Conan (1860–1936), from Dublin, was not an engineer but trained as a tailor after graduating from Blackrock College, in order to take on his father's tailoring business with his brother. Arthur Conan Doyle, the author of the Sherlock Holmes series of novels, was a cousin of his father. Their tailoring business specialised in hiring out academic gowns to students for graduations.

However, Conan was an amateur inventor. He created the combination lock, an apparatus for preserving meat, devices for preventing airlocks in pipes and a type of gas lamp. But his passion was explosives, in particular detonators. He may have had a form of pyromania. He developed the Conan submarine fuse, which could be set to explode in a prescribed depth of water. This fuse has become central to the anti-submarine depth charge used by the British Navy.

Conan subsequently became the inspiration for Brian O'Nolan's (1911–1966) – aka author Flann O'Brien's – eccentric inventor De Selby in *The Third Policeman*. O'Nolan wrote *The Third Policeman* between 1939 and 1940. That wasn't an auspicious year for producing books as the Second World War had just gotten under way. He failed to find a publisher. He made up an excuse that the typescript had been lost in the confusion of the conflict. He was so convincing that the script wasn't "found" until 1967 when it was published to unqualified critical acclaim. Unfortunately, at that stage, O'Nolan was dead.

Nautical Coffins

I would rather spend an evening with a vampire than a night submerged in one of Holland's early model submarines. Henry Hugh Gordon Dacre Stoker (1885–1966), or Harry to his forgetful friends, was Bram Stoker's[111] nephew and a pioneer submariner during the First World War. Harry joined the British Navy when he was fifteen. Maybe his superiors thought he was genetically suited to dark coffin-like places because he was transferred to submarines in 1906. In 1915 he passed through the Dardanelles Straits in his AE2 submarine. The Straits were protected by patrol boats, shore batteries, minefields and nets. His boat was caught in a searchlight as it cruised on the surface and was forced to dive. Stoker then had to evade mines, a cruiser and a destroyer while submerged. He fired a torpedo, missing the cruiser but hitting the destroyer. He eventually ran aground, setting his boat on the bottom of the sea for several hours before letting it float on the currents. When at last he surfaced, he discovered that he had actually drifted through the channel, making him the first ever Allied[112] submarine

---

[111] Stoker is the author of *Dracula*, perhaps the most famous Irish book. See Chapter 6 for more details on Irish horror writing.

[112] The Allied Forces were the United Kingdom including the Dominions of the British Empire, France and Russia, with America

commander to force the Dardanelles. He attacked Turkish shipping in the Marmara before his boat was sunk. He was taken to a Turkish prisoner of war camp where he remained for the next three years. While he was a prisoner he became interested in acting, which was one of the few distractions allowed.

His wife had three children while he was in prison. Being amongst the minority of Irish at that time who didn't believe in immaculate conception, he sought a divorce. When he left the service in 1920 he took up acting professionally. In 1925 he even married an actress. He was a successful Dr Watson in a series of plays based on Sherlock Holmes stories. In 1925 he wrote *Straws in the Wind*, which was an account of his submariner days. He became a successful stage and screen actor before having to return to the navy for the Second World War. After that, he got into television, film, theatre and writing. He died on the day of his eighty-first birthday. Turkish marine archaeologists found his boat, the AE2, in 1998.

Following Currents

A life at sea is best suited to the impetuous. Charles McGuinness's (1893–1947) fate embodied the haphazard, nomadic, adaptable, join-whatever-is-happening-at-the-time devil-may-care attitude of many Irish at sea. Despite his various escapades, he is perhaps best remembered for what may have been his most lasting achievement – bringing the first monkey to Derry. He was the original Forrest Gump. His life shows us that, no matter what your circumstances, you can make the most of them. He was an adventurer at a time when there were many opportunities for adventure. Like all adventurers, he encountered an improbable number of scrapes, any of which could have been his last.

---

joining them in 1917.

McGuinness was the son of a sea captain, which helps when planning to run away to sea, which he did in 1908 when he was fifteen. He travelled throughout the world. He was shipwrecked when he was seventeen, drifting for two weeks on a lifeboat until rescued near Tahiti. He became a pearl fisher in the South Seas for a year before going back to his wanderings.

In 1913 he travelled across Canada, panhandling for gold and joining the militia. In 1914, at the beginning of the First World War, McGuinness joined the British Navy and served in the Dover Patrol and in Cameroon. Following the Easter Rising in Dublin in 1916 and its aftermath, he became so disenchanted with the British forces that he deserted and joined the South African Army. While serving with them in East Africa, he was captured by a German force but escaped through the jungle. At that point he abandoned the global war to continue his travels.

In 1920 he returned to his hometown of Derry to join the IRA during the War of Independence, where he became the leader of a flying column. He was central to the daring escape from gaol of the IRA Sligo Brigade Commander Frank Carty (1897–1942). Next he went on the run when he was accused of the murder of a police inspector in Glasgow. The British Army actually captured him in June 1921 while he was participating in a bungled bank raid in Donegal, but he escaped from custody before they could establish his identity.

He then smuggled arms from Germany to Ireland. After the 1922 Treaty split, which caused the Irish Civil War between the pro-treaty Free Staters and the anti-treaty IRA, he continued smuggling for the IRA but eventually left them when he became disillusioned with their incompetence. He had both soles of his feet tattooed with the Union Jack flag so that wherever he went he could trample on the flag of the British Empire. He claimed that he was arrested in Berlin for conspiring with Bulgarian revolutionaries and released only on condition that he left Germany. He spent time with Chiang Kai-Shek's forces in China before ending up in New York where he became a building contractor, like many Irish before and after him.

In 1928 he joined Admiral Byrd's Antarctic expedition as a navigation officer. In 1930 he invested his entire fortune in smuggling rum from Canada to America during prohibition. He lost everything when his boat and cargo were impounded in 1931. Broke, he emigrated to the Soviet Union and worked as a harbour master in Murmansk. But he didn't like the Soviet Union.

He published an autobiography in 1934 called *Nomad*. In 1936, he joined the International Brigades in the Spanish Civil War but deserted after falling out with the Spanish republicans. He documented his experiences in a sensational exposé of the Brigades in an article called "I Fought with the Reds" published in the *Irish Independent*. By 1942 he was a chief petty officer in the Irish Naval Service at Haulbowline in Cork. He offered his assistance to the German legation to assist them smuggling spies out of Ireland. He was arrested and sentenced to seven years in prison but was released at the end of the "Emergency", the name given to the Second World War in Ireland.

After many close encounters with death, he was eventually presumed drowned in December 1947 when his ship ran aground off the Wexford coast. But we cannot be sure because he may have gone aboard a passing pirate ship.

That Sinking Feeling Again

We built the *Titanic*, which is not in any way a metaphor for our history. Many of us went down on the *Titanic*, some stoically and some complaining loudly. The ship's Captain Smith apocryphally advised his passengers and crew to "be British" as the ship went down. Was this useful advice in the circumstances, or just confusing? But many things, including the size, nature and location of icebergs, confused Smith. I assume that he meant his passengers should go down without complaining and maintain stiff upper lips, facilitated by the freezing North Atlantic water.

Thomas Andrews (1873–1912), from Co. Down, was chief designer in 1903 and managing director in 1907 of Harland & Wolff, the Belfast shipyard that built the *Titanic*. When he became an apprentice at that company, he rose every morning at 4.50 a.m. to arrive at work at 6.00 a.m. He studied every evening when he got home. He was on board on the night of 14–15 April 1912 when the *Titanic* hit an iceberg. When he inspected the damage, he knew better than anyone else on board that the unsinkable ship would soon sink. He advised against panic and assisted the crew in helping women and children, and some men dressed as women, into lifeboats. He didn't disguise himself as a woman and sneak off, like some. He was last seen throwing deckchairs from the *Titanic* into the ocean to act as improvised flotation devices, rather than re-arranging them, which has since become a popular form of distracting activity. He then stoically went down with the ship.

*

Apart from sinking on unsinkable ships, the principal inconveniences of a life at sea were the nuisance of having your head blown off by a cannonball, or the embarrassment of being captured by a pirate in drag. Apart from these, it was generally an appealing life, offering many opportunities for an ambitious Irish person to go down in history practically anywhere in the vast oceans.

6

Irish Writers: The Chicken-Leg Effect and Other Forms of Inspiration

Irish painters were a relatively tame lot compared to their Continental counterparts. We have to look to France or Holland for people drinking absinthe and cutting off their ears. However, with writers we have done better. Per capita, we have definitely produced more drunken authors per pub, more Nobel Prize laureates per page and perhaps those with the worst lungs. But the life of the writer in the past in Ireland was trying. Many had to emigrate in order for their genius to be ultimately recognised at home. If an Irish writer couldn't win a prize or get away, the next best thing was to have their work banned. But the prestige of being banned was historically undermined as a literary challenge when it became only a matter of mentioning the word "sex", even in a biology book.

We know from chaos theory, popularly known as the butterfly effect, that seemingly insignificant events can give rise to a chain of unpredictable consequences. Thus the inspiration for great literature can come from innocuous incidents. From the example of James Johnston Abraham (1876–1963), we learn that the smallest episode can inspire a literary genre. He set a chicken's broken leg when he was a child. This made him decide to become a doctor. He also read a book when he was ten. That caused him to discover "real literature" and be aware of what it was he was ignoring in his own writing. He combined these two inspirations to shape his literary future.

After graduating in medicine from Trinners, he promptly found himself on a banana boat writing what by his own standards was "unreal literature" – his first book, *The Surgeon's Log* (1911). This was quickly followed by his chick-lit work, *The Night Nurse*, in 1913. This work was adapted for the big screen as the 1935 film *Irish Hearts*. This was reviewed as "the most ambitious and daring film" to have been made in Ireland at the time – moderate praise, considering it was probably the fourth film to be made in the country.

The army reasonably rejected Abraham in 1914 for being over-qualified, because getting oneself killed in the First World War demanded little natural talent, and surely no training. He joined the Red Cross instead. In between operating on people, broadcasting and holding many distinguished offices, such as the president of medical societies, he wrote history, biography, journalism, medical articles and an autobiography – in case he was forgotten.

Genteel Chick-Lit

Historical chick-lit thrived out of the reach of the censors because it never involved actual sex. The genteel heroines may have been thinking about sex all the time but they weren't doing it on the pages. Marguerite Gardiner (1789–1849), from Tipperary, who was an early proponent of the principles of chick-lit, knew a lot about sex but didn't write about that sort of thing.

She married a violent bully, Captain Farmer, but left him after three months and returned home. She then became "just friends" with Captain Thomas Jenkins in whose house she spent five years studying and reading. I am not an authority on chick-lit but I believe that the genre allows for its characters to enter into credible "friendships" with the opposite sex, because it is a form of fiction. She was such "just friends" with Jenkins that her future husband Charles Gardiner paid Jenkins £10,000[113] compensation to allow Marguerite to live with him, Gardiner, as "new just best friends". Soon after this, Captain Farmer died in a lucky drunken fall, so Gardiner was able to marry her.

They moved to London where their home became a leading social venue for artists, politicians and writers. Marguerite was known as "most gorgeous" but she was also intelligent and witty. In 1822 she anonymously published her first work, which was a collection of essays. The couple went on a continental tour that lasted ten years – and why not? Gardiner died in 1829, leaving her with diminished funds and an increasing number of her own relations who had become part of her entourage. A recurring feature of marriage in the past was your entire family moving in with you if you just happened to marry someone rich.

She turned to writing to make money. Her book *Conversations with Lord Byron* (1834) is her most significant literary work. Her fiction is notable for her shrewd observations of high society. Despite a prodigious literary output, she went bankrupt during the Famine.[114] The stress of the literary life finally killed her in 1849.

---

[113] About €450,000 in contemporary currency values.

[114] The Famine, or the Potato Famine, as it is known outside Ireland, was a period of mass starvation and forced migration principally caused by the failure of the potato crop in Ireland between 1845 and the early 1850s. Surprisingly, despite our disastrous historical relationship with this tuber, we remain loyal to the spud as our staple food in the form of boiled potatoes, floury potatoes with a knob of butter, chips, new "soapy" potatoes, *patatas bravas*, shoelace chips,

A Musing

While a chicken leg might shape a notable literary career, it was more common for writers to be inspired by love. If you couldn't write, you could become the object of literary affection in the form of a semi-professional muse, like our most famous literary stimulus, Maud Gonne (1866–1953).

Gonne was the subject of most of the love poetry of William Butler Yeats (1865–1939). Yeats was fascinated by the occult and in that sense Irish literature missed out by his choosing poetry over horror writing. By 1890 he was completely immersed in the supernatural, having joined the Hermetic Order of the Golden Dawn, a Rosicrucian and Kabbalistic esoteric society that practised ritual magic. He was a member of the Theosophical Society, the principal prophet of which was Madame Helena Petrovna Blavatsky. From 1912 he attended many séances. Those were the days because currently it is impossible to find a reputable medium in Dublin.

During his honeymoon, Yeats discovered that his new wife, George Hyde-Lees (1892–1968), who he married in October 1916, did not have muse qualities; however, she did have a capacity for automatic writing, whereby she claimed she was inspired by a spiritual source. For several years Yeats and his wife contacted spirits together, who provided them with an account of the forces governing historical change in Ireland, because spirits always know what is going on at a teleological level. This period even saw him win the Nobel Prize in Literature in 1923.

By 1934 he was trying to revive both his poetry and his libido with several new muses, including the

---

colcannon, mashed potaotes, chips with curry sauce, wedges, spicy wedges, crisps, baked potatoes, baked potatoes with fillings, roast potatoes, handmade chips, mashed potatoes on pies, seaside-caravan chips with little black spots, and so on.

soon-to-be-insane actress Margot Collins, the novelist Ethel Mannin and the poet Dorothy Wellesley. But Gonne remained his constant inspiration throughout his literary life.

Gonne was born in England, the daughter of Captain Thomas Gonne. Understandably, as an ardent Irish nationalist, she wanted to be Irish. She produced paperwork to prove it, eventually becoming more Irish than us Irish ourselves. Our genealogy office rarely disappoints. And what harm? She was the ultimate blow-in.

In 1868, when Gonne was two, Thomas Gonne was appointed brigade major of the cavalry in Ireland, which was stationed at the Curragh. When she was six she was sent to live in London. From there, she went to live in the South of France, where she became fluent in French. When he returned from India in 1879, Thomas Gonne travelled around Europe with his daughter Maud. She spent time with her great-aunt Mary in France and Germany. Mary had ambitions to launch Gonne as a professional beauty, which would have condemned her to a life of attending literary salons. Gonne wouldn't have any of it. She wanted to become a muse. Musing meant a life of attending literary salons. But her father rescued her from her great-aunt by taking her to Bayreuth in Germany for the Wagner Festival, and then back to Dublin.

When her father died in 1886, Gonne and her sister Kathleen spent an unhappy time in London with their uncle, William Gonne. As no one remembered to tell Gonne that she would inherit a fortune when she was twenty-one, she tried to make a living by becoming an actress. But before she could develop her thespian skills, she met and began a passionate affair with Frenchman Lucien Millevoye, who was a married journalist with extreme right-wing political views.

In December 1887 she hit the jackpot when her inheritance came through. Back in Dublin from 1888, she established herself in nationalist circles. Gonne was extremely rich, extremely tall,[115] extremely beautiful, fairly intelligent and extremely independent. By contrast, the nationalists were quite a dowdy lot. She became surrounded by a buzz of excitement and gossip because the nationalists had never seen anything like her.

In London, Gonne stunned Yeats when he first met her in 1889. He fell instantly, madly, insanely and irreversibly in love: it was the love of the poetry nerd for the rock-star model. He wrote about her in fifty poems and many critics argue that she can be found in everything he wrote after meeting her, and maybe even before. She didn't write reciprocal poems about him. But she did mythologise herself and her role in the formation of a nationalist consciousness in Ireland in her 1938 memoir, *A Servant of the Queen*.

In 1890 she gave birth to Millevoye's son, Georges, in Paris. She kept the baby but never mentioned him to her Dublin nationalist circle because she knew that they were prim revolutionaries. She was aware they weren't plotting a sexual revolution. Indeed, she wasn't allowed to join the nationalist organisations, the Gaelic League, the Irish Republican Brotherhood and the National League, because she was a woman.

In 1891, Georges died. Gonne wrote to Yeats informing him that she was devastated by the death of an adopted child. By coincidence, she travelled back to Ireland dressed entirely in black on the boat that was carrying Charles Stewart Parnell's (1846–1891) coffin, so the nationalists believed that she was in mourning for Parnell. This added to her mythology. At that time she may have actually been engaged to Yeats but nothing happened.

---

[115] When Maud was fifteen, she was supposedly 6 feet, 4 inches tall, but as she didn't fall into the hands of the dreaded anatomists we don't have a precise measurement.

In 1893, hoping to reincarnate their dead child, Gonne and Millevoye had sex in the crypt of the mausoleum that she had built for her dead son. Nine months later Gonne gave birth to Iseult Gonne (1894–1954), who she brought up in France but didn't initially publicly acknowledge as her daughter.

In May 1897 Gonne started her own journal, *L'Irlande Libre*, to present the Irish cause in Continental Europe, and opened a branch of the Young Ireland Society in Paris where she became intensely engaged with Irish nationalism among expatriates, providing support in the form of salons, writing and money.

She eventually agreed to marry Yeats on another planet, according to their shared astral beliefs, but she wouldn't marry him on Planet Earth. I am ignoring the many rumours about drugs having any role in this arrangement. But in 1898 Gonne eventually told Yeats about her children. This confession seems to have really shocked him. At that point she was willing to marry him on this planet, but he actually said no. Then he changed his mind, but by then she had also changed hers back again. Close!

In 1902 she appeared as the lead in Yeats's play *Cathleen Ní Houlihan*. In 1903 he begged her not to marry the Irish rebel John MacBride.[116] But Gonne converted to Catholicism on 17 February 1903, and married MacBride in Paris on 21 February. MacBride, like many Irish getting married before and after him, vainly hoped that she would change after the ceremony. She travelled to Ireland to get "some space". Conveniently, he couldn't follow her because he was wanted by the authorities there.

In Dublin she flew black petticoats from her home to mourn the death of Pope Leo XIII. This is typical of the

---

[116] See The 1916 Battle for the Biscuits in Chapter 1 for details of MacBride's military and revolutionary career, and his relationship with Maud Gonne.

ardent behaviour of the recent convert. However, she could not have chosen a more inappropriate garment to mourn the pope, unless she was a) making a deeply sardonic statement; b) it was a feminist declaration; c) her understanding of the papacy was flawed; or d) she knew some secret about the Vatican nuns. We can't prove that drugs influenced her garment choice. She then protested against all the insidious foreign influences, except hers, in John Millington Synge's (1871–1909) play *The Shadow of the Glen*.

In 1904 in Paris, her son Seán MacBride (1904–1988) was born. She confessed to Yeats that he had been right all along about the prospects of her marriage. She told him that she had made John MacBride into a hero in her own over-active imagination. She sued for divorce. To support her litigation, she didn't plead insanity. Instead, Gonne accused her husband of sexually assaulting practically everyone in her household or anything that moved. When James Joyce (1882–1941)[117] read of the scandalous divorce proceedings in the French newspaper *Le Figaro*, he wrote to his brother that he was confident that Pope Pius X would alter Catholic regulations to accommodate this Irish Joan of Arc. But when the scandal reached the pious revolutionaries in Dublin, who were more orthodox than the pope, it instantly undermined Gonne's standing amongst them. She was even hissed at in the Abbey Theatre in 1906 and not because of her acting talents. The divorce was a disaster for her Irish identity. Her "bohemian" circle in Dublin fled at the sight of her.

After 1906 she lived mainly in France where Yeats was a regular visitor to her Normandy home. They had another affair on an astral plane in June 1908, followed by a brief liaison on Planet Earth. By 1916 she was back in vogue as the widow of a national hero. She might have asked what

---

[117] See the next section, Sticking with Joyce, for details on his muse, Nora Barnacle.

the British had ever done for her, but in 1916 they shot her ex-husband. She could hardly have hoped for more. The 1916 Rising saved her career as an Irish person. She wore black and called herself Maud Gonne-MacBride and forgave her executed husband all his transgressions, real or imagined.

In a burst of exhilaration, Yeats proposed to the new merry widow in July 1916, whose bullet-riddled husband was still warm in his unmarked prison grave. Gonne rejected him. In 1910 Gonne's daughter Iseult had proposed marriage to Yeats but he turned her down because their horoscopes were incompatible. But after Gonne's rejection of him in 1916, he then proposed to Iseult. Iseult turned him down in August of that year, after consulting with her mother. She said no, not on this planet.

Yeats married George in October 1916. However, Iseult continued to inspire his poetry between 1918 and 1919. She also inspired a poem as late as 1938, the year before he died. In 1920 Iseult married the writer Francis Stuart (1902–2000). She seems to have been a less successful muse in that relationship because the two fought violently – but maybe that was what was needed.

Gonne was gaoled in Holloway Prison in 1918 for an alleged pro-German conspiracy. Yeats and her son, the fourteen-year-old Seán MacBride, spearheaded the campaign to have her released and returned to Dublin, which she was.

Yeats and his wife George had been living an unsettled nomadic life. Gonne allowed them to use her house in Dublin when she was not there – whenever she was in prison, for instance – on the condition they move out by the time she came back. When she was released from gaol in 1918, she arrived home to find Yeats still living in her house, along with his sick pregnant wife, who looked like she was about to die. A massive row broke out, and things were never the same again between Gonne and Yeats, on this or any other planet. After all the musing that they had been

through together, the idyllic inspiration sank on the prosaic
rock of the parsimonious poet overstaying his welcome.

Sticking with Joyce

Much of our literary history seems to be the product of a
series of apparently chaotic accidents of love. But are these
as random as they appear? James Joyce ultimately became
obsessed with the idea that he didn't meet his true love and
muse Nora Barnacle (1884–1951) by accident. From their
separate beginnings, he in Dublin and she in Galway, it
seemed improbable. He convinced himself that it was in fact
incredible, and that his friends had set him up.

Joyce was a bookish nerd; Barnacle wasn't. After
finishing school, Barnacle became a school porter and a
washerwoman. She was a notably rebellious teenager for the
conservative Galway of that time, frequently dressing up in
men's clothes, which seems to have been the pastime of half
the women in Irish history. She may have borrowed them
from the laundry. She thought it was fun to pass herself off
as a man around the quiet dull streets of Galway.

Her uncle, who seems to have been a pious busybody,
and we can assume that Galway was crammed with that
type at that time, beat her up over her relationship with a
local boy. I imagine that same interfering uncle eventually
came to regret his intervention after she eventually hooked
up with Joyce. But his influence was crucial to Irish literary
history because she left Galway in 1904 to become a cham-
bermaid in Finn's Hotel in Dublin.

She met Joyce on 10 June 1904, and again on 16 June, the
day on which *Ulysses* is based. As mentioned, Joyce came
to believe that the initial meeting might not have been the
chance encounter it initially seemed but was arranged by
his friend Cosgrave, who may have already been having an
affair with Barnacle.

Barnacle ran away with Joyce to Zurich, Switzerland in October 1904. They moved between Zurich, Trieste and Rome before going back to Trieste, where they settled. She washed and ironed while he wrote books and taught English, as you do. She became interested in opera and fashion. He became interested in booze and other women. She tried to ignore his drinking and womanising. In what is probably the most imaginative intervention in the history of addiction, she threatened to baptise their children if he didn't stop drinking.

But theirs was the kind of torturous relationship that was ideal for an aspiring literary genius. He was obsessively jealous over her former boyfriends, real or made-up. By 1909 they even split up for a while because of their constant rows over Joyce's obsessive belief that Barnacle had been having an affair with his friend Cosgrave when they first met in Dublin in 1904. Joyce was not the kind of man who could let such an idea go. But perhaps we would never have had *Ulysses* if Joyce hadn't been obsessed with the tiniest inconsequential details, real or made-up.

Barnacle married Joyce in London in July 1931. This came as a shock to her virtuous mother, Annie Barnacle, who had been led to believe that they were already married. It was embarrassing for her to find out through the media that they hadn't been. Whatever about Joyce's happiness, Barnacle seemed to have been happy in Paris with Joyce when he had become successful and recognised. I assume marriage to Joyce was measurably better than washing and ironing piles of laundry.

Barnacle never read *Ulysses*, which makes her typical of most Irish people. Critics hold this against her, which is unfair. Between disparaging his writing, making him jealous, the poor standards in ironing and the constant arguments, she produced in him creativity born of anxiety and misery that inspired his writing. What more could he have wanted?

Shot of Love

In Irish romantic history love and violence often go together like a horse and carriage full of armed servants. Violent love is the perfect inspiration for poetry. George Fitzgerald (c.1746–1786) was both Ireland's leading duelist, with over twelve recorded duels, and a writer of one poem, "The Riddle" (but it is a long one). He had the right attributes for dueling – a short temper combined with being a womaniser. While stationed with the army in Galway, he was ready to quarrel over the slightest insult, real or, the even better kind, imagined.

He left the army to marry Jane Connolly, against her brother's wishes of course. They moved to Paris to lead decadent lives funded by borrowings because credit was scarce in Galway, and decadence was not yet in vogue in the West of Ireland. He had the brilliant business idea of killing one of his creditors in a duel. However, his opponent was a better shot so Fitzgerald had to run from the dueling field. In London in 1773, Fitzgerald tried to redeem his reputation as an honourable scoundrel by challenging Captain John Scawen to a duel. Scawen chose pistols but, as Fitzgerald already had had unhappy experiences with pistols, he wanted to use sabers. An unofficial fight ensued between the pair over which weapons they would use in their official conflict. The duel finally got under way with pistols. When Fitzgerald missed with his shot, he was obliged to throw himself on his knees and beg for mercy, which is preferable for the professional scoundrel to getting a bullet through the skull.

In 1776 Fitzgerald returned to Ireland to live off his father. While the father was campaigning for a seat in Parliament, the son shot and killed a popular member of the constituency in a duel in Ballinrobe, thereby alienating many of the voters. He then fought fellow scoundrel (but non-poetry-writing) "Buck" English with swords in St Stephen's Green in Dublin. Fitzgerald had to be rescued by his seconds when English skewered him several times with his sword. When his father became less enthusiastic about maintaining his son's dissolute lifestyle, Fitzgerald chained him to his bed and forced him to support him. His brother Charles sued over his treatment of their father, and was awarded £500, which probably came out of the old man's funds. Fitzgerald was sentenced to two years in gaol. He escaped and took his father hostage. I admit that he had a limited imagination for a potential poet. He was recaptured and eventually released early for good behaviour.

In 1782 he was back in funds, allowing him to pursue his poetic ambitions. He had married a wealthy heiress after his wife agreeably died in 1779. He anonymously published his magnum opus, "The Riddle".[118] He then had a final duel against animal rights activist and lawyer "Humanity Dick" Martin (1754–1834).[119] The only case Humanity Dick ever took was to prosecute Fitzgerald when he shot the wolfhound of Lord Altamount. When Fitzgerald was convicted, he challenged Humanity Dick to a duel to get revenge against justice. By now Fitzgerald had become skeptical about his abilities with sabers, so the two fought

---

[118] This long poem later appeared under the title "The Riddle by the Late Unhappy George-Robert Fitzgerald Esq. with notes by W. Bingley formerly of London, Bookseller". It is difficult to single out one verse from this classic but the following conveys the gist:

Just punishment! When poor despised,
When rich, not a jot from it:
Nature ne'er long remains disguised;
The dog can't leave his vomit.

[119] Humanity Dick's devotion to animals was such that he persuaded his tenants to each vote three times for him for election to Parliament so that he could legislate for animal rights. In order to vote more than once without being detected, his voters wore elaborate disguises to the voting booths. Perhaps some of them dressed in gorilla suits.

with pistols. Humanity Dick wounded Fitzgerald twice; he himself was wounded once.

Fitzgerald murdered an attorney in 1786, an act that apparently was against the law. But we should remember that attorneys were actually writing the laws so were bound to look after their own interests. Fitzgerald was imprisoned but the gaol was attacked by a surprisingly large mob of friends of the dead attorney, who were probably other attorneys. Fitzgerald was beaten to a pulp. However, he survived long enough to be hanged, quartered and beheaded at Castlebar, Co. Mayo.

You Don't Have to Be Mad . . .

His many critics, including the influential later writers William Makepeace Thackeray and Thomas Babington Macaulay, thought Jonathan Swift (1667–1745) was insane. Seemingly, only a madman could have written *Gulliver's Travels*. However, we now know that he suffered from the then unrecognised form of labyrinthine vertigo known as Ménière's disease.

Swift was a conservative who wrote radical books without being radical himself. In this he was like the creator of Dracula, Abraham Stoker (1847–1912), who wrote about a vampire without being one himself, though he had first-hand experience of bloodsuckers, having trained as a barrister in 1890. Stoker had been a clerk. He wrote *The Duties of Clerks of Petty Sessions in Ireland*, in which some horror fans have seen a foreshadowing of some of the means used to defeat Dracula in his best-known book.

Swift was born in Dublin. There is mystery around his parentage but we do know that his mother left him in Ireland with an uncle, Godwin Swift, when he was three. He studied at Kilkenny School, and then entered Trinners when he was fourteen. He graduated with a BA "by special grace", which we now call "passing by compensation", so we know that he didn't impress his examiners. But in 1702, a mere twenty years later, he took a degree of Doctor of Divinity.

Swift proposed to Jane Waring, who turned him down because he wasn't rich enough for her. Despairing of ever having the resources to marry, he settled for having a girl-friend, Esther Johnson, known to history as Stella.

Swift worked as a personal secretary, and was ordained while completing his studies. He nearly always published anonymously. His first satire, *Tale of a Tub*, appeared in 1704. After a period in Parliament in London, he became a member of the Scriblerus Club, which was dedicated to the satirical arts. While in London, he corresponded daily with Stella in Dublin. He eventually returned to Stella when he became dean of St Patrick's Cathedral, Dublin in 1714, a post that turned out to be a huge disappointment to him.

Perhaps to cheer him up, Dublin Corporation made Swift a freeman of the city as a reward for his political pamphlet-eering. In 1726 *Gulliver's Travels – Travels into Several Nations of the World, by Lemuel Gulliver* was published. It was an instant success all over Europe. However, Stella died in 1728, dampening his new happiness because, unusually for the times, he lived with Stella for love rather than money.

In 1729 he wrote the last of his political pamphlets, on the Irish human economy, which was a savage attack on admin-istrative failures. He then wrote satirical poetry about the potential reaction of the public to hearing of his death. He was declared to be of unsound mind but not insane because he had aphasia, which is the intermittent loss of the ability to speak or understand speech. Besides, he hadn't killed anyone, which was the principal diagnostic criterion for insanity at that time.

Having endured so much public speculation about his sanity, he was willing to do something to help the actually insane. In his will Swift left £12,000 for the establishment of a "lunatic asylum", St Patrick's Hospital, which opened for business in 1746, the year following his death.

Like Swift, Charles Robert Maturin (1780–1824) was both a Protestant clergyman and a writer. Maturin was obsessed from youth with religiously motivated torture, which inspired his gothic horror stories. However, no one doubted his sanity. He went to Trinners in 1795, which was a time of exciting political tension in the college caused by the United Irishmen who were on campus.[120] His 1808 novel, *The Wild Irish Boy*, denounced the union with Britain, and his 1812 work, *The Milesian Chief*, is ambivalent towards the United Irishmen. However, ambivalence at that time was practically the equivalent of hysterical support.

He really wanted to be an actor rather than either a writer or a clergyman. But he was persuaded that acting and giving sermons were closely related occupations, so he entered the Church instead of the theatre in 1803. He rightly neglected his parish duties to concentrate on his writing.

He married the extraordinarily beautiful Henrietta Kingsbury in 1803. He was tremendously proud of both her looks and her musical accomplishments. However, their poverty and his frequent public insistence that she wear even more make-up at parties were the principal marital strains. The make-up issue was his second obsession after religious torture. But his marital life was happy enough to cause him to denounce clerical celibacy and recommend early marriage to everyone. His son Basil William Maturin (1847–1915) ignored this advice. Basil became a celibate Catholic priest and a writer, sadly not of gothic horror like his father but on spiritualism and self-discipline.

On those few occasions when he did turn up for work and preach from the pulpit, Charles Maturin was interested in

---

[120] See A Missing Revolutionary in Chapter 1 for details of several United Irishmen who attended Trinners.

promoting moral conformity. However, in his novels he was fascinated by moral deviance. He wrote the gothic novel *The Family of Montorio, or, The Fatal Revenge*, which is set in Italy in 1807. He published under the pen name Denis Jasper Murphy to avoid shocking his parishioners.

Maturin, along with his wife and children, lived off his father. But that was an appropriate financial strategy for the struggling gothic author of that time, or any time. However, the father became impoverished after being falsely accused of embezzlement, so he had, in turn, to try to live off his son. But while this financial inversion was underway, Maturin guaranteed a huge loan for his brother, who promptly defaulted, as you do when a family member helps you out, leaving him with a massive liability. In response, Maturin opened a school that specialised in tutoring students for entry to Trinners, from which he occasionally made money.

When his play *Bertram* became a hit, Maturin revealed his true identity and travelled to London for the adulation. However, the money was absorbed by his debts and the necessary extravagances typical of the poverty-stricken author who suddenly makes good. The poet Samuel Taylor Coleridge wrote a famously scathing review of the play, so that was that.

Having come out of the closet as the clerical author of a semi-sympathetic portrayal of an adulterous anti-hero in *Bertram*, he added to his reputation as a suspect cleric by satirising evangelicals in his next work, *Women; or, Pour Et Contre*, in 1818. But then he immediately brought out a book of sermons to offset the growing risk of being sacked. The Church authorities were understandably confused.

His next two novels and a play were not positively received. However, his novel *Melmont the Wanderer* became famous in 1820. The hero, Melmont, sells himself to the devil in return for 150 years of life, and can only be redeemed by persuading someone else to take up the bargain in his place. When Maturin's critics accused him of being the devil they churlishly drew the conclusion that, as the devil, he was not deserving of promotion within the church. Maturin protested that these were only stories, but his clerical colleagues didn't believe him and thought that he had written himself into the book in the form of the devil. He argued that he was interested in writing about and exploring evil without being so. His fellow clergymen didn't understand any such distinction between life and art.

However, many of his fans still see him as a Faustian figure secretly enthralled by the devil. A recurring theme in his work is the disturbing attraction of a man to another man who turns out to be a woman in disguise. This may be evidence that he was a suppressed homosexual heterosexual. Another constant theme is night fears and how to resist them. We haven't suffered from these kinds of fears since the invention of the light bulb, so it is difficult for the contemporary reader to relate to this important theme in his work. In general, electricity has ruined the gothic genre.

The money Maturin made from his work did nothing to help his finances because he was so deeply in debt. He died from an overdose of laudanum, which sadly is no longer available over the counter at the apothecary. But despite the manner of his leaving it, and the suspicions of his fellow clerics that he was Beelzebub, Maturin's literary life was not the best model of dissolution. Others achieved higher standards of moral decay.

For example, James Clarence Mangan (1803–1849) practically singlehandedly invented the model of the dissipated Irish nationalist poet. His family ran a grocery shop on Fishamble St in Dublin but property speculation wiped them out. Property speculation, a rare example of a historical constant in Irish history, remains an ineluctable cause of ruin. If you don't lose your shirt in chancery[121] you could try losing it on property.

Following his family's ruin, Mangan managed to attend school but only with the help of his mother's relations. In 1818 he became an apprentice scrivener.[122] In the same year he adopted the name Clarence as his *nom de plume*, under which he published his first verse.

Mangan had a distinctive appearance. He dressed in a blue cloak in summer and winter, and a fantastically shaped hat. He had long golden unkempt hair framing a pale face – the de rigueur style for the romantic poet – and blue eyes sometimes hidden under green goggles. When it rained he carried two umbrellas. He was extremely shy and reclusive. He proposed marriage once to Margaret Stackpoole in 1834. She said no, and so ended his interest in all women.

In all, Mangan wrote nearly 1,000 poems. His reputation rests on twenty-two separate articles, *Anthologia Germanica*, that were translations from the German romantic poets. These were accompanied by witty prose commentaries. He was self-taught in German, though he had never visited Germany and never met a German. In fact, he never got further than Meath. He also published a series of oriental "translations" called *Literae Orientales*, which he purported to be from Persian, Turkish and Coptic verse. But these were either originals that he composed himself or loose adaptations of actual German poems. He described this technique as the "antithesis of plagiarism", that is, original work that he claimed to belong to someone else. He anti-plagiarised Serbian, Polish, Chinese, Hindostanee, Chippewawian and

---

[121] For details of the risks involved in being thrown into chancery and other forms of lengthy litigation see A Missing Revolutionary in Chapter 1.

[122] Scrivener is a historic form of clerk. If you are a clerk try calling yourself a scrivener at parties: it is more erudite.

Tartarian compositions. He used these supposed translations of both real and unreal peoples to comment on Irish
history and identity. Who would have thought that the
Tartarians were obsessed with Irish affairs?

Mangan became a legal copyist in 1826. This was employment that understandably drove him to excessive drinking.
While drinking on the job, he contributed pieces to a wide
range of periodicals. He wrote his most substantial work for
the *Dublin University Magazine*. Heroically, his friends got
him a job as a copyist at the Ordnance Survey Office from
1838 to 1841 when even they couldn't justify his relevance
to mapping. He wasn't competent in Irish so he confined
himself to giving poetic translations to the literal translations from Irish into English that were handed to him. When
that didn't suffice he made up whatever he couldn't understand to fill in the gaps. His friends were obliged to move
him from the Ordnance Survey Office to a job cataloguing
books in Trinners library, where he spent his time reading.

While at Trinners, he wrote depressingly political poems
and inventive verse satires under titles such as "To the
Ingleezee Khafir Calling Himself Djaun Bool Djenkinzun".
He had a dysfunctional younger brother who depended
on him, and who lived with Mangan whenever he had
somewhere to live himself. We can only imagine what this
brother was like to be classed as dysfunctional by Mangan.
Eventually, Mangan became homeless, sick, depressed and
alcoholic, all of which he readily admitted to. But he denied
being an opium addict. He was actually fired from Trinners
library in 1846. He was reduced to writing poems for immediate payment, perhaps the lowest occupation imaginable.
In 1849 he was found in a state of malnutrition and admitted
to Meath Hospital. There he wrote his last poems. His impa-
tient nurse, who may have been moonlighting as a literary
critic, burned these. When he died after a week under her

care, three people attended his funeral. Such obscurity is real proof of his genius.

Like many after him, his death was a massive career move. His life was easily rendered into that of a romantic nationalist martyr. Yeats described him as "our one poet raised to the first rank by intensity".

Dublin-born Joseph Thomas Sheridan Le Fanu (1814–1873) started his professional life as a lawyer but began writing novels in 1845. His wife, Susan Bennett, suffered intense depression and a loss of faith before she died. She dreamed of her father's ghost inviting her to join him in the family vault, which she promptly did. Such a spouse can be an inspiration for the horror writer. These macabre troubles had a role in inspiring his lesbian vampire story, *Carmilla*, which was made into the film *The Vampire Lovers* in 1970, after lesbians had been officially invented.

Le Fanu wrote sixteen novels in the final ten years of his life. He wrote horror and detective novels, including the first-ever novel with a plot based in plastic surgery, *Checkmate*, in 1871. His reputation, however, is based on his ghost stories. His character Dr Martin Hesselius, from the 1872 collection *In a Glass Darkly*, is the model for Abraham Stoker's Van Helsing character in *Dracula*.

Le Fanu's son became his publicity agent after his death. To increase his father's gothic credentials, he claimed that Le Fanu had become a recluse. "Reclusing" was an essential career move for the horror writer. His son did such a good job in promoting his father that, even today, Le Fanu is highly regarded amongst fans of gothic literature and ghost stories.

But Irish fathers and sons don't always support each other like the Le Fanus. Writer and professional liar Thomas Reid's (1818–1883) father wanted his son to follow him into the Church, but Reid had other plans. He emigrated to America in 1839 to escape his narrow spiritual environment. First, he was a corn factor, or dealer, in New York but left because he refused to whip slaves. He then worked as a teacher, a clerk and an Indian fighter, on the basis that shooting Indians was more in keeping with his literary integrity than hitting slaves. He met the American gothic writer Edgar Allen Poe, and they became close friends. Poe, who was impressed by Reid's brilliant storytelling, said of him that he was a "colossal but most picturesque liar".

Reid joined the army and fought in the Mexican–American War from 1846 to 1848. In 1849 he wrote *War Life*, which was a suitably embellished account of his heroic war experiences, because straight reality would not suffice. He wrote under the name Captain Mayne Reid. However, he wasn't a captain, only a colossal liar.

In 1849 he sailed to England with a group of Hungarian radicals. He settled in London while the rebels travelled on to Hungary. Prolific writing years followed. He wrote the successful *The Rifle Rangers* in 1850, followed by *The Scalp Hunters* in 1851, *The Desert Home* in 1852 and *The Boy Hunters* in 1853. During his lifetime, he became one of the most popular novelists of his generation, producing over sixty bestsellers that were translated into ten languages. He had one winning theme so he stuck with it – all of his stories concern young men faced with overcoming overwhelming odds against the backdrop of a romanticised American Wild West. Franklin D. Roosevelt, Leon Trotsky, Robert Louis Stevenson and Arthur Conan Doyle were all fans.

Perhaps his most famous novel was *The Headless Horseman* (1856). He also wrote *The Quadroon*, which was plagiarised by Dion Boucicault[123] for his *The Octoroon*, a book about the interbreeding of different races. However, like Boucicault,

---

[123] See The Non-Applications of Engineering in Chapter 7 for the details of Boucicault's life and work.

he went bankrupt in 1866 because he had spent all of his considerable income on building a Mexican hacienda, "The Ranche", in England. He toured America and wrote the hugely successful novel *The Helpless Hand* in 1868 to try to recoup his losses. In examining our literary history, it seems there would have been fewer Irish novels without the spur of bankruptcy, which perhaps is second only to dysfunctional love as a literary motivation. From around 1870 he became acutely depressed and suffered doubts about his art.

Good Bellows

If a potential poet hadn't the energy for a wild or degenerate life, they could have cultivated a decaying respiratory system as a traditional alternative mode of poetic being. Edmund Armstrong (1841–1865) lived the traditional bronchial life of the poet to the full, expiring of tuberculosis at the height of his powers, as you should do as a poet.

Armstrong grew up in a large house in Dublin where he had a happy childhood. Contentment is a disaster for a potential poet. He went to Trinners in 1859. He was one of our few poets who prioritised perspiration over inspiration. Not for him the unrequited love of a muse, insanity or alcoholism: he made do with his tuberculosis. Besides, he couldn't stay out late pursuing debauchery because he rose every morning at 3.30 a.m. to study. This enthusiasm gained him a reputation as one of the college's best scholars and poets. He won prizes for Latin, Greek and Hebrew poetry.

He had a shotgun-blast approach to verse: he composed huge numbers of poems during his examinations. However, the effort nearly killed him because a blood vessel in his lung burst from the strain in 1860. He went to Jersey to recover, and undertook an inspirational walking tour of France with his younger brother, who idolised him. It was poetically inspiring because they had just £7 between them for the entire tour. His brother still idolised him when they eventually got back, shattered from the experience.

In 1863 he was fit enough to return to college. His normal routine was to write five poems per day. He was a poetry factory. He wrote nature poems and poems about his love for Ireland, which surprisingly are no longer popular. But he also wrote humorous poems and one about prostitution from a strictly theoretical point of view. He lost his religious faith, as a romantic poet must, and this caused him considerable existential suffering, which he appreciated would help his poetic output after his appallingly happy childhood. He studied theology as a bizarre way back to faith. He died of tuberculosis in his mother's arms. His brother edited his collected poems, letters and essays for publication in three volumes in 1877. He deserves our recognition as Ireland's hardest working poet because sheer output is not valued enough in poetry.

Family Ties

If an Irish writer didn't have tuberculosis or a miserable childhood, or if they were not in an obsessive relationship or bankrupt, they might have found the inspirational misery they needed in their family. The Irish family was invented to incite writing.

The Wildes were a literary family who are best remembered for the witty aphorisms and plays of Oscar Fingal O'Flahertie Wilde (1854–1900). But there were other scribblers in the Wilde family who were overshadowed by the attention-seeking Oscar.

Oscar's father, William Robert Wills Wilde (1815–1876), from Roscommon, was a doctor and a writer. On graduating in medicine in 1844, he took a post as a physician to a wealthy invalid who was going on a cruise on his private yacht, *Crusader*. William wrote a travelogue about the voyage that earned him £250, which he used to fund his study of eye and ear surgery in London, Vienna and Berlin. When he returned to Dublin, he set up a private practice but also opened a dispensary for poor patients in a converted stable. He was editor of the *Dublin Journal of Medical Science*, to which he contributed articles on eyes and ears. He was commemorated eponymously with two surgical procedures: "Wilde's snare" and "Wilde's incision". When not inventing surgical sewing techniques, he wrote guidebooks, memoirs and biographical articles. He wrote movingly on Swift, arguing that he wasn't insane, as everyone had believed.

However, William Wilde was only one half of a notably literary marriage. William's wife and Oscar's mother, Jane Francesca Agnes Wilde (1821?–1896) was known to her contemporaries as "Speranza". She was a poet, national-ist and feminist, which is probably the last thing you want your own mother to be. Speranza wrote an introduction to Charles Maturin's gothic masterpiece *Melmont the Wanderer* in 1892. In her twenties she published translations of works in German and French. She also knew Italian, Spanish, Polish, Russian, Latin, Greek and Gaelic. She contributed prose under the name John Fanshawe Ellis and poetry as Speranza to the Irish nationalist newspaper *The Nation*. She wrote the first poetic response to the Famine, which must have been a boon to the starving masses. But she then agitated for rebellion in *The Nation* when its editor Charles Gavan Duffy (1816–1903) was in prison awaiting trial. The paper was subsequently suppressed.

In 1864 a probable mistress of her husband sued her for libel. Mary Travers, described as an hysterical former patient, accused William Wilde of seduction. But her real case was against Speranza. She used the name Speranza to sign a scurrilous pamphlet about herself in a twist on the traditional pamphlet war.[124] Travers then hired newspaper boys to wave placards about the Wildes at them while they were holidaying in Bray. One conscientious boy got into their house in order to wave his placard at them while they sat at their dinner table. When the real Speranza confiscated the placard, Travers responded by threatening to sue for larceny. Speranza protested to Travers' father, alleging that the campaign was designed only for financial extortion. This accusation resulted in a suit for libel against the Wildes. The attorneys were delighted with the pamphleteering and placarding campaign, which went beyond their wildest hopes. While Travers won costs and damages of a farthing,[125] public sympathy lay with the Wildes. Speranza actually gave evidence to exonerate her husband. But he did not defend himself. Oscar should have followed his father's example years later at his own disastrous trial for libel by not turning up in court.

Speranza moved to London in 1876, when her husband died. There she became a successful prose writer and kept a literary salon. However, the money ran out when Oscar went to gaol and was predictably bankrupted from the associated law suits. Like many before and after her, Speranza died in litigation-originated poverty while Oscar was in gaol.

Oscar had an older brother, William (Willie) Wilde (1852–1899), who was one of the world's most efficient journalists. In school he excelled at drawing and piano but his talents were neglected in favour of those of his younger brother, who was the family pet. His mother said of him, "Willie is all right; he has a first-class brain. But Oscar will turn out

---

[124] See footnote 1 in Chapter 1 for details on the nature of pamphlet wars.

[125] A farthing was a quarter penny, about 40 cent in contemporary currency values.

something wonderful." Can you imagine having to grow up with that smug spoilt little narcissist, as well as having to listen to such discrimination from your mother? Oscar was spoilt rotten. No wonder he ended up in gaol.

Willie won a gold medal in ethics at Trinners, where he was also a leading debater. He had poems published as an undergraduate, and may have achieved even more than Oscar with a little encouragement from his mother, which he didn't get. He was called to the bar but never practised law – that's how sophisticated he was. Instead of the life of a lawyer, he chose the more ethical path of drunkard and pursuer of rich heiresses. He was the expert in ethics, after all, so who are we to judge him?

When Oscar was gaoled, loyal Willie publicly defended his younger brother's reputation regardless of how he may have privately felt. When Oscar heard that Willie was supporting him, he put the needs of wit ahead of fraternal gratitude and said, "My poor brother; he would compromise a steam engine." When Oscar was released on bail in 1895 he was reduced to living with Willie, who rightly exacted revenge for the privilege by lecturing him on ethics.

Willie inherited the family home in 1876 but was forced to sell it to raise funds because he had failed to find an heiress, despite dedicating himself full time to the project. In May 1879 he moved to London with his mother to live in the shadow of Oscar's celebrity. The brothers looked alike. This sibling similitude understandably upset Oscar, who was pursuing a career in individuality. He paid William to grow a beard and mustache. Nice work if you can get it!

Willie was popular company because he had a genial humour rather than the caustic rapier wit of his brother that was in vogue at that time. He was taken on as a correspondent with the *Daily Telegraph* newspaper, where he excelled at churning out succinct pieces on a huge range of topics. He boasted that he could arrive at his desk at noon, come up with an idea, and then go for lunch and a stroll before retiring to his club to write the article in an hour. He'd then spend the rest of the evening in the Café Royal.

In 1891 Willie Wilde achieved his life ambition, allowing him to retire from his arduous writing career. He found an heiress who was willing to marry him: Mrs Frank Leslie, who was fifty-five and had been married three times before. They married in New York.

It is mandatory to relate pithy Wilde-isms whenever the Wildes are mentioned, so here is my favourite. Because the best man at Willie's wedding was Marshall P. Wilder, the magazine *Town Topics* joked that the groom was wild, the best man was wilder, but the bride was the wildest. Willie ignored Oscar's rare piece of practical advice that he should get a pre-nuptial contract, so he was duly divorced and destitute within two years. I cannot imagine what went wrong in the relationship or why a divorce was necessary because Willie had spent the entire marriage in New York's Lotos Club, entertaining its members with drunken parodies of Oscar's poems. He also wrote a negative review of his brother's play *Lady Windermere's Fan* for the *Daily Telegraph*. This was perhaps his masterpiece. When Oscar found out about the review and the poetic parodies, there was a falling out.

Willie married again in London in 1894. It must have been love because his new wife was not fabulously wealthy. The couple had a daughter, Dorothy Ierne Wilde (1895–1941). Dorothy had the misfortune of inheriting her uncle's looks without his original intellect. She divided her time between London and Paris, where she was the toast of salons for looking like Oscar. She even dressed up as him and reproduced his maxims. Naturally it was all a bit confusing for those attending the salons. The importance of being Oscar had its demands. She became a lesbian because, I assume, she believed that Oscar would have been a lesbian if he had been a woman, in which case he would have stayed loyal to his long-suffering wife. She also became a morphine addict, I imagine based on Lady Bracknell's advice on the importance of having an occupation in *The Importance of Being Earnest*. She became a recluse in London, as she should have, and died in 1941 at the age of forty-six – the same age at which both her father and uncle had died. Her literary legacy consists of witty letters and reminiscences printed as *In Memory of Dorothy Ierne Wilde: Oscaria* in 1951.

The catastrophic end of the Wildes did not discourage other erudite families from forming. Stephen and Kathleen Behan were the core of another such family. Like the Wildes, the family is best remembered for the literary contributions of one overbearing member, Brendan, but his brothers also contributed to Irish literary life.

The Behans ran a different sort of familial literary salon. Their neighbours in Crumlin, Dublin called the home "the Kremlin" because it engendered militant trade unionists, republicans, communists and anarchists. The mother, Kathleen (1889–1984), was the daughter of a prosperous businessman who owned a grocer shop, a pub and a row of houses on Dorset St. However, the business failed because he spent all of his time in the courts, obsessed with the general minutiae of legal proceedings. He was yet another victim of the law. Kathleen and her sisters were placed in an orphanage when he died. Her eldest brother, Peadar Kearney (1883–1942), composed the lyrics of "The Soldier's Song" ("Amhrán na bhFiann"), which became the Irish national anthem.

Kathleen married Jack Furlong in 1916. Furlong fought in the Jacob's Factory garrison[126] in the 1916 Easter Rising, while Kathleen was a courier at the bullet-riddled GPO.

---

[126] See The 1916 Battle for the Biscuits in Chapter 1 for details of the week-long conflict in the biscuit factory.

After Furlong died in the global influenza epidemic of 1918, Kathleen married Stephen Behan (1891–1967). He was a house painter and republican. They had five children, Brendan, Seamus, Brian, Dominic and Carmel. Kathleen wrote a bestselling autobiography in 1984 called *Mother of All the Behans*.

The eldest Behan son, Brendan (1923–1964), was addicted to attention and storytelling from his earliest years. He trained to be a house painter like his father. He joined Na Fianna,[127] the youth organisation of the IRA, when he was eight, graduating into the IRA proper when he was sixteen. Many members of that organisation were worried that he was too flamboyant for covert operations.

In 1939 he travelled to Liverpool on his own initiative, where he was arrested carrying explosives. He was sentenced to three years' detention in Hollesley Bay Borstal, and was deported back to Ireland in November 1941. Within six months he was involved in a shoot-out with gardaí in Dublin and sentenced to fourteen years' penal servitude. He served five of those in Mountjoy Gaol, Arbour Hill Prison and the Curragh Camp before being released on a general amnesty. He began to write in prison because being locked up limited the distractions of a social life.

When he got out, he emigrated to Paris in order to try to put his past behind him. There he wrote twelve poems in Irish and three highly regarded short stories. He made a living as a journalist and as a professional "character". He sang, and did dramatic parodies and grotesque dramatisations of Brian Boru, Toulouse Lautrec and Maud Gonne, amongst others, in Paris cafés. He established his reputation as a drinker during his time in France.

---

[127] The term "Fianna", which was used in the names of various organisations, derives from the name for the warriors of Irish mythology, the Fianna.

His play *The Quare Fellow*, which was first performed in Dublin in 1954, was a hit in London in 1956. Brendan appeared drunk on British television, thereby establishing his public persona and enthralling the delightedly outraged English viewers. He wrote the play *An Ghiall* in 1958 in gratitude to the Irish language organisation Gael Linn for their support when he was in prison. But while this was well received in Irish by a potential audience of eleven native speakers, its English-language production, *The Hostage*, was an international hit.

His most famous work, the autobiographical *Borstal Boy*, which he had originally started in Mountjoy Gaol, also appeared in 1958. But, perhaps as a result of his time in prison, he had become addicted to public adulation and socialising, and wasn't able to focus on writing. He became famous around Dublin pubs in the early 1960s for being the most violent and repetitious of the dipsomaniacs, a role for which the competition was intense at that time.

It is now traditional to repeat Brendan's many repetitions, especially when one is drunk in a Dublin pub. Here is the one I like to repeat: Brendan vanished immediately after arriving on a ship in New York Harbour. Three weeks later he turned up and, when asked where he had been, he replied, "I saw a sign that said 'Drink Canada Dry', so I did." He wasn't able to write because he was consistently drunk. And, naturally, he got drunk because he couldn't write. His funeral was one of the largest in Dublin, ever.

Brendan's brother Brian Behan (1926–2002) was sent to Artane Industrial School when he was twelve just because he didn't like going to school. Since its formation in the 1920s, the Irish State has been practising this outrageous tyranny on its young citizens without criticism or even mild public outrage. Imagine – not going to school is against the law. This is unjust because what child can afford to sue? In revenge against authority, Brian organised dairy workers into a farm-workers' union. That was also illegal at the time. He enlisted in the Irish Army in 1945 to avoid gaol, and then emigrated to London in 1950. There he joined the Communist Party of Great Britain. He met both Joseph Stalin and Mao Zedong in 1951 but, disillusioned with party elites, he quit the communists to join the Trotskyite Socialist Labour League but was soon expelled for "deviationism". He was thrown out of the British Labour Party and two trade unions. He was even expelled from an anarchist organisation.

He wrote a novel, *Time To Go*, in 1979 and ghosted his mother's bestselling 1984 autobiography. He recycled this as a novel, *Kathleen: A Dublin Saga*. In 1988 he turned his creativity to the stage with a series of plays which gave substance to his claim that "being stage-Irish was a trade like any other." His first play, *Boots for the Footless*, was a success. He also wrote *The Begrudgers*; *Hallelujah, I'm a Bum*; *Brother of All the Behans*; and *Barking Sheep*. Being thrown out of an anarchist organisation was a special achievement in contrariness. But Brian is now best remembered for his televised fight with his brother Dominic, with whom he maintained a feud.

The youngest son, Dominic Behan (1928–1989), was influenced by the republican and intellectual life in "the Kremlin". He joined the republican youth movement Fianna Éireann, and became a prominent member of the Dublin Unemployed Movement, being frequently unemployed himself. He emigrated to London to pursue the dual family businesses of house painting and writing. By accident he became a broadcaster in 1956, and wrote and recorded songs. He wrote plays, novels, biographies and periodical pieces for newspapers, and a cantata on the life of Christ.

The Behan siblings had learned how hard it is to escape the influence of our parents. It is difficult, even when such parents are securely locked up. Dublin-born Elizabeth Bowen's (1899–1973) father was a barrister and was also occasionally insane. This combination, probably not as rare as you might imagine, made for both an exciting childhood and an essential grounding in the gothic. It would have been ideal if he had been confined to the attic but disappointingly he wasn't because no one prioritised the literary formation of his daughter. Whenever her father was actually mad, Elizabeth, or Bitha as she was called, along with her mother, was obliged to stay with relatives in Kent. To add to her woes, her mother died when she was eight. The displaced, or orphaned, child became a theme in Bowen's short stories, which were often gothic in tone.

Bowen was a serious child who didn't like silliness. Sadly, silliness has fallen completely out of fashion. She developed a fashionable stammer when her mother died. Again, sadly, stammers are no longer chic. People now go to great lengths to get rid of them when once they were so trendy in the literary salons.

Bowen married Alan Charles Cameron in 1923, which ironically was silly, the same year as the publication of her first volume of short stories. Cameron's party piece at their literary dinners was to be a deliberately extremely boring storyteller. During the 1930s they lived in Oxford, New York, Italy and London, where she wrote books and had many silly affairs, including one with the Irish writer Sean O'Faolain (1900–1991).

Bowen really enjoyed the Second World War. She became an air warden in London. Because people could be killed at any moment during the London air raids, life was intense and that intensity was an excuse for her to engage in reckless silly love affairs.

However, her London house was bombed. In Bowen's writings, houses often take on sentient qualities and influence the identity of her characters. In *The Death of the Heart* even the furniture is alive. I assume she blamed the German airforce, the Luftwaffe, for killing her table and chairs.

She became a journalist for the Ministry of Information, which in practice was really disinformation. She lived between London and her ancestral home at Bowen's Court in Cork. In the 1940s and early 1950s her literary output was enormous. She wrote short stories, novels, articles, broadcasts, criticism, introductions, prefaces, reviews and travelogues. She wrote on a wide range of subject matters, including London, ghosts, children and hotels. The actor Richard Burton débuted in her play *Castle Anna*.

When her husband Cameron, by then a long-time alcoholic, died in 1955, she started to spend more time in Cork, but she found it difficult to maintain Bowen's Court. It was eventually sold to a farmer in 1960, who demolished it. She then moved back to Oxford. She died in 1973 and is buried with Cameron in Cork.

Getting Ahead in an Oven

The Behans may have all been semi-professional contrarians but they were never incredibly annoying like their fellow republican writer Darrell Figgis (1882–1925). Figgis didn't understand the exquisitely fine creative distinctions between being contumacious, which deserves artistic recognition, and annoying, which deserves a fist in the face. Unfortunately for him, his republican comrades were clear on the difference.

Figgis, from Dublin, was the son of a tea merchant. He spent his early years in Ceylon, contemporary Sri Lanka, and joined his uncle's tea business in London in 1898. He spent ten years in the job, which he hated. In 1909 he published his first volume of poetry, *A Vision of Life*, and became a professional writer the following year. But he felt the need to move to Ireland, dividing his time between being annoying in Dublin and irking the natives on Achill Island. In 1913 he joined the Irish Volunteers.

After the 1916 Rising he was arrested in Achill and interned in England. While locked up he wanted to become the prisoners' spokesperson, but instead became the most unpopular inmate. He had a natural talent for irritating other people, a gift that came to the fore in prison. His cell-mates hated him, regardless of politics, and fought amongst each other to get away from him. To their inordinate relief, he was freed in December 1916 under a general amnesty.

In 1917 he wrote a self-aggrandising account of his time in prison, *A Chronicle of Jails*, because no one else was going to do it. He was arrested again in 1917 and deported to Oxford, probably with the active assistance of the Volunteers. But failing to take a hint, he returned to Ireland and was re-arrested. To the despair of the hardcore republican prison population, he was sent to join them in Durham Gaol. There he irritated them until his release in March 1919.

He continued to write in parallel to being annoying. *Children of the Earth* attracted positive critical reviews in 1918. *A Second Chronicle of Jails* appeared in 1919, again giving himself a constructive role amongst the republican prisoners. In Durham he had been even more unpopular as a cellmate. He was the cause of much bickering and a collapse in morale. Everyone just hated him.

However Arthur Griffith (1872–1922), who was the leader of Sinn Féin, trusted and promoted him within the party. This was despite, or maybe because of, the fact that Figgis's *The Economic Case for Irish Independence* of 1920 was largely plagiarised from Griffith's own work. Perhaps Figgis knew that there was no downside to telling a politician what they wanted to hear or to repeat their own opinions to them. In 1922 he was vice-chair of the committee established to draft the Free State Constitution. This committee split – you may have seen that coming – due to committee members falling out with Figgis because he was annoying them. One of the sub-committees resulting from the split eventually produced three draft reports. Most of Figgis's "Draft A" found its way into the Constitution, to the exasperation of many.

During the 1922 elections, in which he was standing for a seat, he was so unpopular with his fellow republican candidates that a group broke into his house and shaved off half his beard, of which he was extraordinarily proud. He won the sympathy of the public, who didn't really know who he was. The attack allowed him to top the poll. However, in his latter days in the Dáil, the chamber would quickly empty whenever he stood up to speak. He published *The Return of the Hero* under the pen name "Michael Ireland" in 1923. Probably those who had never met him praised it.

Sometimes unpopular people marry popular people to compensate. This was the case with Figgis. His extremely popular wife Millie shot herself with a pistol given to her by the revolutionary leader Michael Collins (1890–1922) in 1922. Everyone blamed the suicide on Figgis, who had started an affair with twenty-one-year-old dancing teacher Rita North. We don't know if the affair began just before or just after his wife's death, but either way it dented his already fatally undermined popularity. He was on a downhill roll. North died in 1925 from a botched abortion that made Figgis even more unpopular, if that was possible. He gassed himself in rented rooms in London in October of that year. While Mick Jagger couldn't get any in 1965, there was widespread satisfaction amongst the republicans in 1925.

Positions for Female Companions

Writers are symbiotically related to readers: without one we wouldn't have the other. It was common for women in the past with time on their hands to sit together in companionable pairs reading edifying books in their literary salons. Two women in Irish history, Eleanor Butler (c.1738–1829) and Sarah Ponsonby (1755–1831), may have taken this kind of literary companionship one step further.

(Charlotte) Eleanor Butler was both a so-called female companion and a famous recluse with a hectic social life. She was born into old gentry in Kilkenny but was educated in Cambrai in France by Benedictine nuns. This experience turned her off religion for the rest of her life. The nuns tend to have that effect on their pupils. She returned to Ireland when her brother John became the 16th earl of Ormond. She didn't want to marry, so she spent ten years sitting at home twiddling her thumbs. Everything changed for Eleanor in 1768 when thirteen-year-old Sarah Ponsonby visited the Butlers in Kilkenny Castle. Initially, the two became secret correspondents, sharing an interest in the arts and the writings of Rousseau.[128]

Sarah Ponsonby, like Butler, was a professional diarist, which was a career that required the financial support of her upper-class family. When Ponsonby left Miss Parke's boarding school in Kilkenny, she became busy deflecting the unwanted attentions of a middle-aged guardian. At that time, any self-respecting middle-aged guardian would strive to marry their young ward. By now, the Butlers, who were relatively poor even if they lived in a castle, were fed up with Eleanor's lack of interest in rich men and were considering sending her back to France.

The two women ran away together in the same carriage, dressed as men and toting pistols. Sarah brought her dog, Frisk, on this escape attempt. She leaped out the window of her house at Woodstock, Co. Kilkenny with him in her arms, which was disturbingly unladylike behaviour. They got as far as Waterford before their frustrated families caught up with them. Eleanor was sent to cousins in Carlow, but she

---

[128] See Made in France in Chapter 1 for details of what happened to Lord Edward Fitzgerald as a result of Rousseau's writings.

promptly escaped from there to find Ponsonby. Eventually the relatives' resolve was worn down. They gave up and allowed the two to officially become female companions.

They settled in Llangollen in Wales with a maid in a rented cottage called Plas Newydd. But their families were assured that they were definitely not lesbians; they were reclusive female companions.

For the "Ladies of Llangollen", as they became known, being recluses involved reading, keeping journals, collecting books to read, and house and garden renovations. They went in for a gothic look for the cottage with matching landscaped gardens. In time, their refuge became a popular visitor attraction and they often had guests out of a vast circle of high-profile artistic and intellectual friends. As female companions, they were obliged to wear men's clothes, and to cut their hair short and powder it.

Prince Puckler-Mukau described them as "certainly the most celebrated virgins in Europe". Female visitors to the cottage were reluctant to spend a night alone with them because they were such convincing female companions. It became fashionable for those in the gothic-bohemian set to visit, little realising that frequent house calls are inconvenient for a recluse. Everyone who was anyone visited the ladies: Charles Darwin, Sir Walter Scott, the Duke of Wellington, Josiah Wedgewood, Edmund Burke and Lady Caroline Lamb, amongst others. So frequently did visitors call that it caused Butler to lament in her journal, "When shall we ever be alone together?" Pamela Sims,[129] Lord Edward Fitzgerald's wife, visited. Soon after Fitzgerald's death in the 1798 Rebellion, Sims visited again but was encouraged to move on after a cup of tea. The two may have been recluses and female companions, but they were definitely not rebels.

---

[129] See Made in France in Chapter 1 for details of the relationship between Fitzgerald and Pamela Sims.

The two were always short of money because being recluses was costly. They had the highest catering bills of any hermits in history. They did have an allowance from their families, but Butler received nothing from her father's will. Charlotte, Queen Consort of the United Kingdom and wife of George III, gushed her admiration for the gothic eccentricities of their house and garden but, typical of those living it large on the taxpayer, she didn't make a financial donation. From their retreat they closely followed European politics, and knew what was going on all over Europe. Byron thought that the adulation they received from France, where they supported the Bourbons in the French Revolution, went to Butler's head, making her a haughty and imperious recluse.

Butler was regarded as being clever. At the time, no self-regarding woman would have wanted to be that. She was also regarded as odd, which again was a traditional preserve of men. An anonymous contemporary silhouette shows two fat ladies in traditional riding gear. An article in the *General Evening Post* of 24 July 1790, entitled "Extraordinary Female Affection", outrageously suggested that their relationship might have been unnatural. Butler, Ponsonby and their loyal maid are buried together at Llangollen Church. I wonder if the maid is in the middle. Out unnatural thoughts!

While they have only contributed diaries to the canon of Irish literature, Butler and Ponsonby were the objects of much gossip and letters, and they naturally inspired poetry, because everything inspired poetry back then: female companions, fits of passion, Greek vases, various bird species, country lanes, storms and daffodils. Both Anna Seward and William Wordsworth wrote poems celebrating the companionship between the two women.

Geraldine Cummins (1890–1969) was an Irish female companion with an occult connection to literature: she was a psychic medium who was in contact with dead writers, some of whom dictated books to her.

She became telepathic after an unsuccessful stint as a suffragette. Cummins was stoned by a mob because she was a suffragist. Being stoned on the streets of Cork meant something entirely different in 1914 than it does now for undergraduates from University College Cork.

She received training as an oracle under the Irish medium Hester Dowden (1868–1949), who was in regular contact with Oscar Wilde and William Shakespeare. One needs training to communicate with the dead, especially dead wits and playwrights.

A spirit called Silencio dictated several books to Cummins, including *Paul in Athens* (1930) and *The Great Days of Ephesus* (1933). She was also a contributor to the *Occult Review*. She lived in Chelsea in London with her female companion, Beatrice Gibbs. In 1950 her ownership of Silencio's books was legally challenged. But Cummins won on the grounds that a spirit, even a literate one, could not own copyright.

*

I never saw a man who looked
With such a wistful eye
Upon that little tent of blue
Which prisoners call the sky,
And at every drifting cloud that went
With sails of silver by.

From *The Ballad of Reading Gaol*,
written by Oscar Wilde (1854–1900)
after his release from prison

7

Irish Science and Thought: Life In (and Out of) the Laboratory

Anyone who has ever had a chemistry set knows the joy associated with trying to blow up the cat. But few of us have our own laboratory in our basement, a lightening conductor on our roof and a convenient nearby village filled with boorish rustics ready to surround the house at the slightest hint of a scientific breakthrough. The best scientific progress has only ever been possible in the face of the recalcitrant resistance of the local small farmers.

Ah, I am nostalgic for the mob of peasants! Peasant mobs occur all over Irish history, and are usually to be found surrounding castles, wielding pitchforks and burning brands while shouting threats and abuse at those inside who are usually aristocrats, or "doctors", in the process of re-assembling dead bodies. Peasant mobs normally dispersed home for supper in the evening before it got dark because they couldn't imagine what might come out of the castle. It is one thing to complain about scientific progress; it is another to do something about it.

If you want to go down in Irish history as a scientist, try making something in a laboratory that doesn't involve too many complicated calculations. Something hideous would be easier to build, and more memorable, than something useful. Consider the success of Doctor Victor Frankenstein. However, when it comes to the sciences, we Irish lack that killer scientific instinct typically found in remote nineteenth-century Transylvanian castles. This is true not just in reconstructive anatomy. In general, we seem to have been better at fighting and writing poems than thinking and doing sums. However, we have had a few worthwhile scientific breakthroughs.

Doctor Strangelove

Trinners could have had the atom bomb in the 1940s. They had the man who could have built it in Ernest Walton (1903–1995), but they didn't have the funds or ambition. In any case, Walton became a pacifist.

Walton is our only Nobel Prize laureate in science. He was the first person in history to split the atom. In 1951, almost twenty years after their world-changing experiments, the Nobel Prize for physics was awarded jointly to Walton and the British scientist John Cockcroft for their pioneering work on the transmutation of atomic nuclei by artificially accelerated atomic particles. Their experiments pioneered a new branch of physics that produced nuclear interactions in a controlled way. Any controllable interaction can be used as a bomb, which is perhaps the point of physics. It was the first direct verification of Albert Einstein's famous mass–energy relationship in a nuclear reaction, in which the destruction of just a tiny amount of matter released a huge amount of energy. Walton proved that E does equal mc^2. The bombardment of uranium with neutrons and the discovery of the key nuclear-bomb-related neutron itself followed directly from Walton's research in 1932.

By 1934 Walton was so highly regarded that he could have gone to any leading physics laboratory in the world. Instead, he chose to return to his *alma mater*, Trinners, which was underfunded and particularly depressed at that time. During the Second World War, the Physics Department was down to just three staff; the rest may have been supporting the allied national war effort and building bombs. Walton stayed in Dublin because he patriotically decided that the needs of the students, our future physicists, were greater than those of the free world. In other words, he wasted his time teaching.

In fact, Walton became a dedicated pacifist following media speculation about the potential of his famous experiment for military applications. But imagine what Trinners could have achieved with an atomic bomb. Imagine what our leader at that time, Éamon de Valera (1882–1975)[130] could have done with a bomb. Come to think of it, maybe Walton was right not to build one because it would surely have fallen into the wrong hands – de Valera's. He could have ultimately terrified even North Korea.

Pick a Number, any Number

William Rowan Hamilton (1805–1865) was arguably our best person in history at doing sums. Like me, he was born on the stroke of midnight, if that means anything. His father was an apothecary who had become an attorney, if you can imagine such a conversion. The Hamiltons had become bankrupt because of the involvement of William's godfather

---

[130] For more on de Valera see The 1916 Battle for the Biscuits in Chapter 1.

in the United Irishmen.[131] Hamilton was sent to his uncle's
school in Trim, Co. Meath when he was three years old.
The school had a reputation: the building had at one time
been owned by Jonathan Swift,[132] and the Duke of Wellington, who was thick,[133] had been a student there. Hamilton's
uncle was a classicist rather than a mathematician. Therefore, Hamilton was exposed to a torrent of Hebrew, Greek,
Latin and the classics. However, when he was sixteen he got
an analytic geometry book that ignited his interest in mathematics, something that never happens in school nowadays.

The mathematics syllabus at Trinners in 1823, when
Hamilton enrolled, had been updated to reflect the massive
Continental developments in that discipline. His initial
attempt at originality was in geometry, in which field he
produced his first famous paper, "Theory of Systems of
Rays", which was read before the Royal Irish Academy in
1827.

Following this success, he was elected to the Andrews
chair in astronomy[134] while he was still an undergraduate.
He effectively became the "Royal Astronomer of Ireland".
He moved to the observatory at Dunsink,[135] and, not

---

[131] See The Dis-United Irishmen in Chapter 1 for information on the
members of this fractious political group.

[132] See You Don't Have to Be Mad in Chapter 6 for details on the life
and work of Jonathan Swift.

[133] See Our Waterloo in Chapter 3 for details on the academic abilities
of the Duke of Wellington, the Irishman Arthur Wellesley. Amongst
his many achievements, he also popularised the Wellington boot.

[134] Currently the Andrews Professorship of Astronomy is an honorary
chair at Trinners. It used to be the title given to the astronomer in
charge of Dunsink Observatory. From 1792 to 1921 the holder of this
chair was also given the title "Royal Astronomer of Ireland".

[135] The observatory at Dunsink, Co. Dublin was endowed by Francis
Andrews, who was a provost of Trinners. The observatory was
opened in 1785.

knowing anything about astronomy, he wisely employed his two sisters as his assistants to do all of the work.

While pretending to be an astronomer, Hamilton became aware of a feature of the extremely complex geometrical nature of wave structures. It seems obvious to us now, but he was the first to notice that, for a particular direction of the incident ray on a biaxial crystal,[136] each incident ray gave rise to a complete cone of refracted rays rather than a double refraction, as you might expect. It's simple when these things are actually pointed out to us. He described this discovery to his colleague at Trinners, Humphrey Lloyd, persuading him to perform a complex experiment in optics, which he did. The resulting observation of conical refraction was a clear proof of the underlying hypothesis of Augustin-Jean Fresnel's important wave theory. Fresnel had devised a model for the propagation of transverse light waves in crystals that in turn supported Christiaan Huygen's model

---

[136] Crystals are classified according to the number of optic axes they have. Thus, a biaxial crystal has two. Crystals are used in the study of optics which – in a particular light – may be illegal. I refer you to the case of *Tisdall versus McArthur & Co. (Steel & Metal) Ltd and Mossop* [1950] 84 I.L.T.R 173, heard in the Supreme Court before Judges Maguire and Murnaghan O'Byrne Black, where it was suggested on behalf of Tisdall's injunction to prevent McArthur & Co blocking up three windows in his premises that in some way the whole nature of light was altered by its passage through glass (a type of crystal) – "a proposition which would seem to involve some novel theories in physics. Light may be reflected, refracted or blocked, but the light which emerges from one side of a pane of glass is essentially the light – or part of the light – which impinges on the other side." The court affirmed the judgment of Kingsmill Moore that all arguments based on physics should be dismissed. In Ireland, the laws of physics must yield to the laws of the land. Therefore, as I understand this judgment, you are legally obliged to ignore physics so don't even enquire about bi-axial crystals for fear of arrest.

of wave propagation.[137] Anyway, Hamilton was an instant success. The Lord Lieutenant knighted him in 1835.

Hamilton next shifted his attention to dynamics. It wasn't until the twentieth century that the relevant mathematicians were bright enough to appreciate what he was on about at the time. A hundred years after his discoveries in dynamics, Erwin Schrödinger used Hamilton's formulations as the basis of his quantum mechanics. Again, as clear as day when someone else has pointed it out.

Hamilton changed focus once more, this time to algebra. Perhaps his greatest achievement was his discovery of a complex number[138] system in 1843 which he called quaternions. Quaternions have been useful both in the control of spacecraft and in 3-D computer modeling. In other words, they are basic rocket science. His discovery of quaternions, along with the recognition of their non-commutativity, was

---

[137] I wouldn't lose sleep over this unless it was the night before a big examination on the physics of light for which I had forgotten to study (the popular stuff of nightmares). From the seventeenth century, the question of the nature of light did keep physicists awake. There were two opposing theories of light. The great Isaac Newton championed the idea that it was composed of particles. On the opposing side, Christiaan Huygens published his wave theory in 1690. He proposed that light was emitted in all directions as a series of waves. Augustin-Jean Fresnel had also independently worked out his own wave theory by 1817. Hamilton's work in optics contributed to the ever-growing support for the wave theory. However, weaknesses persisted on both sides into the twentieth century when a boring compromise or wave–particle duality position was reached, so that we can now all sleep soundly in the dark – where I remain when it comes to the physics of light.

[138] Complex numbers don't get their name just from being difficult to understand. These types of numbers are composed of real and imaginary parts. Apparently they are very useful in quantum physics and applied mathematics. It is best to just rub your chin knowingly when you see one.

just what was needed for the development of algebra as an abstract axiomatic discipline. Hamilton was inspired by reading the German philosopher Immanuel Kant's *Critique of Pure Reason*, which, in my opinion, is the most difficult book in the world, ever. If you can understand that book you don't need to understand anything else.

On 16 October 1843, as he was walking from Dunsink into Dublin City to attend a meeting of the Royal Irish Academy, Hamilton had what he called "a feeling" of the solution to the formulation of an equation that had been haunting him for fifteen years. He recorded his equations that give us the multiplication law for his new complex numbers on the stones of Broom Bridge in Cabra. There is a plaque on the bridge now with the equation. Like me, you can go there and study his formula, nod sagely, rub your chin knowingly and mutter, "Ah, the old quaternions! So simple. So elegant. Why didn't I think of them?" But we can console ourselves that, like most brilliant people, Hamilton was miserable: his brilliance was inversely proportional to the square root of his melancholy.

Hamilton had a penchant for unrequited love: the kind guaranteed to depress him. He seemed determined to love the one whom he wasn't with. He loved Catherine Disney, who had been forced into an unhappy marriage. Years later when she was dying, Hamilton, on his knees at her death-bed, offered her a copy of his book, *Lectures on Quaternions*. While that must have cheered her up, it must also have made her repent those lost years spent apart. He married Helen Bayly. Helen was frequently ill and away from home, which was good for promoting his depression. Better still, they were usually stressed over money and Hamilton often drank too much. He had intended to propose marriage to Ellen de Vere but he didn't because that might have made him happy. He was a friend of Oscar Wilde's mother,

Speranza (1821–1896),[139] who asked him to be Oscar's godfather. He declined, perhaps imagining it might be too much effort keeping up with that child's wit. He was also a friend of the poet William Wordsworth, who visited Hamilton at Dunsink. Hamilton came to believe that he could have been somebody in the world of poetry. Therefore, he regularly treated Wordsworth to his compositions. Despite Wordsworth's prudent diplomatic discouragements, he wrote many poems, specialising in sonnets. Fortunately, he scratched none of them onto Dublin's bridges for posterity.

We Don't Need No Education

Many of our most accomplished Irish minds are proof of the advantages of avoiding school, where you will most likely be turned into just another peg for a peg-shaped hole. Mandatory education is a contemporary outrage that is never debated because the world is run by adults who want children to suffer as they did. In the past, if you were bright and didn't want to be ruined by school, a fashionable alternative to formal education was to get yourself bedridden for years as the result of a horrible accident or a chronic illness.

Robert Murphy (1806–1843) was fortuitously run over by a cart while he was playing near his home in Mallow, Co. Cork. His thighbone was badly smashed, joyfully confining him to bed for a year. He had books on geometry and algebra with him in bed. How common is that nowadays? Meanwhile, Timothy Mulcahy (dates unknown), a schoolteacher from Cork whose son John (1810?–1853) became the first professor of mathematics at Queen's College Galway, was posing mathematical teasers in the local newspaper. Murphy impressed Mulcahy with his ingenious solutions.

---

[139] See Family Ties in Chapter 6 for details of the life and work of Oscar Wilde's mother, Speranza.

Mulcahy came to Mallow to investigate who the mathematical genius might be, and found thirteen-year-old Murphy
at the end of his quest. The mean Mulcahy then insisted on
sponsoring the poverty-stricken Murphy's education.

However, in 1823, Murphy, despite being a genius, was
denied entry to Trinners to study mathematics because of
his lack of formal education combined with his ignorance
of the classics. It is nice to know some things never change.
Murphy published a refutation of a supposed construction
of a cube root of two that had been produced by a young
priest at Maynooth with a classical education. This paper
came to the attention of Robert Woodhouse, the Lucasian
professor of mathematics at Cambridge. Woodhouse agreed
to admit Murphy to Cambridge in October 1825 on a fee of
£60 paid by the cruel Mulcahy. Murphy was soon recognised
as a significant mathematician, producing twenty scholarly
papers. He was appointed junior dean of Gonville and Caius
College, Cambridge between 1831 and 1833, where, with no
irony on the part of the college authorities, he taught classics.

However, invoking the inverse law of misery, he quickly
showed his college fellows that he was a drunk and a
gambler. His newfound success and relative prosperity
went straight to his head. Just after being elected a Fellow of
the Royal Society, which Hamilton never was, he returned
to Cork to avoid his creditors. In West Cork he became a
cobbler. But he pulled himself together and returned to
Cambridge in 1835; he moved to London in 1836 where he
wrote "popular mathematics" books and became an exam-
iner in mathematics at the University of London. He died of
tuberculosis in 1843.

While there is frequent reference to alcohol in the history
of Irish erudition, there are disappointingly few accounts of
drugs before the rock n' roll scene of the 1960s and 1970s.
John Henderson (1757–1788) is a welcome exception, being
a forerunner of the twentieth-century celebrity drug addict.

Limerick-born Henderson was quickly recognised as a genius. He was a Latin teacher when he was eight, moving on to teach Greek at twelve. He attended Pembroke College in Oxford. Henderson's father, who was a lay preacher and later owned a private lunatic asylum in England, was devastated by his refusal to join the Church. To facilitate his calling as a drug addict, he resolved to become a life-long student.

After graduating, I assume by accident, he remained in his student rooms and kept up an interest in languages, "medicine" and science. Just like future rockers, he spurned the fashion of his day, that is the powdered wigs, neck cloths and large shoe buckles; except, ironically, the rockers would embrace the powdered wigs, neck cloths and big buckles. He drank and became an opium addict, regularly consuming in one go enough dope to kill twelve average addicts. He also experimented, as you must, with other drugs, including mercury. There is no account of what music he listened to, but Mozart's *Eine Kleine Nachtmusik*, which became a massive hit, was released in August 1787. This was before record players, so he would have had to hire an orchestra to perform in his rooms or just hum the tune to himself.

He provided free "medical" treatments to the poor, who were indifferent to his being a "doctor". He promoted sleeping in a wet shirt while lying in a wet bed. Contemporaries such as Dr Johnson and Hannah More hung out at his place. Hannah More, a friend of Johnson's, was a religious writer and a do-gooder. Can you imagine dealing with her when out of your head on drink, opium and mercury? Eventually, setting the template for the future heavy-metal rock n' roll lifestyle, he became both a recluse and obsessed with the occult. He communed with spirits and developed an interest in physiognomy, which is the art of judging a person's character from facial features.

He died, allegedly of an overdose, in his college rooms on 2 November 1788, a day his fans will never forget. I suspect foul play. We know his father shared my suspicions because he had his son's grave opened in case he had come back from the dead, like Elvis, or was in fact still alive, like Jim Morrison. I suspect he may still be alive. His obituary, which could have been that of many of our more contemporary rock n' roll heroes, read – "with as great and good talents as most men … he had lived two and thirty years and had done just nothing." At least he didn't set the fashion for dying at the age of twenty-seven. Robert Johnson, Brian Jones, Jimi Hendrix, Janis Joplin, Jim Morrison, Kurt Cobain and Amy Winehouse all died aged twenty-seven. Perhaps mercury gives you that extra few years.

Thomas Grubb (1800–1878), from Co. Waterford, was another autodidact with no formal education in the field in which he excelled, and he, too, had no grasp of the classics. He established a factory near Charlemont Bridge in Dublin to make billiard tables. One of his two hobbies was astronomy. He built a small observatory in his garden, equipped with a 9-inch reflecting telescope that he built for relaxation, as you do. Thomas Romney Robinson, the director of Armagh Observatory, was so impressed when he saw this telescope that orders for more followed.

In 1834 Grubb built an equatorial mounting for a 13.3-inch lens for an observatory in Co. Sligo. At that time, this was the world's biggest telescope. In 1835 he produced a 15-inch reflecting telescope for Armagh Observatory. Grubb designed a triangular system of balanced levers that distributed the weight of the primary speculum that was used on the world's biggest telescope in 1845, the 72-inch reflecting telescope that was known as the Leviathan of Parsonstown, kept at Birr Castle, Co. Offaly. Other major commissions included telescopes for the Royal Observatory, Greenwich;

West Point Academy, New York; and a 48-inch equatorially mounted reflecting telescope for Melbourne, Australia.

However, building the world's biggest telescopes in his back garden wasn't Grubb's most passionate sideline: his other hobby was his real delight. He loved making money-printing machines for the Bank of Ireland. He designed and built the machines for engraving, printing and sequentially numbering banknotes. He developed the novel idea that all banknotes of the same face value should be identical, a breakthrough that upset forgers who up until then were passing their own idiosyncratic efforts off as legitimate promissory notes. He also designed microscopes and developed ray-tracing lenses that are still used in computer graphics. He was one of the earliest photographers, patenting a camera lens in 1858. He is an example to us all of the advantages of avoiding school.

However, some people just like studying, and there is little enlightened people can do to stop them. It is probably a disease. David Torrens (1897–1967) was an eternal student, a genial lecturer and the world's foremost authority on clock collecting. His enlightened parents wanted him to stay at home and work the farm but he wanted to study. He enrolled in a diploma in agriculture in 1915. After graduating, he studied for a degree in natural sciences, and eventually became a medical student. He graduated as MB (*Medicinae Baccalaureus*) in 1934, a mere nineteen years of study later. He became vice-dean of the Medical School at Trinners. He was popular with his students because he loaned them money without hope of ever getting it back.

But, as usual, what he studied wasn't his passion: clocks made him tick! Unknown to most of his friends and colleagues, Torrens accumulated the largest private collection of horological material in the world in his house. In clock circles, he was recognised as the greatest living authority on horological tools. In 1967 he was admitted to the freedom of the Worshipful Company of Clockmakers of London. Most of his vast knowledge was lost when he died because, as an amateur, he wrote little about clocks. The practice of raving about subjects like clock collecting in pamphlets had died out by the 1960s.

Boyle at a Constant Temperature

Robert Boyle (1627–1691) was one of the most eminent and accomplished chemists of his day. He even has his own law:[140] P [pressure] and V [volume] are inversely proportional for a fixed amount of an ideal gas at a fixed temperature. Boyle was born in Lismore Castle in Waterford. In 1644 he started his scientific career by writing about morality. It was usual back then for scientists to get a run up to physics and chemistry by writing about religion. But in 1649 he built a laboratory, not a chapel, and started experimenting. His motivation was to use chemistry as a defence of religion. From 1650 he fell under the influence of the American chemist George Starkey and subsequently became obsessed with alchemy. Alchemists searched for the philosopher's stone, which possessed special powers, the most important of these being the capacity to turn common metals into gold. Another substance that alchemists sought was the elixir of life, which would confer eternal youth on whoever drank it. It is ironic how many

---

[140] Boyle is the only Irish scientist to have a law called after him. Murphy's Law – "Anything that can go wrong, will go wrong" – doesn't count. There are two theorems named after Irishmen. John Stewart Bell (1928–1990) developed Bell's Theorem in quantum physics, which deals with hidden variable theories, whatever they might be. There is also William Hamilton who gets a mention in the Cayley–Hamilton Theorem, which states that every square matrix over a commutative ring satisfies its own characteristic equation, which must be a great relief to all of us.

alchemists were killed from drinking substances that weren't after all the elixir of life. Boyle owes some of his later fame as a chemist partly to his habit of not drinking his own concoctions.

Boyle was one of the first to discover air. He devised a vacuum chamber for experiments involving observing the consequences of withdrawing air from lighted candles and animals. He set up and published novel experiments. This was the dawn of laboratory-based research with the subsequent development of the familiar figure of the mad scientist laughing insanely in his lab surrounded by bubbling test tubes. In other words, Boyle invented the experimental method of modern chemistry.

Peter Woulfe (1727–1803), from Limerick, invented the Woulfe bottle, which was an apparatus used for capturing poisonous gases, making laboratories relatively safer places for chemistry experiments. However, for Woulfe, his invention came too late. Due to all his experimentation with noxious fumes before he perfected his bottle, he turned into the archetypal nutty professor. He breakfasted at 4.00 a.m., often inviting his friends to join him. When they arrived they could only get into his house by knowing his latest secret code. He became convinced that a return trip on the London to Edinburgh mail coach was marvellous for his health. In 1803 that trip killed him when he caught a cold and died from inflamed lungs.

From the interests of some of our earlier chemists it is difficult to avoid the conclusion that they had too-easy access to fumes and other exotic substances. John Grattan (1800–1871), from Dublin, became a successful apothecary in Belfast, having served a seven-year apprenticeship in the Apothecaries' Hall, Dublin. He made an initial sober impression by making aerated mineral waters, including ginger ale, which he claimed to have invented. However, his real interest was in phrenology and craniology.[141] Both phrenology and craniology are now extinct disciplines, which is a pity. Grattan published methods for measuring and recording human skulls using a craniometer that he invented himself. With this unique device he drew links between lumps on the skull and specific individual human characteristics, values and morals. Basically, he could read your personality from your skull. He carried out a case study on the skull of the Reverend George Walter, who was governor of Derry during the 1688–1689 siege, whose skull he must have had to hand.

When not playing with skulls, Grattan could be found behind the counter handing out drugs at Grattan & Co. Medical Hall in the Corn Market in Belfast. I suspect business was brisk. The Belfast Museum holds his personal collection of skulls.

Chemistry has other uses, especially in the making of beer. Cornelius O' Sullivan (1841–1907), from Cork, became the first brewer's chemist with Bass & Co., which had the slogan, "Aaah, that's Bass!" O'Sullivan learned the chemistry of brewing in 1865 in Berlin, where they made exceptional beer. When war broke out between Germany and Austria in 1866, he volunteered for ambulance work but retired when someone threw a limb at him during a visit to an anatomy department, which was just typical anatomist behaviour at the time.

His duty as a brewer's chemist was to taste the ales at 11.00 a.m. and play sport for the afternoon. Unbelievably,

---

[141] There are important differences of focus between these two fields which, if ignored, might have brought their enthusiastic practitioners to blows. Phrenology is the detailed study of the shape and size of the cranium as a supposed indication of character and mental abilities. Craniology is the study of the shape and size of the skulls of different human races.

O'Sullivan was unhappy with this workload, and he wanted to do more. Obviously, he didn't taste enough of the brew. He applied science to the challenge of producing a consistent and predictable quality beer, which is exactly what we have come to expect from our ales. "Aaah, that's Bass!"

Just a Little Prick

There were some notable Irish contributors to the development of contemporary medicine and public health. Francis Rynd (1801-1861) was probably the first doctor in the world to administer a hypodermic injection. In June 1844 he was treating a patient with a pain in the face, an affliction we now know to be caused by the too-close proximity of an annoying person. But Rynd didn't know that. Instead, he devised a special instrument that allowed him to inject a solution of acetate of morphine, dissolved in creosote, under the patient's skin. The guinea pig made an instant recovery.

Next, Rynd used injections to cure a bed-ridden patient with sciatica who was soon up and walking twenty miles. It wasn't until 1861 that he actually published a pamphlet in time to contribute to a raging medical debate about who had actually invented the syringe.

Another notable medical achievement is that he encased Philip Crampton's (1777-1858) corpse in cement, as requested in his will. Crampton had been Rynd's tutor. He helped establish "the bedside manner" for doctors, for which Dublin became famous in the nineteenth century. This probably involved muttering platitudes about the weather as a prelude to sawing off the limbs of the patient in the bed, without anesthetic. Anesthesiology was developed later as a response to the failure of the bedside manner. Crampton was also famous for saving the life of a choking diner in a restaurant by opening the diner's windpipe. He could swim across Lough Bray, ride his horse into the city,

244

chat at a patient's bedside and amputate a limb – all before breakfast. He had an avian eyemuscle and an extinct reptile named after him. Crampton ordered his body to be encased in cement, probably to avoid the dreaded anatomists.[142]

Rynd knocked down a pedestrian while out riding in his carriage in Clontarf. He wasn't adept at the roadside manner because a fight broke out between himself and the pedestrian. The row resulted in Rynd suffering a fatal heart attack.

The Hazards of Hygeine

A notable contributor to the field of public health was Mary Mallon (1869–1938), who became known to posterity as "Typhoid Mary". This was not because she found a cure for typhoid but because of her fatal participation in improving our understanding of its transmission.

However, she didn't transmit it in Ireland. Thankfully, Mallon emigrated to America when she was fourteen, where she worked as a domestic cook in New York. In August 1906 she was working for a banker when six members of his family became ill with typhoid fever. The investigating epidemiologist, George Soper, applied a radical new idea from Europe to the case. He believed that a healthy carrier might have caused the outbreak. Soper discovered that Mallon had been present at seven previous outbreaks of fever at her former employers' homes, accounting for twenty-two victims, including one fatality. He confronted Mallon where she was working preparing food, and demanded samples of her blood, urine and faeces, there and then. She chased him from her kitchen with a carving fork. She resisted all further attempts to compel her to submit samples.

---

[142] See The Dreaded Anatomists in Chapter 2 for details of the noble profession of stealing bodies and chopping them up in the interests of science.

Poet, Madman, Scoundrel

Eventually she was arrested and forced into hospital where the samples were collected under duress. Tests proved that she was a carrier of typhoid bacilli, which she harboured in her gall bladder, excreted in her faeces and transmitted via her hands to the food she cooked. Just in case you were wondering, toilet paper was invented around 1880 but there were many traditionalists who resisted using it. This was also before the widespread recognition of the importance of hand washing after using the toilet.

Consequently, Mallon was detained in isolation at Riverside Hospital. In 1909 she lost a court case for her release. However, in 1910 she was freed after agreeing by affidavit to change jobs and to consistently observe hygienic precautions. However, she resented both her new life as a laundress and the enormous inconvenience of having to wash her hands every time she went to the loo. She returned to cooking and not washing her hands in 1912. In 1915 she was discovered cooking in a maternity hospital under an assumed name. The hospital had experienced an outbreak of typhoid fever, resulting in two deaths. Mallon was sent back to isolation in hospital. She eventually became a laboratory assistant at the hospital. She died, still in isolation, in 1938 – a forgotten protester against the tyranny of the new-fangled hygiene.

Scientettes with Pipettes

In the good old days women were understandably barred from membership of the royal scientific societies. Men needed their own space in which to do their deep thinking about the movement of objects on inclined planes, noxious fumes, the nature of light, bi-axial crystals, complex numbers, rehearsing a new bedside manner, and so on, without being asked if they remembered to put the cat out or if a bum looked big in an eighteenth-century bustle.

246

Of course it did! The serene daydreams of these men in relation to having laws named after them or future atomic bombs were brutally interrupted by gender equal opportunists. These state-of-the-art women weren't content to be operated on by eminent "surgeons". They insisted on making their own contribution to science.

Cork woman Mary Ball (1812–1898) came from a family with a shared interest in natural history. She achieved the distinction of being both a scientist and a woman without, like her sailing sisters Anne Bonny (1698?–1782) and Grace O'Malley (c.1530–c.1603), having to resort to drag.[143] Ball specialised in collecting invertebrates and shells because she lived beside the sea. She was a friend of Baron de Sélys-Longchamps, who was an international authority on dragonflies. Ball was the first person ever to record the shrill sound made by corixidae water bugs rubbing their legs or wings together. This contribution is surely proof of the advantage for science of the equality of gender representation. I don't know what technology Ball used to record these sounds because the phonautograph, which was the earliest recording device, was only available from 1857. That medium consisted of smoked paper onto which a stylus traced a wavy line. Perhaps she wrote them down phonetically. Her brother published her observations, or stridulations, if you want to get very technical, in 1845. She had a mollusc and a seaweed named after her.

Alice Perry (1885–1969) was the first woman to obtain an engineering degree in Ireland and the UK. She won a scholarship to Queen's College, Galway where she initially enrolled on an arts degree like the few other women in the college. However, when she excelled at mathematics in her first year,

---

[143] See Dressing for all Weathers in Chapter 5 and Battle Dresses in Chapter 3 for details of the lengths to which women will go to enter professions traditionally reserved for men in Irish history.

she transferred to engineering. Perry graduated first in her class with a first-class honours degree in 1906. Her younger sister, Molly, was considered to be the most distinguished mathematician of her time in Queen's College. Perry became Galway's county surveyor when she graduated, making her Ireland's first female county surveyor. However, it couldn't last. She ended up writing spiritual poems in Boston.

George Boole (1815–1864) was an eminent mathematician and logician at Queen's College Cork. He invented Boolean logic, which became the basis of modern digital computing. He can be regarded as "the father of computer science". However, he was also the father of three impressive daughters. Boole died young, leaving his girls to the care of his wife Mary, an educational psychologist who pioneered modern pedagogy and an eccentric philosopher (as opposed to the normal kind), who ran a bohemian home for her daughters.

The Boole sisters, who were the grand-nieces of George Everest, after whom Mount Everest is named, were bursting with brains, and each left their mark on history. When her husband died in 1864, Mary returned to London, leaving her daughter Alicia (1860–1940) in the unhappy care of her grandmother in Cork. Alicia followed her mother to London in 1871, and attended the Queen's College school where her mother was both librarian and mathematics teacher. It is an outrageous oversight that the Boole Library in University College Cork is named after George, who was not a librarian, rather than Mary, who was.

Alicia Boole Stott's formal mathematics education could only stretch to the first two books of Euclid, which was all they had at home. However, she experimented with wooden cubes to develop an understanding of four-dimensional geometry. On her own she constructed cardboard models of the three-dimensional cross-sections of all the six regular four-dimensional figures, using only rulers and a compass. She introduced the term "polytope" to describe the figures represented by the models. After marrying in 1889 she gave up her mathematical interests to become a devoted house-wife. Before you start getting outraged, it was actually her husband who got her interested in work that was being done on polytopes at Groningen University, Holland in around 1900. He was very proud of her cubes. On his insistence, she sent photographs of her models to and was invited to collab-orate with Pieter Schoute, a Dutch mathematician known for his work on polytopes and Euclidean geometry. Schoute persuaded her to publish her work, under her married name of course. In 1914 she was awarded an honorary degree and her models were publicly exhibited. Following Schoute's death, she collaborated with H.S.M. Coxeter. Together they investigated the four-dimensional polytope of the amateur mathematician Thorold Gosset. She introduced new produc-tive methods, which are beyond me, and made two further discoveries relating to polyhedral constructions.

Boole Stott's son, Leonard Stott, was a pioneer in the treat-ment of tuberculosis. He invented a portable X-ray machine, and devised a system of navigation based on spherical trigonometry. Boole Stott's sister Lucy (1862–1905) was a chemistry autodidact who never attended university. She became a lecturer at the London School of Medicine for women. She was the first woman to be elected a fellow of the Institute of Chemistry in 1894.

Boole Stott's other sister was the novelist Ethel L. Voynich (1864–1960). Between the ages of fifteen and twenty-seven, when she married, Voynich dressed in black as an outward sign of her being in mourning for the state of the world. She was the original goth. She studied music in Berlin between 1882 and 1885. She then studied Russian with an exiled revolutionary in London. She travelled in Russia between 1887 and 1889, giving music lessons in St Petersburg. Back in London in 1891, she married a Polish exile. In 1894 she travelled alone to Ukraine to organise a smuggling ring for banned books. She also translated books from Russian. At that time she had an affair with a British spy who supposedly had eleven passports and eleven wives. They travelled to Italy together. He left her in Florence to return to one of his wives.

Voynich wrote her first and most successful novel in 1897, *The Gadfly*, which was drawn from her own life experiences. Her heroine was inspired by the life of Charlotte Wilson, mistress of the Russian anarchist Peter Kropotkin. The book was a bestseller, especially amongst international revolutionaries and anarchists, of whom there were many in the late nineteenth century, except in Ireland. It was translated into over thirty languages, adapted for the theatre and the cinema, and made into an opera. A 1955 Soviet film version, with a score by Shostakovich, won an award at the Cannes Film Festival. When this reignited Russian interest in her, excited Russian literati extracted her from retirement in New York.

The Non-Applications of Engineering

Traditionally it is difficult for Irish people to stay focused on the sciences. If we don't concentrate we tend to drift into dangerous areas like poetry. It is even more difficult for us to apply science in the form of engineering because we tend to start playing music or writing plays. The history of engineering is peppered with many illustrious engineering students who never became successful engineers.

Dennis Lardner (1793–1859), from Dublin, contributed to raising national engineering consciousness by making technology available to a mass readership. Changing his first name to Dionysius, he entered Trinners in 1812 where he won sixteen college prizes. He lectured and wrote on philosophy, mathematics and steam engines, producing the first popular accounts of the new steam technology. He wrote encyclopaedias, pamphlets, as you would expect, and lectures dealing with popularising the sciences, including Charles Babbage's computing machine[144] and steam travel.

Lardner was annoyingly self-confident and stubborn, which is typical of those who are almost always mistaken in their opinions. His predictions on the future of technologies were consistently wrong. He was widely regarded in the scientific community as being an ass. William Makepeace Thackeray called him "Dionysius Diddler". However, he didn't care because he made a fortune from lecture tours, and his books went into at least fifteen editions. In 1845 he settled in Paris where several railway companies employed him as an expert witness in law cases involving steam. He wrote *Railway Economy* in 1850, a book that supposedly influenced Karl Marx.

While he successfully raised popular awareness of engineering wonders, albeit in a faulty way, he is best remembered for his contribution to the arts rather than the sciences by illegitimately fathering a playwright who made Shakespeare look like a slacker. Lardner married Cecelia Flood while he was still an undergraduate in 1815. However, he had a son, Dion Boucicault (1820-1890), with Anna Boursiquot in 1820 (that family was not obsessed with the consistent spelling of their name). At the time of her affair with Lardner, Anna was married to a Dublin wine merchant, Samuel Boursiquot, and was the sister of George

---

[144] Charles Babbage is considered to be "the father of computing". He developed the concept of a programmable computer in the 1820s. The design for his first computer had 25,000 parts. If it had ever been built, it would have weighed 13,600 kilogrammes and been 2.4 metres high. He later designed the improved "Difference Engine No. 2", which was not constructed until 1989–1991. It was built using his plans and the original nineteenth-century manufacturing tolerances. It actually worked. It can calculate to thirty-one digits, which is more than a pocket calculator.

Darley (1795–1846) who was the then fashionable combination of poet, critic and mathematician. Cecelia left Lardner after denouncing his affair in front of a group of dinner guests. I love those kinds of dinners.

Lardner moved in with Anna and her husband Samuel to start writing his *Cabinet Encyclopaedia*, which appeared over twenty years from 1829. He co-wrote twelve volumes with contributions from Mary Shelley, Sir Walter Scott, and the Irish writer and musician Thomas Moore (1779–1852). However, the *ménage à trios* didn't last. He left that pair to elope with a "lady of mature years", the not-ironically named Mrs Mary Heavyside. Her husband, Mr Heavyside, was awarded a generous £8,000[145] in damages against Lardner for the seduction of his wife. But he could afford it because Lardner brought out a second set of encyclopaedias called *The Museum of Science and Art* in twelve volumes, which had 50,000 subscribers.

Dion Boucicault was sent to London by his mother to become an apprentice engineer. Thanks to his training, he became an actor, a playwright and a theatre manager. His career was distinguished by a roller coaster of unprecedented successes followed by spectacular failures, nervous breakdowns and bankruptcies. In other words, he made yet another distinguished contribution to Irish civil engineering.

His first play, *Lodgings to Let*, was performed in 1839 when he was nineteen. When his second play failed, he moved back home to his mother in Dublin, as you do. His next play, *London Assurance*, was a hit. However, success went to his head, and he quickly squandered his earnings. He was reduced to writing and selling poems, if you can imagine such a humiliation. He made a mess of editing *Maestro*, failed with his feminist play, *West End*, abandoned

---

[145] About €450,000 in contemporary currency values.

a three-volume novel and wrote a couple of awful plays. At the age of twenty-two, he was declared bankrupt.

However, resorting to a traditional form of fundraising, he married a wealthy French widow. He threw her off a mountain, allegedly, during a holiday in Switzerland. Anyway, whatever happened, she was satisfactorily dead. He became enthusiastic about French theatre during his brief marriage in Paris so, using his deceased wife's money, he opened a French theatre in London. But it was closed due to rioting because, at that time, Londoners were quite rightly sick of French dramas. He was bankrupt again in 1848, aged twenty-eight. He rebuilt his career in part by inventing popular stage devices. Queen Victoria, who was a fan, commissioned a watercolour of him to hang on her bedroom wall and blow kisses at.

He went to America in 1853 with a young actress, as you do in the theatre, with whom he had six children, as you shouldn't do when you are trying to scrape a living in the theatre. After a run of bad luck, coupled with mismanagment of a string of theatres, he wrote another hit almost by accident. By 1860 he was back in London acting in *The Colleen Bawn*, which he also wrote. That play was the biggest sensation for decades. A successful opera was produced from it. Boucicault managed to sue a variety of producers for breach . of copyright. He toured Britain and Ireland, crowning his triumph with an adultery scandal in 1862 that destroyed his newfound reputation. He was bankrupt again in 1863, aged forty-three.

In 1856 his play *Arrah-na-Pogue*, staged at the Theatre Royal in Dublin, was a huge success. He collaborated on a weekly instalment novel that was received each week to cries of plagiarism. Finally, he announced his retirement from show business and had a nervous breakdown. The following year he wrote *Formosa* for the London stage. He then produced the most costly dramatic failure of the entire nineteenth century, *Babil and Bijou*. After that, he fled to America in 1872.

In 1874 in New York he had unprecedented success, even by his own erratic standards. As proof that you cannot suppress an engineering training forever, he pioneered fireproof scenery in 1877. He had another nervous breakdown in 1879 following a series of successes and failures. It must have been stressful wondering if one of his plays would be sensationally wonderful or unbelievably bad.

He was sued for divorce in 1880 and gaoled. A flop in London in 1881 necessitated his fleeing back to America. He entered a bigamous marriage in Australia, as you do in show business. The novelty of a bigamous couple filled theatres in New Zealand for a few months, where they were desperate for any form of distraction. When he died of heart failure he was buried at Woodlawn Cemetery in New York City. Not surprisingly, he was then dug up and moved to Mount Hope Cemetery in Rochester, New York, where, surprisingly, he remains to this day. In all he wrote over 150 plays, and invented the matinee, the sensational scene and fireproof scenery. He was the first to pay attention to ensemble playing and the first engineer to be credited with anticipating the Russian theatre director Constantin Stanislavski because of his many modern directorial innovations and his professional approach to the theatre.

The father of the Irish songwriter Percy French (1854–1920), under the common false impression held by many Irish parents that mathematics is their offspring's leading talent, convinced Percy to enrol in a civil engineering course after he graduated with an arts degree from Trinners in 1876. While "studying" engineering he impressed his classmates with his virtuosity on the banjo, learned to play the piano and tennis, and organised concerts. He amazed his rapidly growing number of college friends with his comic song "Abdul Abulbul Amir", which was a massive hit. He expanded his audience beyond the classroom to include audiences at cricket matches.

He passed his final engineering examinations after just four years of musical distractions. He became an apprentice in the Midland Great Western Railway Company, after which he took a job with the Board of Works as an inspector of drains. He deserved that fate for passing his examinations. However, to mitigate this setback in his career, he used his office at the board to store banjos, paints, paintings and sports gear, and dressed outrageously on his drain inspections. He formed a music troupe called the Kinnypottle Komics and wrote his next smash hit, "Phil the Fluther's Ball". Predictably, the board did not renew his contract.

Finally happily unemployed, French unsuccessfully edited a journal while writing his next hit, "Slattery's Mounted Fut", which was a song celebrating the ambiguous military achievements of some of my own forebears. He lacked ambition – a disposition often maligned in our contemporary world – especially engineering ambition.

From the 1890s he began to drift into a hugely successful musical career in collaboration with the classical musician Houston Collisson. He cycled everywhere, and gave away his watercolour paintings to those who would actually take them. His famous song "The Mountains of Mourne" appeared in 1896. Drawing on his railway experience as an apprentice, he wrote "Are Ye Right There, Michael?" in 1902, which was a song about the punctuality of the West Clare Railway Company. He toured London, Canada and America. He frequented large London theatres in winter and Irish seaside resorts and small towns in summer. In 1915 he did eighty one-night concerts in Ireland alone. He sometimes toured with Collisson, or on his own when, I assume, Collisson couldn't keep up. Between 1877 and 1915 he wrote about sixty-three songs and fifty-one poems, as well as parodies and plays. He performed in France for British troops during the First World War. However, he achieved little in engineering despite an unpromising start.

If Trinners had built the atomic bomb it is probable that nothing would be different in our history because the engineers in the common rooms wouldn't have known how to work the buttons, being too busy with their plays and musical instruments. Ironically, failed Irish engineers have made some of the most important contributions to the arts, which means that we either had the most inspired or the most misguided engineers in the world.

Classical Applications of Engineering

Perhaps the engineers may not have known what to do with a bomb, but the classicists might well have. In the eighteenth century, one of the most exciting innovations was in air travel. Richard Crosbie (1756?–1800?) was a balloonist. We don't know when he died because he seems to have just drifted up, up and away in one of his balloons. We do know that, while he was a student at Trinners, his aptitude for mechanics came to the fore in his classics studies. He was noted for preparing reliable dueling pistols for his classmates. It seems he was practical precisely because he didn't study engineering.

Crosbie began experimenting with the new-fangled hot air and hydrogen balloons that were becoming the rage. Inspired by a short flight in Dublin in 1784, Crosbie planned to cross the Irish Sea by balloon. To raise money for this feat, he charged admission to his exhibition of balloons at Ranelagh in Dublin, where he released several into the sky, carrying animals. This resulted in Crosbie becoming embroiled in a lengthy public spat in the newspapers with his balloon rivals over the principles of large balloon design.

On 19 January 1785, in front of 30,000 spectators at Ranelagh, Crosbie won the argument by ascending in an elaborate gondola or wicker basket. He eventually landed at Clontarf to a heroic reception. This was the first recorded balloon flight in Ireland.

In May 1785 Crosbie, who was tall and heavy, was seriously worried about a public ascent in his balloon so he wisely asked a lighter Trinners undergraduate called Richard McGwire, who he seemed to have judged as hardly a significant loss to the scientific world, to go up in his place. But McGwire proved to be a more resourceful engineer than Crosbie imagined. While drifting into oblivion, he punctured the balloon to descend into the sea. Crosbie was furious when McGwire was knighted for his innovative efforts on behalf of Irish aviation.

Following this drama, the Mayor of Dublin banned ballooning because the new mania was interfering with commerce with balloons crash-landing and burning all over the city. But Crosbie himself ascended from the lawn of the Duke of Leinster's house in Dublin, now the home of the Irish Parliament (Dáil), on 19 July 1785. The balloon hit the Irish Sea about halfway to England. Crosbie was rescued by a specially commissioned barge but was not knighted. He made another flight from Limerick in April 1786 before eventually disappearing from history into thinning air.

There is evidence from the history of computing in Ireland that those who didn't study engineering made the most progress. Percy Ludgate (1883–1922), from West Cork, was Ireland's first computer nerd, even before we had information technology. As a suitable preparation for nerdiness, he studied accountancy, becoming an auditor with Kevans & Son in Dublin. During the First World War he was on a committee formed by his company to control the production and sale of oats for cavalry horses. Ludgate shone at the complicated organisation involved in this.

He is the earliest successor to Charles Babbage, who in 1834 invented the fundamental concepts of what would become the digital computer of the twentieth century. Ludgate's work is known from just one surviving paper that he published in 1909. This paper describes his plans for a machine that incorporated fully automated mechanisms for storing and accessing nearly 200 28-decimal numbers, and executing a sequence of arithmetic operations on these numbers under the control of instructions entered on a punched paper tape. His machine was different from Babbage's. He indicated a sliding rod to represent a decimal digit instead of Babbage's rotating gear wheel. Ludgate claimed that he learned of Babbage's designs only during the final stages of his own plans. His techniques in what have become known as programme control and storage addressing were more advanced than those of Babbage.

Ludgate never built his machine, nor did anyone else. If you have a few million hours on your hands it would make an interesting hobby. However, he did point the way for all future computer geeks and nerds who would follow. He lived at home with his mother, spending all his free time in his bedroom, where he died in 1922. Sadly, none of his papers or drawings survived. It seems that after his death his mother did a thorough spring clean.

Is There a Real Doctor in the House?

Between 1772 and 1782 Patrick Joyce from Kilkenny was known as Achmet Boroumborad. He is described for posterity as a professional quack and fraud. He was what we would now call an entrepreneur.

Being a swindler was a common career in eighteenth-century Ireland, so he had to do something more noteworthy to stand out from the crowd of imposters. He dressed in what passed at that time in Dublin as being a Turk on the run from Istanbul. This went down exceedingly well with the local gentry. In 1769, centuries ahead of his time, he was promoting the benefits of steam baths in Finglas, in Dublin. Sometime during his Turkish career, when he dressed as a Turk and recommended Turkish baths, he assembled a group of politicians and local gentry to demonstrate the benefits of his hot and cold baths with the hope of attracting funding for expanding his enterprise. Unfortunately, the assembled local dignitaries fell en masse into one of the baths.

However, the character of the eighteenth-century fraudster is necessarily robust. Joyce quickly bounced back from that setback by throwing off his Turkish robes and marrying the sister of a "surgeon". At that time the difference between a quack and a "surgeon" was well understood: a "surgeon" would have trained in the most efficacious methods by which to kill their patients, while a quack would have killed theirs by improvisation. Joyce later became an heir to the estate of William Gregg, who we can be confident expired with convenient speed after this. He even gets a mention in James Joyce's (1882–1941)[146] *Finnegan's Wake* as "an Indian sahib and aural surgeon".

You didn't have to be a "surgeon" or "doctor" in the past. You could have been an actual doctor. For example, the famous conjurer Doctor Lynn was hugely popular with his audiences. It seems a doctor's popularity was directly proportional to his willingness to perform illusions. He toured Dublin every year at the end of the nineteenth century, and every year his audience looked forward to being bewildered and delighted by him. He specialised in pulling bowls of fish from the air. Demonstrating another improbable skill, he would ask a member of his audience to select any pear from a bowl of pears that he would present

---

[146] For more details on James Joyce see Sticking with Joyce in Chapter 6.

to them with a flourish. Once selected, the audience member would be invited to take a slice from the pear with a knife, presented for that purpose, and to eat the slice before handing the partly consumed pear back to the amazing Doctor Lynn. He would take the pear, throw it in the air and when he caught it as it fell he would hand it back to the audience member whole and sound. Fantastic.

The Father of Turpentine

Ah, the past! Then, if you didn't have any medical qualifications you could simply claim to have them – and if you were caught you could defend yourself by claiming to be an eccentric. Sadly our modern laws ignore eccentricity as a medical exoneration. There were definite circumstances in the past when you might have wanted to become an eccentric. These included being illegitimate, too cerebral, too rich or not having enough to occupy your time. The latter was a typical historical manifestation of being too rich.

John Brenan (1768–1830) was a satirist, accomplished classicist, "physician" and proficient eccentric. He began his career writing verse for Dublin magazines before coming up with the not-entirely-original idea of claiming to have medical qualifications from Glasgow University. Having thus qualified himself, he started practising medicine at the turn of the nineteenth century, and quickly cornered the market in turpentine cures.

Brenan claimed to be the first to use turpentine as a treatment for puerperal fever,[147] having seen it used on a horse to treat colic. In an unexpected development for medical

---

[147] This is better known as child-bed fever and was contracted by women during childbirth; it could develop into septicaemia. Famous victims of puerperal fever include King Henry VIII's mother, Elizabeth, Henry VIII's wives Jane Seymour and Catherine Parr, the

standards of the time, he was fired from the Rotunda Maternity Hospital for dosing everyone with turpentine during an epidemic. He then did the appropriate thing. He wrote a few pamphlets, *Thoughts on Puerperal Fever and its Cure by Spirits of Turpentine* (1814) and *Reflections upon Oil of Turpentine, and upon the Present Condition of the Medical Profession in Ireland* (1817). These were essentially ravings against the establishment in which he compared his own genius to that of Jenner, Harvey and Galileo. As Edward Jenner discovered the smallpox vaccine, he can be regarded as the "father of immunology". William Harvey discovered the circulation of blood and may be looked upon as the "father of anatomy". Galileo Galilei discovered the orbit of the Earth around the sun and consequently enjoys the title the "father of modern science". Perhaps Brenan can lay claim to being the "father of turpentine".

After falling out with his magazine editors, Brenan started his own, the *Irish Monthly Gleaner*. Being an eccentric, naturally he didn't publish this monthly every month. This magazine was dedicated to establishing the benefits of turpentine.

But turpentine wasn't his only obsession. He was also a fanatical wrestler and organiser of wrestling bouts. He regularly broke the shins of his wrestling opponents, and then offered to fix them using his medical skills. Obviously, this involved rubbing them with turpentine.

When his father died, Brenan sued his mother for his father's land, and the matter was dragged through the courts with the opposing attorneys getting all the money in the estate. Not surprisingly, Brenan's mother died penniless in the poor house, which was one condition that defied his turpentine treatments.

---

philosopher Mary Wollstonecraft, and Mary Shelley, the author of *Frankenstein*.

The "Science" of Healing

Valentine Greatrakes (1628–1683), from Affane, Co. Water-ford, began to feel, as you do, that he might have the power to cure people of scrofula,[148] also known as the king's evil. On one occasion, Greatrakes met King Charles II of England who didn't like him because he, the king, couldn't cure the king's evil, while Greatrakes, not the king, could.

Greatrakes's first patient was a boy from Lismore, Co. Waterford who had disease around his eyes, face and throat. People started to flock to Greatrakes's house for cures when the boy improved. He was called "the stroaker" because he healed by rubbing his spittle onto the affected area.

Apart from curing people, he was a busy man. He was a farmer and one-time justice of the peace so he was only able to set aside three days a week for curing. The Dean of Lismore wanted him to stop healing because it was against the teachings of the Church to help people without a licence.

Greatrakes got himself into a pamphlet war with his many critics. His defence included testimonials from fifty-three people whom he had cured. He eventually became disillu-sioned with the public's lukewarm response to his healing, and retired to his farm.

Greatrakes visited Florence Newton (d.1661?) in Youghal, Co. Cork when she was in gaol on charges of witchcraft. She had been accused of bewitching Mary Langdon, who was a servant. Langdon claimed that she had been bewitched shortly after refusing to give Newton some of her employ-er's beef at Christmas. She fell victim to fits and trances so violent that four men were needed to hold her down. She vomited needles, straw and pins. Stones also rained down on her that instantly disappeared. The fits stopped as soon as Newton was safely chained in prison.

---

[148] This is a form of lymphatic tuberculosis.

Greatrakes undertook a variety of well-established tests to decide if Newton was actually a witch, including, I assume, determining if she had a cat. But she didn't; she was a dog person. Newton confirmed that she had a familiar in the form of a greyhound, and that she had "overlooked", or put a spell on, Langdon.

Local busybody David Jones tried to teach her the Lord's Prayer while she was in gaol because it was a fact that witches couldn't recite the Lord's Prayer in gaol, or anywhere else. She kissed his hand in gratitude and, sure enough, he was dead within a fortnight.

We don't know what happened to her or how Greatrakes's evidence affected her case. Maybe she just vanished or turned into a greyhound.

If There Is No Cat Is It Really Magic?

Biddy Early (c.1798–1874) was a clairvoyant from Co. Clare who had a genius for healing. She established her occult reputation when she was a teenager by predicting the murder of her employer. With her employer dead as foretold and her reputation established, she settled in Kilbarron, Co. Clare, where she opened her clairvoyant and healing business. She treated thousands of people for various illnesses, disabilities and possession by fairies, which, though a common ailment at that time, has since been completely eradicated as a medical condition, just like smallpox.

Fairies are the spirits who remained neutral during the conflict between God and Lucifer. In other words, they couldn't decide whether they were unambiguously on the side of good or evil. When God won that fight, they were punished for their ambivalence by being sent to live under fairy mounds, deserted castles and graveyards, ruined churches, glens, lakes and caves all over Ireland. They usually congregated in large societies. Fairies could change shape and make themselves so ugly that you would faint if you saw one. It is not known for certain if they had wings but their apparel was agreed upon. Lady fairies wore pure white robes with long hair flowing untied over their shoulders. Married female fairies wore their hair tied up in a bun, signifying their marital status. Male fairies donned green jackets with white breeches and stockings.

In fairness, fairies were in Ireland before Irish people so we respected their prior claim on the country. It seems they engaged in savage fairy wars, and may have wiped themselves out. But in the absence of their written records, we will never know. Whatever happened, we definitely didn't do it. We can take credit for the dodo, the woolly mammoth and our cousins the Neanderthals, but not fairies. We were too terrified to go near them.

Fairies specialised in stealing beautiful peasant babies and replacing them with young, ugly, red-faced leprechauns who would bawl non-stop. Interestingly, no one has ugly babies these days. This pulchritudinous improvement in our infant stock seems proof that fairies are no longer operating in Ireland.

Obviously, any ugly, red-faced mewling baby was a changeling who had to be brought to Biddy Early for a swap because no normal couple could have such a monster naturally. Any sudden changes in mood were deemed cases for Early. For example, a wife falling out with her husband after he slapped her around was obvious proof that she had been swapped with a replacement wife under the management of fairies. She would have to visit Early for treatment. Early also healed sick animals.

As a traditional healer, she didn't charge a fee but accepted gifts of food and alcohol from her clients. She used her famous "dark bottle" as a crystal ball for foretelling future events, such as imminent murders. She married an unknown number of men who all died from alcohol abuse, which unaccountably she didn't specialise in curing.

Ireland was a fairly humourless place in 1865, the year she was accused of witchcraft. She was put on trial in Ennis. However, she wasn't convicted because witnesses were reluctant to testify against her. Also, while we know she owned a bottle, there is no record of her owning a cat, and we know that all witches have cats.

Her final husband, who was much younger than her, died soon after their wedding. She died in poverty in 1874, having dedicated her life to helping others and the promotion of health, especially relieving the locals from possession or kidnap by fairies.

A Man Walks into a Bar ...

Our world-beating achievements in science are not exhausted by physics, chemistry, mathematics, engineering, medicine, "medicine" and healing. We have also achieved wonders in philosophy, which is regarded as the "mother of the sciences".

Do you ever look out the window of an airplane at 36,000 feet and find it impossible to imagine that the people down below in the tiny towns and villages are real and have real lives like you? If so, then you are at the starting point of an important philosophical awakening, or disorder, depending on your point of view.

Worries about the reality of other people bothered philosopher George Berkeley (1685–1753). Perhaps only an Irish person could funnel such an individual anxiety about the existence of other people into a philosophical question – if a tree falls in the forest when no one is there to hear it, does it make a noise?

Berkeley was born near Kilkenny. He went to Trinners in 1700, where he studied mathematics, logic, philosophy,

Greek, Latin, French and Hebrew. Berkeley's fame rests on his acclaimed book, *A Treatise Concerning the Principles of Human Knowledge*, which appeared in 1710. He developed his philosophy, known as idealism,[149] essentially because he didn't believe that other people were real.

Here is how his philosophy works in practice (though you might be wondering why I'm bothering with this at all because on the basis of this argument you don't exist either): stand beside a man at the bar in your local pub, preferably someone big, and tell him that you are convinced, because of idealist principles, that he doesn't really exist, despite the fact that you are talking to him, which might seem like a contradiction. Don't worry about these small annoying details because contradictions are the life-blood of philosophy. We can ignore the small, if significant, quirks in what would be an otherwise coherent argument. Assure the large man at the bar that you know from Berkeley that general ideas, like "other people", are merely a product of the operation of the mind – your mind, in this case. Berkeley believed that God's mind produced all of our ideas. This is typical of philosophy in the eighteenth century. Every time a philosopher got his philosophical knickers into a contradictory twist, he dragged God into the argument as a kind of metaphysical trump card. Why bother, you might ask. Why not just call on God to strike your philosophical opponent down with a bolt of lightning? I presume God was rolling his eyes, but not up to heaven exactly. Anyway, I digress, as one should do in philosophy. But digression is vitally important to the progress of human thought. If you doubt

---

[149] Idealism is the view that there is no reality independent of imagination; we can only know a world constructed by the mind. Berkeley believed that other people are just mere ideas in the mind and have no real existence independent of one imagining them.

that, then you just don't have the wherewithal to appreciate the subtleties of modern philosophy.

At this point in the pub you might laugh smugly to yourself at your complex metaphysical thoughts, which even you don't understand because they are so bewildering. Once you have thus proved to your own satisfaction that the large man at the bar doesn't exist, his standard response should be the subtle metaphysical antithesis of hitting you in the face. He might politely enquire if you now think he doesn't exist as you slump to the floor clutching your broken nose. Perhaps this traditional response to the merits of metaphysical debate in the Irish pub reveals the reason for our relative historical philosophical retardation. Surely it is this kind of gauche impulse that has made us so bad at philosophy. But what about the tree, you are probably still wondering: does it make a noise or not? It is not as simple as yes or no. It never is, or philosophers would be out of business. An ideal tree does make noise in an ideal forest, probably neither of which exists. How would I know? I will let you work out the details.

Berkeley's materialist[150] rivals accused him of being insane or hilarious, as you do when you are a philosophical rival. He ignored them. He wrote his ideas in a new book that took intellectual London by storm. He was invited to write for *The Guardian* newspaper, to take coffee with wits and to dine at Oxford, where the conversation was famously superior to the food. Ah, sweet success! Being a wit is another historically redundant profession no longer appreciated by

---

[150] Here is my philosophy thesis: for every seemingly absurd philosophical idea there is an equal and opposite absurd position. If you think Berkeley's ideas are rubbish it might be evidence that you are a materialist. Materialists believe that nothing exists, including the mind, except matter and its movements and modifications. In other words, it is the opposite to idealism.

the contemporary boorish pub goer. Berkeley toured exten-
sively in Italy before travelling to America with a plan to
establish a college in Bermuda. While his plans ultimately
failed, the state of California later established its university
in a town named after him.

In 1734 he was made bishop of Cloyne. He returned to
Ireland to commence his medical idealism phase. While
bishop, he championed the plight of the poor, encouraging
local industries in workhouses. He even opened a spinning
school, which was practical for such a famous idealist. The
foundation stone of his medical idealism was his belief in
the virtue of tar-water as a cure-all remedy. Tar-water is a
particularly disgusting medieval medicine, even by the
standards of medieval medicines, composed of pine tar and
water. But tar-water may have been better than nothing in
the context of there being no medical infrastructure what-
soever at that time. He wrote *Siris, A Chain of Philosophical
Reflections and Inquiries, Concerning the Virtues of Tar-Water*
in 1744, which sold extremely well. He loved concerts. He
retained the famous Italian musician Pasquilino for four
years to give concerts in his house in Cloyne.

Berkeley's philosophical contemporary competitors
included Sir Richard Bulkeley (1660–1710), who was one of
the earliest members of the Dublin Philosophical Society,
founded in 1683. He spent most of his time there trying to
convince his fellow members to use a singular carriage of
his own invention. This carriage had the appealing feature
that it could not be turned over under any circumstance.
Picture the scene during a typically contemplative evening
at the Society, when Bulkeley interrupts the abstract lectures
to drag the members out to the street to vainly attempt, en
masse, to capsize a sample carriage. He is definitely the
answer to critics of philosophy who protest that the discipline should be more practical.

Berkeley is Ireland's greatest philosopher. However, Ludwig Wittgenstein, who may be the world's greatest philosopher, came to Ireland in 1947. He sat on the steps in the glasshouse of the Botanic Gardens in Glasnevin, Dublin and had thoughts. The steps bear a plaque marking the site of this rare esoteric thinking in Ireland, which tells us that the Viennese philosopher "liked to sit and write at these steps". Thankfully it doesn't say "write on these steps" because Wittgenstein was a philosopher of language: one must be exactly precise in describing their behaviour.

*

J.B. Hall, in his *Random Records of a Reporter*,[151] wistfully recalls how the famous Greek philosopher Socrates used to turn up at a highly respectable séance in Dublin at the end of the nineteenth century speaking poor English with a Cork accent. Who could have imagined that Socrates would have moved to Cork after drinking the hemlock in Athens in 399 BC?

---

[151] See The Wrong Place at the Right Time in Chapter 1.

Postscript: Giants of Irish History

High King of Ireland Brian Boru had supposed descendants who he could look up to because they were, literally, giants. One alleged descendant was Derryman Charles Byrne (1761–1783). While alive, his height was estimated to be 8 feet. He was actually 8 feet, 4 inches when measured after his death. He formed a double act with the 3-foot Count Joseph Boruwlaski. Boruwlaski was obviously another descendant of the great king, only shorter.

Byrne made a lot of money from exhibiting himself as O'Brien Boru. But he invested all his earnings in one £700 bank note that was stolen from his pocket while he drank in a pub in April 1873. He was carrying the equivalent of approximately €40,000 of today's money while he drank in a pub. Understandably he was upset, though you would wonder who would ask for change from a £700 note.

He died in June of that year, apparently from excessive drinking brought on by "vexation at the loss of his savings". Fortunately, vexation is one of those historical conditions that don't affect us any more.

He was terrified of the anatomists.[152] He wisely requested that he be buried at sea. However, his wishes were ignored. When he died, surgeons surrounded his house in London

---

[152] See The Dreaded Anatomists in Chapter 2.

like a peasant mob. After frantic bidding, his corpse was purchased by the famous anatomist Doctor John Hunter for either £500 or £800. Byrne could have sold himself in advance to recoup his lost bank note and thereby have alleviated his vexation. He obviously had poor financial advisers. His skeleton is preserved in the museum of the College of Surgeons in London.

Patrick Cotter (c.1760–1806), from Cork, reached a height of over 7 feet while he was still a teenager. He worked as a plasterer and roofer because he could plaster walls and slate shed roofs without using a ladder. His father was bribed by a showman in 1779 to allow Patrick to be shown as an exhibit in a fair. Patrick fell out with that showman when he discovered that he had been sublet to another show. His original manager had him thrown in gaol for breach of contract because Patrick was sulking. He was released through the kind intervention of a man called William Watts, who was obviously a supporter of the tall. Patrick eventually became a popular attraction at fairs in Bristol. He was amazed to make £10[153] a day on his first three days. He invested the money in a pub called The Giant's Castle.

Cotter also took the stage name O'Brien Boru and claimed direct descent from King Brian Boru. However, according to his detractors, while Byrne may have been a descendent, Cotter only saw a way of cashing in on an association with the name.

His advertising claimed that he was 9 feet tall but he never allowed himself to be measured. Sober audience members guessed his height at 7 feet, 10 inches. As this O'Brien Boru became rich from his showings, his health deteriorated. Fearing that the dreaded anatomists would dig him up after death, he arranged to have himself buried in three coffins placed inside each other like Russian dolls. These

---

[153] Approximately €800 in contemporary currency values.

coffins were then buried in a 12-foot grave protected by iron bars. Even though he was buried at 6.00 a.m., 2,000 people attended the funeral. His grave plaque gave his height as 8 feet, 4 inches.

However, curiosity about his genuine height did not decline. Public debate raged on, with guesses putting him between 6 feet, 10 inches and 8 feet, 1 inch. It was like a national lottery. He had to be dug up in 1906 and again in 1972 just to satisfy public curiosity. Measurements of his skeleton showed that he was between 7 feet, 10 inches and 8 feet, 1 inch tall. We do know that his walking stick was 53 inches.

For the record, Patrick Murphy (1834–1862) who, unconventionally, did not claim descent from Brian Boru, outgrew both Byrne O'Brien Boru and Cotter O'Brien Boru. According to parish records, Murphy reached a height of 8 feet, 1 inch, or, in other estimates, 8 feet, 10 inches. He refused to allow himself to become a paid exhibit, and walked freely around Dublin to the delight of passers-by. He amused children by lighting his pipe from the village gas lamp. Only once did he settle a dispute in a football match by hoisting the two quarreling players into the air and banging their heads together. However, he was eventually persuaded to tour Europe in a travelling circus, becoming a celebrity in France. He died of smallpox which he caught while touring in Marseilles. Just the bad luck of the Irish giant!

Bibliography

Clancy, Tomás, "The Four Courts Buildings and the Development of an Independent Bar of Ireland" in Caroline Costello (ed.) *The Four Courts – 200 Years: Essays to Commemorate the Bicentenary of the Four Courts*, Dublin: Incorporated Council of Law Reporting for Ireland, 1996.

Daly, Gerald J., "Captain William Bligh in Dublin, 1800–1801", *Dublin Historical Record*, Vol. XLIV, No. 1, spring 1991.

Ekin, Des, *The Stolen Village: Baltimore and the Barbary Pirates*, Dublin: The O'Brien Press, 2006.

Gregory, Lady Augusta, *The Voyages of Saint Brendan the Navigator and Tales of the Irish Saints*, Buckinghamshire, UK: Colin Smythe, 1973.

Hadden, Victor, "The Gordon Bennett Race of 1903", *Books Ireland*, No. 76, 1983.

Hall, J.B., *Random Records of a Reporter*, Dublin: The Fodhla Printing Company, 1928.

Harvey, Robert, *Liberators: Latin America's Struggle for Independence, 1810–1830*, London: John Murray, 2000.

Haverty, Anne, *Constance Markievicz: An Independent Life*, London: Pandora, 1988.

Herbert, Ivor, *Arkle: The Story of a Champion*, London: Pelham Books, 1966.

Irish Migration Studies in Latin America, Vol. 4, No. 2, March 2006.

le Brocquy, Sybil, *Brendan the Navigator: A Synopsis of the Legend of His Westward Voyage*, pamphlet © P.J. Carroll and Company Ltd., Dublin: Royal Irish Academy, 1964.

McAnally Jr., D.R., *Irish Wonders: The Ghosts, Giants, Pookas, Demons, Leprechawns, Banshees, Fairies, Witches, Widows, Old Maids, and Other Marvels of the Emerald Isle; Popular Tales as Told by the People*, illustrated by H.R. Heaton, Boston and New York: Houghton, Mifflin & Company; Cambridge: The Riverside Press, 1888.

McGarry, Fearghal, *Rebels' Voices from the Easter Rising*, Dublin: Penguin Ireland, 2011.

McGuire, James and Quinn, James (eds), *The Dictionary of Irish Biography from the Earliest Times to the Year 2002*, Dublin and Cambridge: Royal Irish Academy and Cambridge University Press, 2009.

MacLean, Heather, Gentles, Ian and Ó Siochrú, Micheál, "Minutes of Courts Martial Held in Dublin in the Years 1651–1653" in Thomas O'Connor (ed.) *Archivium Hibernicum*, Vol. LXIV, 2011.

Madden, Richard R., *The United Irishmen: Their Lives and Times. With Numerous Original Portraits, and Additional Authentic Documents; the Whole Matter Newly Arranged and Revised*, First Series, Second Edition, Dublin: James Duffy, 1857.

Magee, Sean, *Arkle: The Life and Legacy of "Himself"*, UK: Highdown, 2005.

Matthew, H.C.G. and Harrison, B. (eds), *Oxford Dictionary of National Biography from the Earliest Times to the Year 2000*, UK: Oxford University Press in Association with the British Academy, 2004.

Smith, Micheal, *An Unsung Hero: Tom Crean – Antarctic Survivor*, Cork: The Collins Press, 2009.

Stradling, Robert A., *The Irish and the Spanish Civil War 1936–1939: Crusades in Conflict*, Mandolin, 1999.

Thompson, E.A., *Who Was Saint Patrick?* Suffolk, UK: The Boydell Press, 1985.

Tone, William Theobald Wolfe (ed.), *The Life of Theobald Wolfe Tone, the Founder of the "United Irishmen", Written by Himself and Extracted from His Journals, from the American Edition of His Life and Works*, Dublin: James McCormick, 1846.

Index

Note: 'n' following a page number indicates a footnote, a number following 'n' indicates a footnote number if there is more than one footnote on the page.